A Sounding of Women

A Sounding of Women

❖

Autobiographies from Unexpected Places

Martha C. Ward

University of New Orleans

Allyn and Bacon

Boston • London • Toronto • Sydney • Tokyo • Singapore

Series Editor: Sarah L. Dunbar
Editor-in-Chief, Social Sciences: Karen Hanson
Developmental Editor: Sylvia Shepard
Editorial Assistant: Elissa Schaen
Marketing Manager: Karon Bowers
Production Coordinator: Thomas E. Dorsaneo
Editorial Production Service: Melanie Field, Strawberry Field Publishing
Manufacturing Buyer: Suzanne Lareau
Cover Administrator: Suzanne Harbison

Library of Congress Cataloging-in-Publication Data

A sounding of women : autobiographies from unexpected places /
   [collected by] Martha C. Ward.
       p.   cm.
   Includes bibliographical references.
   ISBN 0-205-27015-8
   1. Women — Biography.   2. Autobiographies.   3. Ethnology.
   4. Feminist anthropology.   I. Ward, Martha Coonfield.
HQ1123.S69   1997
305.4'092'2 — dc21
                                         97-4169
                                           CIP

*This book is dedicated to the men who are so much
a vital, endearing, and enduring part of my own life story.
Here is "A Sounding of Men":*

My dear brothers (alphabetically and in order of birth):
Hugh A. Coonfield ("Butch") and Ted Coonfield ("Teddy John")

Dr. Malcolm C. Webb, Chairman, Chairperson, and Chair
of the Department of Anthropology, University of New Orleans

My father, Hugh Arley Coonfield, once again with love.
And two grandfathers, Claude C. Biard and Hugh Albert Coonfield

Teachers who made a difference:
Joseph Vandiver, Marshall Durbin, Dan Hughes, and Jack Fischer

Siegfried de Rachewiltz, esteemed colleague

All former or aspiring "boyfriends" and one ex-husband

Friends Forever. Thank you all.

CONTENTS

Introduction

All women have a story — the story of their lives. Generally, however, women's stories remain untold, unheard, and unrecorded. It is always remarkable, therefore, when we have the chance to hear each other's tales. So here is a collection of seven such stories, autobiographies from unexpected places, times, and cultures. I call them "soundings."

My dictionary defines the word *sounding*, first, as emitting or producing a sound, and then as the act of examining a body of water below its surface or the atmosphere above the reach of our eyes. A sounding may be the result of a test or measurement with a simple lead and line or may involve more sophisticated equipment. A whale plunging downward through ocean depths is sounding. When humans make tactful inquiries or indirect investigations, we are sounding out a situation.

For these soundings, I selected "self-steering stories." That means women tell the tales of their lives in their own words. They may have received help from translators, anthropologists, anthropologists' wives, publishers, interpreters, or others. But the story line belongs uniquely to them. I looked for stories of women who grew up and experienced adulthood, because girlhood or coming-of-age stories are another type of autobiography.

None of the women in this book "represents" anything. Each is special if only because she exists in print. None is just a voice, because that implies stories are only a body part.

Each story is embedded in many complex and even contradictory cultural settings. Each story is filtered somehow by the teller, again by the recorder, and again by the listener. We cannot look for factual truth; inevitably there are gaps, forgetfulness, suppression, repression, and probably some deliberate distortions. All these women have constructed or built their lives from their own blueprints. Frequently, they did not work under conditions of their own choosing.

Writing Women's Lives

Why are autobiographies or personal narratives so important? Why should women bother to tell their stories? Why would anyone bother to collect them? Anthropologist Marjorie Shostak, who collaborated with a !Kung Bushwoman named Nisa to write her life history, offers, these answers:

> No more elegant tool exists to describe the human condition than the personal narrative. Ordinary people living ordinary and not-so-ordinary lives weave from their memories and experiences the meaning life has for them. These stories are complex, telling of worlds sometimes foreign to us, worlds that no longer exist. They express modes of thought and culture often different from our own, a challenge to easy understanding. Yet, these stories are also familiar. It is just this tension — the identifiable in endless transformation — that is the currency of personal narratives, as they reveal the complexities and paradoxes of human life. As we cast our net ever wider, searching for those close as well as those far away, the spectrum of voices from otherwise obscure individuals helps us learn tolerance for differences as well as for similarities. What better place to begin our dialogue about human nature and the nature of human possibilities?[1]

Anthropologists have a long and special tradition of ethnographic autobiographies or person-centered ethnographies. These books are as well known and often cited in anthropology as the autobiographies and biographies of writers and diarists are to literary scholars. You will find a number of examples included or cited in this book.

For anthropologists, life history methods are part and parcel of doing fieldwork — whether or not we publish our research as autobiography. Describing the lives of ordinary people within their cultural settings has produced sensitive ethnographies and moving accounts of the endlessly varied ways of life on the planet. As two anthropologists who promoted the life history method most eloquently say,

> There continue to be hundreds of biographies of and autobiographies by all kinds of people and about all kinds of people published each year. We seem never to lose our curiosity about each other and our desire to know the myriad details, occasional disasters, and constant turnings that combine together in different contexts to make up what we perceive as our "lives."[2]

Scholars in history, literature, and other disciplines also look to biography, autobiography, and stories for understanding about how we live within ourselves and with each other. Here is another example: a group of women headed by anthropologist Riv-Ellen Prell and historian Susan Geiger gathered like-minded women around them and began to study women's life histories in other societies. They affiliated with the Center for Advanced Feminist Studies at the University of Minnesota. After a long series of collective efforts and individual struggles — the kind that seem to characterize women's work — they held a conference. It was cross-disciplinary, cross-cultural, and collective. These are humane and meaningful criteria. When they published the results of their work, they alphabetized their names and published under a group title, the Personal Narratives Group.

These scholars uncovered four features that characterize women's autobiographies, wherever and whenever they appear. I find their analyses extremely helpful.

First, narratives exist in a specific time and in a specific place. Particular social, cultural, and historical contexts are crucial to understanding a person's life. We are not talking about a stylized, idealized "EveryWoman."

Second, narratives are not just brute facts about dates of birth or what happened in such and such a year. Instead they are special ways of talking to each other about what matters to us. They encode abstract concepts about the meaning of life for human beings as well as the why of a particular person's existence in a certain time and place. Moreover, they demonstrate the many varied but firm ideas we have about how a good story should be told.

Third, no narrative is pure — whatever that might mean. It is the product of complex negotiations between a narrator and the interpreters, and within the individual speakers themselves. Power relations always surround the production and publication of a life history, biography, or autobiography. These hidden hands include, but are not limited to, gender, class, colonialism, ethnicity, religion, politics, economics, and sexuality. In reading or producing such a work, ethics, identities, and ownership come into play in both obvious and subtle ways.

And last, narratives are about respect — the kind that forms between people who work together — as well as about truths. Here is what the Personal Narratives Group concluded:

> We were not talking about *a* truth or *the* truth. We had developed a healthy disdain for reductionist approaches that would have us determine the "truth" of a woman's words solely in terms of their exact factual accuracy, the representativeness of her social circumstances, or the reliability of her memory when it was tested against "objective" sources. We were talking about *truths*, a decidedly plural concept meant to encompass the multiplicity of ways in which a woman's life story reveals and reflects important features of her conscious experience and social landscape, creating from both her essential reality.

As feminists we wanted to hear these truths and to understand them. We wanted them to inform our own realities, and to learn what we could from the experiences of other women. These truths were necessary to our work, and to our lives.[3]

There is a growing interest in, even hunger for, knowledge about women's lives. Over the last quarter of the twentieth century an explosion of scholarship in women's studies has provided us new ways of looking at our lives. We have reflexive, multicultural, and postmodern ways for women's life-writing. Marilyn Yalom, who is editing a book series called Women's Life Writings from Around the World, says that "I" stories have long been part of human culture and women's culture around the world. Just now are we finding them, seeing them, hearing them, and gathering them for each other to read.

Once the stepsister of both literature and history, autobiography was considered too close to reality to be the former and too fanciful to be the latter. Today, literary works called "memoirs," "autobiographies," or "personal narratives" are widely appreciated for a variety of reasons, including their psychological revelations and their documentary value. In our largely impersonal, often overgrown, and frequently uncomfortable world, the first-person story offers reassurance to countless readers eager to discover how someone else has found a way through the hazards of life.[4]

A Sounding of Women came into being as I was writing a longer book called *A World Full of Women*.[5] I wanted to use short quotes from women's autobiographies to illustrate certain points such as the surreptitious use of birth control. But I learned very quickly that women allowed to talk about their lives weave long and complex stories. It proved impossible to find "sound bites" or short takes. Our critics are correct, women are very good at talking; most of us like to tell stories.

Then I thought about the trajectory of women's lives for a long time and concluded that somehow they are different from men's. So I started a search for women's autobiographies. This was not as easy as it may sound. No central listing or bibliography of women's autobiographies exists. Many autobiographies are not routinely available to American readers. Sometimes they are too long, out-of-print, or published outside the United States. Even the information highway has few if any signs leading to women's life stories.

Life history narratives about women are not as numerous as those about men. Women's lives are often presented only in reference to men's lives, as the "other side," or even as a kind of deviancy. As a token woman, one is enough to represent "women's lives" in Culture X. In many accounts or representations, men have the "real" lives. Women are exceptions that prove the rule.

Women often have no experience in examining their personal lives, no vocabulary for personal experience. As most writers acknowledge, women emphasize personal matters, small objects, fragments of a conversation remembered, or the emotional content of historical experiences, places, or people. Women's stories are anecdotal rather than analytic (a fact for which I am routinely grateful). Indeed, women have discrete and recognizable traditions of storytelling.

> The truths of personal narratives are the truths revealed from real positions in the world, through lived experience in social relationships, in the context of passionate beliefs and partisan stands. They recount efforts to grapple with the world in all of its confusion and complexity and with the normal lack of omniscience that characterizes the human condition. It is precisely because of their subjectivity — their rootedness in time, place, and personal experience, and their perspective-ridden character — that we value them."[6]

Reading Women's Lives

All the accounts in this book were published in English in the twentieth century. Some readers, particularly young ones, may interpret the events of these women's lives as old-fashioned, or unlikely to be of relevance in our "modern" times. So I issue a gentle reminder that history is another unexpected place — just a different country — and women may share common destinies beneath the mottled surfaces of our cultural lives.

We enhance a precious or semiprecious stone when we place it in a gold setting to wear or to give to someone we love. So I have placed each woman's story in its appropriate social and cultural setting. The fact that we have women's autobiographies often seems to be random, an accident of circumstances. So how and why an account comes to exist is also part of its story.

In each selection, women use words from different languages. I left these phrases in the text and, where necessary, added a translation or note in brackets for clarification. They add spice. Consider each chapter a gourmet recipe with unexpected flavors and seasonings added to the dish. In that same spirit, I have left the British spellings: *flavour* for *flavor, colour* for *color, moulding* for *molding, odour* for *odor.* Read right through them.

Colleagues in the Personal Narratives Group were particularly struck by how women in each autobiography they read seem to move back and forth between many different cultures. No one seemed to see herself as marginal to a dominant culture or even as being in any marked categories. Real cultures are very slippery, shambling creatures. They are not just in our heads. So where they come from is crucial to understanding women's lives. Autobiography, like life as we know it, is not one size fits all.

Something else impressed me about these autobiographies. All of these women could recount conversations with a mother, father, husband, or child as though it happened yesterday. Moreover, every woman I read about skipped key parts of her life! Just when I want to know more, there's a blank — sometimes a very big blank. And there seems to be no way I will ever know why or what is there.

Please note that you will not agree with some of the things these women say or the feelings they have. You may not approve of actions the women quoted here have taken or their reasons they give for what they did. But the beauty of autobiography — when we relax and give in to the reality of other people's lived experiences — is that we don't have to predict their actions or be responsible for them. We can't tell them what to do.

Some years ago a friend of mine was dying of cancer. In the nearly two years it took, her friends spent time with her and, as these things work, with each other. With no malice or planning, we each assumed that our dying friend would complete certain tasks, handle certain obvious problems, and tie up the loose ends before she left. Shouldn't she write a letter to each of her children, one friend asked. What about that huge closet with unfinished craft projects? A prayer circle is surely better than a bridge group! Why on earth is she redecorating the living room? And so on.

But our lists of what she needed to do, of course, differed from person to person and, most certainly, from her own lists. Finally, I guess, most of us understood that she got to choose how to die. It was her life and it was her death.

This viewpoint, painfully achieved, underlies each of the autobiographies here. I suggest that you watch very closely for how each woman handles and names her feelings. Today many of us share a belief that feelings are natural — that we will all have the same response to the same event, or that any given event will predictably have the same effect on us. But feelings are not prescribed. For example, a husband dies; a wife is secretly relieved. A husband dies; a wife finds her life torn asunder. Autobiographies are not the truths of objectivity, facts, or science; they are the truths of lived experience, of shared stories. There is no right way or wrong way to be a woman — or to tell a woman's story.

Much as I would dearly love to question each of these women about what really happened, what they really felt, or why they did what they did, I cannot. They have chosen what to say and what to leave out. What they decided to say is all we have.

It is common these days to hear about "speaking out," "voices," or "tongues," and so forth. If we talk about recapturing our voices, then we must talk about reclaiming our ears. The listener counts too. Listening is one of the most profound contributions we can make to each other. The people who helped produce these autobiographies offer us a special space to listen and to hear. To assist you I have added some provocative questions at the end of each chapter. Several women suggested this strategy to me; they thought such questions would help them read, listen, and hear better.

I would also like to acknowledge here those women who reviewed the manuscript and provided insightful comments: Barbara Miller, George Washington University; Rita Ross, San Jose State University; and Mary Jo Schneider, University of Arkansas.

I hope these stories inspire you to write your own lives, to recognize the lives of others, and to collect autobiographies or life histories — just because. When I share these selections with friends, relatives, and students, they react strongly. They seem to bond with the characters; later they quote from them. They say these stories have an immediacy, freshness, and an application to their own lives. I agree. They claim that if these women can make their lives sound so compelling, so can we. I certainly hope so.

Books and Lives

Human lives — the personal and the self — are the yeast that causes the bread of ethnography, literature, theory, or history to rise. Many wonderful books have grown out of the fermentation of the women's movement and feminist scholarship of the last quarter century. Many wonderful books come to us through time-honored ethnographic techniques and fieldwork traditions in the discipline of anthropology. Other wonderful stories just rise up.

Here at the end of the introduction, as at the end of each chapter, I offer some suggestions about autobiographies that relate to or follow the main one of the chapter. Some are classics; others are, of course, unexpected. Some of these books really do have the power to change people's lives.

In that spirit, here are some books you might want to know about. These recommendations may be useful when you need sources of good scholarship, analysis, or critiques about the making of autobiographies.

The following are general works of interpretation and theory about autobiographies and life histories. Some are collections of scholarly articles on specific subjects. These books are the most frequently cited in professional writings on the topic.

L. L. Langness and Gelya Frank, *Lives: An Anthropological Approach to Biography* (Novato, CA: Chandler and Sharp, 1981).

Personal Narratives Group, *Interpreting Women's Lives: Feminist Theory and Personal Narratives* (Bloomington: Indiana University Press, 1989).

Carolyn Heilbrun, *Writing a Woman's Life* (New York: Ballantine, 1989).

Ruthellen Josselson and Amia Lieblich, eds., *The Narrative Study of Lives,* vol. I (Newbury Park, CA: Sage Publications, 1993).

Amia Lieblich and Ruthellen Josselson, eds., *Exploring Identity and Gender: The Narrative Study of Lives,* vol. II (Newbury Park, CA: Sage Publications, 1994).

Carol Ramelb, ed., *Biography East and West: Selected Conference Papers* (Honolulu: East-West Center, 1989).

You may be more interested in one cultural, historical, or geographical area, so included here are some excellent informative sources.

David H. Brumale, *American Indian Autobiography* (Berkeley: University of California Press, 1988).

Arnold Krupat, ed., *Native American Autobiography: An Anthology* (Madison: University of Wisconsin Press, 1994).

Farzaneh Milani, *Veils and Words: The Emerging Voices of Iranian Women Writers* (Syracuse: Syracuse University Press, 1992).

Afsaneh Najmabadi, ed., *Women's Biographies and Autobiographies in Iran* (Cambridge, MA: Harvard University Press, 1991).

Patricia K. Addis, *Through a Woman's I: An Annotated Bibliography of American Women's Autobiographical Writings 1946–1976* (Metuchen, NJ: Scarecrow Press, 1983).

Helen M. Buss, *Mapping Our Selves: Canadian Women's Autobiographies* (Toronto: McGill-Queen's University Press, 1993).

Estelle C. Jelinek, *The Tradition of Women's Autobiography: From Antiquity to the Present* (Boston: Twayne Women's Studies Publishers, 1986).

Here is a list of the autobiographies excerpted in *A Sounding of Women*:

Chapter 1: "The Autobiography of a Fox Indian Woman," *40th Annual Report of the Bureau of American Ethnology* (Washington, DC: Smithsonian, 1925).

Chapter 2: Etsu Inagaki Sugimoto, *A Daughter of the Samurai* (Garden City, NY: Doubleday, Doran and Co., 1934).

Chapter 3: Mary de Rachewiltz, *Ezra Pound, Father and Teacher: Discretions* (New York: New Directions Press, 1971).

Chapter 4: Mary F. Smith, *Baba of Karo: A Woman of the Muslim Hausa,* with introduction and notes by M. G. Smith) (London: Faber and Faber, 1954).

Chapter 5: Oscar Lewis, Ruth M. Lewis, and Susan Rigdon, *Four Women Living the Revolution: An Oral History of Contemporary Cuba* (Urbana: University of Illinois Press, 1977).

Chapter 6: Amiria Manutahi Stirling as told to Anne Salmond, *Amiria: The Life Story of a Maori Woman* (Auckland: A. H. & A. W. Reed, 1976).

Chapter 7: Nawal el Saadawi, *The Hidden Face of Eve: Women in the Arab World* (London: Zed Press, 1982).

Nawal el Saadawi, *Memoirs from a Women's Prison* (London: The Women's Press, 1983).

Endnotes to the Introduction

1. This quote is from an essay called "What the wind won't take away," The genesis of *Nisa — The Life and Words of a !Kung Woman*. In Personal Narratives Group, *Interpreting Women's Lives: Feminist Theory and Personal Narratives* (Bloomington: Indiana University Press, 1989), 239.

2. In the introduction to L. L. Langness and Gelya Frank, *Lives: An Anthropological Approach to Biography* (Novato, CA: Chandler and Sharp, 1981), 18.

3. From the introduction to Personal Narratives Group, *Interpreting Women's Lives: Feminist Theory and Personal Narratives,* 14.

4. This quote is from the introduction to Marilyn Yalom, ed., *Efronia: An Armenian Love Story* (Boston: Northeastern University Press, 1993), ix.

5. See Martha Ward, *A World Full of Women* (Boston: Allyn and Bacon, 1996).

6. From Personal Narratives Group, *Interpreting Women's Lives: Feminist Theory and Personal Narratives,* 263.

A Sounding
of Women

No picture or drawing of a woman named Anonymous exists. In fact, few images of women from these places or these times are available at all. Here is a drawing of Gä-hah-no, a young Seneca woman wearing a costume of the Iroquois nation. The Iroquois, the Seneca, and the Fox (Mesquakie) are also called the Eastern Woodlands peoples.

Caption and art from Lewis Henry Morgan, League of the Ho-De-No-Sau-Nee or Iroquois. Volume II. Human Relations Area Files (New Haven, CT, 1954), frontispiece.

Anonymous

"You Must Dance Vigorously"

In 1918 an ethnographer named Truman Michelson asked a Fox Indian woman to tell him her life story. She agreed to talk with the anthropologist and his two Fox field assistants on the condition that her real name not be used. They honored her request. Michelson was, in fact, only looking for a text of the Fox language for linguistic analysis. Collecting an autobiography was simply his way to insure a long sample of ordinary language.

In 1925 Michelson published the autobiography in the Annual Reports of the Bureau of American Ethnology, one part of the giant Smithsonian museum system in Washington, D.C.[1] Ironically, the Fox text matters now only to a few specialists, but the by-product, a woman's story, endures.

Translations from one language to another and from one culture to another are fraught with problems. For starters, the name "Fox" seems to be a misunderstanding. Apparently a French trading party happened upon a group of Native American men, asked their identity, and were told a clan name, "we're members of the [Renard] Clan." This was translated into English as "Fox." But the members of the group called themselves Mesquakie or "Red Earth People." When we add the difficulties of translating and interpreting between men and women, we may well wonder about the worth and validity of any autobiography acquired under such circumstances.

Reading Anonymous's story today, we have questions with no clues to answer them. What motivated her to tell her story? Why did she ask to remain forever unnamed? Anonymous is speaking at a time of great anguish for Native American peoples. The Fox or Mesquakie, along with similar Native American groups, had farmed the prairie regions in what we now call the Midwest. They had apparently relocated there after European colonization of lands to the east created pressures to keep moving. In the decade after 1833 the U.S. government forced the agricultural Indians of Michigan, Indiana, Illinois, and Wisconsin to remove themselves west of the Mississippi river. The surviving bands of Fox moved westward to Iowa, Kansas, and finally, to Oklahoma. The reservation system, the Dawes Act of 1887, the massacre at Wounded Knee, and many harsh and punitive acts by federal bureaucracies contributed to widespread deaths, diseases, dislocation, and starvation. Alcoholism, suicide, and despair were rampant. Clans were useless to care for their members as they once had done. These were times of terrible traumas and tragedies.

Yet Anonymous utters not one word about the social or political contexts in which her life is set. She is careful to conceal not only her name, but the names of her relatives and husbands.

Instead, Anonymous talks about her first period, her first love, a baby's birth, and how she still feels about a bad husband and a husband's death. She recounts entire conversations with her long-dead mother and her mother's brother. Anonymous gives us one of the fullest and frankest stories about the start of menstruation we have in anthropology. She is secluded in a distant hut to prevent her new powers from harming anyone. Special food and water and other taboos safeguard her from her own power. Older women give her new clothes and advice she must heed. Later in the narrative, she casually mentions the indigenous forms of birth control she used. At that time European-Americans did not understand that Native American women knew how to make and use plant recipes to prevent pregnancies and regulate their menstrual cycles. They systematically regarded such practices as primitive superstitions.

By this point, however, the story sounds entirely authentic to contemporary readers. It seems to transcend the translation and the cultural circumstances of collecting it. It might well be EveryWoman's story. We have had or heard of similar experiences.

Anonymous begins her story with the importance of play in molding adult skills. She makes clothing for her dolls and puts them to work in miniature houses called *wickiups,* a bark-covered, loaf-shaped traditional house. She tends her crops in child-sized fields and gathers firewood with miniature burden straps and hatchets. Throughout her narrative, clan grandmothers, aunts, and uncles appear and give her instructions. In fact, throughout the narrative, she talks to them, argues with them, and remembers their advice as turning points in her life.

The anthropologist and the Fox men who assisted him did not question her or guide this narrative. It appears to be "self-steering." Michelson writes,

No attempt was made to influence the informant in any way; so that the contents are the things which seemed of importance to herself. It may be noted that at times the original autobiography was too naive and frank for European taste; and so a few sentences have been deleted. . . . The English translation is based on a paraphrase written by Horace Poweshiek, supplemented and corrected by a grammatical analysis of the text by myself. The translation has been made as literal as possible without violence to English idiomatic usage. ("The Autobiography of a Fox Indian Woman," P. 295).

For the record, I have used a few contemporary editing conventions such as shorter paragraphs. On occasion, I have cut sentences to preserve the flow. But the story Anonymous tells outshines light editing and Michelson's sometimes stilted translations. It survives the passage of years and vast changes in our sensibilities. You might even consider reading her story out loud; after all, she told it that way.

When I was ten years old I ceased caring for dolls. I still liked to swim. But when I said to my mother, "May I go swimming?" she said to me, "Yes. You may wash your grandmother's waist [blouse] for her, and you may wash mine also."

"That is why I treat you like that, so that you will learn how to wash," my mother told me. "No one continues to be taken care of forever. The time soon comes when we lose sight of the one who takes care of us. I never got to know how my mother looked. My father's sister brought me up. Today I treat you just as she treated me. She did not permit me to just fool around. Why, even when I was eight years old I knew how to cook very well. When my father's sister was busy with something, I did the cooking," she said to me.

I did not believe her when she said that, for I was then ten years old and was just beginning to cook well, and I knew how to sew but I was poor at it. At that time, when my mother woke up, she said to me, "Wake up, you may fetch some water. And go get some little dry sticks so we may start the fire," she said to me. When I was unwilling I was nevertheless compelled. This is the way I was always treated.

Soon, moreover, I was told, "This is your little ax," when a little ax was brought. I was glad. "This is your wood-strap," I was told. My mother and I would go out to cut wood; and I carried the little wood that I had cut on my back. She would strap them for me. She instructed me how to tie them up. Soon I began to go a little ways off by myself to cut wood.

And when I was eleven years old I likewise continually watched her as she would make bags. "Well, you try to make one," she said to me. She braided up one little bag for me. She instructed me how to make it. Sure enough, I nearly learned how to make it, but I made it very badly. I was again told, "You make another." It was somewhat larger. And soon I knew how to make it very well.

She would be very proud after I had learned to make anything. "There, you will make things for yourself after you take care of yourself. If you happen to know how to make everything when you no longer see me, you will not have a hard time in any way. You will make your own possessions. My father's sister, the one who took care of me, treated me so. That is why I know how to make any little thing.

'She is in the habit of treating me meanly,' I thought, when she ordered me to make something all the time. Now as a matter of fact she treated me well.

"And that is why I treat you so today. So very likely when you think of me you think, 'she treats me meanly.' It is because I am fond of you and wish you to know how to make things. If I were not fond of you, I would not order you to do things. If I were not fond of you, I would think, 'I don't care what she does.' If you are intelligent when you are grown and recollect how I treated you, you will think, 'I do declare! My mother treated me well.' Or if you are bad you will not remember me when I am gone. I do not wish you to be that way. I desire that you take care of yourself quietly," my mother told me.

And again, when I was twelve years old, I was told, "Come, try to make these." They were my own moccasins. "You may start to make them for yourself after you know how to make them. For you already know how to make them for your dolls. That is the way you are to make them," I was told. She only cut them out for me. And when I made a mistake she ripped it out for me. "This is the way you are to make it," I was told. Finally I really knew how to make them.

And then a small belt of yarn was put on the sticks for me. A little one was started for me. "Try to make this one," I was told. I began to try to make it. Later on I surely knew how to make it. Then I kept on making belts of yarn. My mother was pleased when I learned how to make anything.

At that time I knew how to cook well. When my mother went anyplace, she said to me, "You may cook the meal." Moreover, when she made mats I cooked the meals. "You may get accustomed to cooking, for it is almost time for you to live outside. You will cook for yourself when you live outside," I would be told.

Soon I was told, "Try to weave; you may wish to make these mats." Then I began to try to weave. Later I knew how to weave very well. Then I began to help my mother all the time. She was proud when I continued to learn how to make anything.

And then I was thirteen years old.

"Now is the time when you must watch yourself; you are nearly a young woman. Do not forget this which I tell you. You might ruin your brothers if you are not careful. The state of being a young woman is evil. The manitous [spirits] hate it. If anyone is blessed by a manitou, if he eats with a young woman, he is then hated by the one who blessed him and the manitou ceases to think of him. That is why it is told us, 'be careful' and why we are told about it beforehand. At the time when you are a young woman, whenever you become a young woman, you are to hide yourself. Do not come into your wickiup. That is what you are to do." She frightened me when she told me.

Lo, sure enough when I was thirteen and a half years old, I was told, "Go get some wood and carry it on your back." It was nearly noon when I started out. When I was walking along somewhere, I noticed something strange about myself. I was terribly frightened at being in that condition. I did not know how I became that way. "This must be the thing about which I was cautioned when I was told," I thought.

I went and laid down in the middle of the thick forest there. I was crying, I was frightened. It was almost the middle of summer after we had done our hoe-ing. After a while my mother got tired of waiting. She came to seek me. Soon she found me. I was then crying hard.

"Come, stop crying. It's just the way with us women. We have been made to be that way. Nothing will happen to you. You will have gotten over this now in the warm weather. Had it happened to you in winter you would have had a hard time. You would be cold when you bathed as you have had to jump into the water four times. Now, today, as it is warm weather, you may swim as slowly as you like."

I was told, "Lie covered up. Do not try to look around. I shall go and make a wickiup for you." I was suffering very much there in the midst of the brush. And it was very hot.

It was in the evening when I was told, "At last I have come for you. I have built a place for you to live in. Cover your face. Do not think of looking any-place." I was brought there to the small wickiup. I was shut off by twigs all around. Brush piled up so that I could not see through it. There was only a little space where I lived to cook outside. My grandmother must have made it so that there was only room for us to lie down in.

"I shall fetch your grandmother to be here with you," my mother told me. It was another old woman [her maternal grandmother was dead so a clanswoman was summoned]. She was brought there to give me instructions. I did not eat all day long. The next day I was told, "We shall fetch things for you to use in cooking." I was not hungry as I was frightened. The next day my grandmother went to eat. I was alone; she took only as long as she needed to eat, but I was afraid. In the evening I was brought little buckets to cook with, some little things to eat, water, and wood. Then for the first time I cooked.

My grandmother would keep on giving me instructions, telling me how to lead a good life. She really was a very old woman. Surely she must have spoken the truth in what she said to me. "My grandchild," she would say to me, "soon I shall tell you how to live an upright life. Today you see how old I am. I did exactly what I was told. I tried and thought how to live an upright life. Surely I have reached an old age," she told me.

"That is the way you should do, if you listen to me as I instruct you. Now as for your mother, I began giving her instructions before she was grown up, every time I saw her. Because she was my relative is why I gave her instructions, although she was well treated by her father's sister by whom she was reared. That is why she knows how to make things which belong to the work of us women. If you observe the way your mother makes anything, you would do well, my grandchild. And this. As many of us as entered young womanhood, fasted. It was very many days: some fasted ten days, some four, five, every kind of way. Today, to be sure, things are changing. When I was a young woman I fasted eight days. We always fasted until we were grown up," my grandmother told me.

My mother only came to fetch me water and little sticks of wood so that I might kindle a fire when I cooked. And we made strings. That is what we did.

"Do not touch your hair; it might all come off. And do not eat sweet things. And if what tastes sour is eaten, one's teeth will come out," my grandmother told me. She always gave me good advice from time to time. "There is another thing. Now the men will think you are mature as you have become a young woman, and they will be desirous of courting you. If you do not go around bashfully, for a long time they will not have the audacity to court you. If you laugh over their words, they will consider you as naught. They will begin bothering you right away. If you are immoral your brothers will be ashamed, and your mother's brothers. If you live quietly they will be proud. They will love you. And your brothers will believe you when you say anything to them. When one lives quietly the men folks love one. And there is another thing. Some of the girls of our generation are immoral. If one goes around all the time with those who are immoral, they would get one in the habit of being so. Do not go around with the immoral ones, my grandchild," my grandmother told me.

"And this. You are to treat any aged person well. Because a person has conducted his or her life carefully is why he or she reached an old age. Do not talk about anyone. Do not lie. Do not steal. If you practice stealing, you will be wretched. Do not act stingy with a possession of which you are fond. If you are stingy, you will not get anything. If you are generous you will always get something. Moreover, do not go around and speak crossly toward anyone. You must be equally kind to every old person. That, my grandchild, is a good way to do," my grandmother said to me. She was indeed always instructing me what to do.

Soon I had lived there ten days. "Well, at least you may go and take a bath," my mother said to me. We started to the river. "Take off your waist [blouse]," I was told. After I had taken it off I leaped into the water. Then, "I am going to peck you with something sharp," I was told. I was pecked all over. "And now on your lower part," I was told. "Only use your skirt as a breechcloth," I was told. I was also pecked on my thighs. "It will be that you will not menstruate much if the blood flows plentifully," I was told. I was made to suffer very much. I put on other garments. I threw away those which I had formerly been wearing around. And then for the first time I looked around to see. And again I had to cook alone for myself outside for ten days. After ten days I again went to bathe. And then for the first time I began to eat indoors with the others.

I told my mother, "My grandmother has always been instructing me what I should do." She laughed. "That is why I went after her, so she would instruct you thoroughly in what is right. 'She might listen to her,' is what I thought of you." And then I was fifteen years old.

"You may now try to sew bead and applique ribbon work. If you know how to sew you are to make things to wear when you dance. If it is known that you can already sew, people will hire you. Not merely that. You will be paid. You will be benefited by knowing how to sew," my mother told me. Then indeed I began to practice sewing. It took me a long time to sew well. It must have taken me two years to sew well. From then I was always making something.

I was sixteen years old when we were making mats in the summer. In the winter we were making sacks and yarn belts, and sewing applique ribbon work and bead work. Behold, it was true that I was constantly asked to make something; then I would be paid.

When I was more than seventeen, late at night while I was still sleeping, someone said to me, "Wake up." The person was holding a match, and lit it. Lo, it was a man. I looked at him. I was as frightened as possible. I trembled because I was frightened. When I ordered him away, my voice did not sound natural when I spoke. I was barely able to speak to him. And from then on, now and then, men tried to come to me. I always had been instructed what was proper. When it was known what kind of a person I was, they began to try to court me.

[In courtship customs of this place and period, young men and women could not be seen talking together. They had to meet at night or in the brush away from the older people. Young girls who giggled too much were believed to be readily available for sexual advances.]

Then I was instructed, "When you are twenty, then you may desire to take a husband. Whoever is the one whom you are going to take as your husband, he alone is the one with whom you are to talk. When you begin to talk with men, do not talk to many. It is not right for women to have many friends. Their husband(s) will not treat them well, as they are jealous when they know what their wives have been doing. That indeed is why women are forbidden to have many [male] friends." That is what I was told.

Then soon when I was eighteen, in the spring at the time when people begin to pick strawberries, I accompanied a young woman strawberrying. "We will see one," she would say to me. Then she would say to me, "I am just joshing you." As a matter of fact, she and one young man had made arrangements to see each other there.

Soon he came over there. They were well acquainted with each other and treated each other kindly. He helped her when she was picking strawberries. She kept coming to me to get me to go with her to places. Soon he came with another young man. Then this young woman got me to talk to his fellow young man. "He will not do anything; you may talk together quietly," that woman told me. As often as we went anywhere those men came. Finally I began to talk to that young man. And then we four went around together a great deal.

Of course many men tried to get me to talk with them. Soon it was known what kind of a person I was. My, but they scolded me severely. Another young man had been selected for me to take as husband.

"You had better take a husband right away," I was told. "'When you are twenty, you shall take a husband,' I told you formerly when I was instructing you. And I forbade you to go around with immoral girls. Surely you are already not doing right. I desired to see you well married while I was still living. The father of the one with whom you talk is evil. He [your lover] might beat you. That is the way his father is. He is always beating his wife. And when anything is taking place, he will not allow his wife to go there. Moreover, that man is extremely lazy. That is why I think the son will be like that. He is always merely walking around. I have never known him to do any work. If you took him as your husband, you would probably then be taking care of him. He would cheat you. You already know how to do all the work that belongs to us women. You really must not take him for your husband. You must take the other one as your husband, the one with whom I think it proper for you to live."

"You must stop talking with the one you are trying to love. If, however, I learn that you talk again with him, I shall not believe anything you say to me. Now I know in the past that you listened to what I told you. That is why I believed you when you said anything to me. That is why I would forbid you to go around with immoral girls. As soon as you began to go around with them we found it out. You are no longer afraid of me. You formerly were afraid to go anywhere because of them. But now you always desire to go somewhere. You will be thought of as naught if you are immoral. The ones who are moral are those whom men want to live with [i.e., marry]. And they will only make sport of the immoral ones. That is why they bother them, to have a good time with them, not to marry them. You might as well quickly take as your husband the one whom I permit you," I was told.

I was nineteen years old. Then I made up my mind to begin talking with the one I was permitted. I did not like him very well. I thought more of the other one. Always I would think, "Would that I might talk with him." I really couldn't stop talking with him. I worried about him. And I again went around with the one I was permitted, when I went anywhere. But I always thought more of the other one, the one they hated on my account.

Soon the one I was permitted tried to take me with him to his home. He always asked me to go with him whenever I saw him. Then I said to him, "I am very much afraid of your parents." He said to me, "We do not speak a different language, so it is not right for us to be afraid of each other. As for me, I am not afraid of your parents. For I have done nothing evil to you. As long as we have been talking together, I have been quiet with you. You know it too. I intend that we shall live quietly with each other. I always think, 'Oh that she were willing.' You are the only one with whom I wish to live. I shall treat you very nicely. Whatever you tell me, I shall do. And I shall always work. And I shall not hate your parents. I am not fooling you. What I say to you this day, I shall surely do," he said to me.

Soon I consented. At night we departed. When it was daylight, I was ashamed to go home with him. The next day when they saw him, he was treated very nicely. I had taken a husband, the one they had wished me to.

[By going to his house, she is married; later, the families exchange gifts such as horses, corn, matting, kettles, and fine clothes.]²

❖

My husband for a long time treated me nicely. And my mother strongly forbade me to keep on talking with the other one. She watched me closely. But I couldn't stop thinking of him, for he was the one I loved. I did not love my husband. That is why I always thought of the other one. When anything was going on, I went around with my mother, as she was watching me so that I should not talk with the other one again. And she forbade me to go anyplace by myself. "Go with your husband when you go anyplace. They might say something about you. Someone might say of you, 'she goes around with another man.' Those who desire to make trouble for married couples are smart," I would be told.

And when I had been living with him for half a year, I ceased having menstrual flows. Thereupon I was given instructions again, "Well, this is what has happened, probably you are to have a child. When anything is cooked and it is burned, it must not be eaten so that children's afterbirths will not adhere. And nuts are not to be eaten, so that the babies will be able to break through the caul [amniotic sac]. And in winter, one is not to warm their feet, so that the babies will not adhere to the caul. And women are not to join their feet to those of their husbands, so that the babies will not be born feet-first. And the feet of no animals are to be eaten. And one must be careful not to touch crawfish. Also, if these are touched when one is pregnant, the babies will be born feetfirst. It is said that women have a hard time when babies are born that way. That is why one believes and fears what one has been told, so that one will not suffer a long time at childbirth. It is better to do what we are told."

"And no corpse is to be touched. If it is touched the babies would die after they are born, by inheriting it. And if the dead are looked at, they are to be looked at with straight eyes. Also it is said that if they are looked at slantingly, the babies will be cross-eyed. And if cranes are touched, the babies will always look upward. The children will not be able to look upon the ground. And when anyone drowns, if he is touched, the babies would die. These are the number of things one is forbidden to do. And it is told that one should carry wood always on one's back so that the babies will be loosened [i.e., born easily]. Again, after a woman knows that she is pregnant, she ceases to have anything to do with her husband. Otherwise, the babies will be filthy when they are born. When their parents do not observe this, the babies move around."

"For we women have a hard time at childbirth. We suffer. Some are killed by the babies. But we are not afraid of it, as we are made to be that way. That is probably the reason why we are not afraid of it. Oh, if we were all afraid of it, when we all became old, that is as far as we could go. We should not be able to branch out to a new generation. So at childbirth we should do only what we are told. The ones who do not do as they are told are the ones who are injured by their children."

Soon my abdomen grew large. I was ashamed. When there was a dance I did not go there as I was ashamed.

After eight months went by, my mother-in-law came. She came to talk with my mother. "Now is the time when she is on the point of giving birth. We should build a little wickiup beforehand for her so that she may be delivered there."

Then I became sick in the evening when lying alone. "I am sick and have a little pain in the small of my back," I said to my mother. "Oh ho," she said, "very likely now is the time when you are to have a child. I shall summon her [the mother-in-law]. For she said, 'you will summon me.'" In a little after she came, she said to me, "Come, go to the little wickiup." Blankets were spread for me. When I sat down comfortably a strap was fastened from above. "You are to hold on to this when you begin to feel intense pain," I was told. I then felt more intense pain. After a while I was told, "Lie down. When you begin to suffer acute pain you are to try to sit up. You are to sit on your knees and you are to sit erect." I did so. I would hold on to the strap. The child could not be born.

After midnight I was nearly unable to get up. The women who were attending me became frightened. Then they said among themselves, "We shall pray for help." My mother-in-law took Indian tobacco and went to a woman skilled in obstetrics for help. And when that woman came, she at once boiled some medicine. After she had boiled it, she said: "Let her sit up for a while. You must hold her so that she will not fall over." After I was made to sit up, she spat upon my head; and she gave me the medicine to drink. After she had given me the medicine to drink, she began singing. She went outside and around the little wickiup singing. When she danced by where I was, she knocked on the side. "Come out if you are a boy," she would say. And she would again begin singing. When she danced by she again knocked the side. "Come out if you are a girl," she would say again. After she sang four times in a circle, she entered the wickiup. And she gave me medicine to drink. "Now it will be born. She may lie down. Only lay her down carefully. You must hold her knees straight up," she said. Lo, sure enough, a little boy was born.

Then I knew how painful childbirth was. After I had borne the child, I was not in pain in any spot. I was well. They cut off the baby's naval with one inch of the cord on it. A brand-new pair of scissors was used. They tied up the place where he was cut. His belly was washed. The next day he was placed in a cradle. And they tied a little piece of meat on his naval with a cloth going around his abdomen. "You must moisten him once in a while so that his umbilical cord will drop off soon," I was told. I did so to him. I did not wash him myself. My mother attended to him for me. In three days his umbilical cord dropped off. He could not draw the milk out for two days when I nursed him.

Then, "You must always keep him in a cradle [swaddled in a cradle board]: otherwise he might have a long head, he might be humpbacked, or he might be bowlegged. That is why they are placed carefully, so they will not be that way. When they are tied that way they will be straight. They are kept in cradles for nearly one year. Again, they are not to be held all the time. They are placed in a swing after they suckle so that they will not be a nuisance. They become trained to be left alone when one goes someplace, if they are not crybabies. And when they are constantly held, some cry when they are laid down. Babies bother people when they get them used to being constantly held," I was told.

I lived outside for thirty-three days.

Then my husband began to act differently. He did not treat me at all the way he had done when he was acting nicely. The fact of the matter is that the young woman with whom I used to go around before I was married had been telling him things. "You are treating her so well, but your wife formerly was the same as married to another man. I know about her. 'We shall never stop talking to each other even if we marry other people,' they said to each other," she kept on telling him. Finally he apparently really believed her. From that time on he began to treat me badly. That young woman was made jealous because he treated me well. That was why she kept on telling him stories. As for her, the men would not marry her as she was immoral. [As her relatives told her, girls with bad reputations cannot find husbands to marry them.] Finally my husband began to beat me.

"That is why I formerly forbade you to talk to any men. That is why I said to you, 'You must talk only to the one whom you are to marry,'" my mother said to me. "Finally you will make your son angry if you are always having trouble with each other. Babies die when they become angry," I was told.

Soon, when our little boy nearly knew how to talk, he became ill. I was full of sorrow. Later on, indeed, he died. It is very hard to have death in the family. One cannot help feeling badly. "That is why I told you about it when you were both unfortunately frightening him," I was told. "That is why children are not struck. One would feel worse if one had beaten the child," I was told. I felt worse after he was buried. The fourth day we fed those who buried him in the evening. We began to make every kind of new finery. After we had made it, I began to think over the one whom we should adopt. I thought of all the babies. I found one as if this way: "This one perhaps is loved as much as I loved my baby," I thought. Then we adopted him, so that we in a way had a son.

And later on my husband became meaner. He was lazy. But my mother for-bade me to be divorced. And then my mother died. I was twenty-five years old. I felt terrible. From time to time I remembered everything she told me.

And from that time, I really began taking care of myself. It was very hard. Work never ended. A person could not just stay around and do nothing. "Surely my mother treated me well in teaching me how to make things. What would have happened to me if I had not known work suitable for women? I should have been even poorer, if my mother had not instructed me," I thought all the while. When-ever I made anything I was given clothing to wear in exchange. And when I made something, I gave it away. In the spring when I planted anything I attended to it carefully. I cooked it when it grew. In winter I did not lack things to cook.

And my husband did nothing but act meanly. When there was a dance he would not allow me to go and see it. Soon I thought, "Well, now that my mother has gone, this fellow treats me meanly. It was because my mother forbade me to divorce that I allowed this fellow to ill-treat me. Besides I do not love him. Now no one would scold me. And I love the other one. I hate this one." I began to see dances in spite of him. He was fearfully angry. "You may see that man; that is why you are perverse in going there," he said to me. "I want to see him," I would say to him. I began to chase him away.

"You may marry other women who are quiet [of good moral character]. We shall never be able to live nicely together. While I was living quietly [morally] with you, you began to act badly. And it was not my idea to live with you. It was because I was told. So now we will be divorced. You must go. You could have behaved nicely if you had wished us to live together always. You know how I have been doing. I have been working quietly. And you without reason began to be jealous. I have not talked to anyone as long as we have been living together. But now we must surely be divorced," I said to him.

"Truly from now on I shall stop acting that way. I shall begin to treat you nicely. And I shall work diligently, I shall not be able to refuse what you ask me," he said to me. "No, I shall not believe you though you may do your best to speak nicely. You have ill-treated me too long," I said to him. I was not able to chase him away. As I was leaving he came and seized me. He held me there. "You are not going off anyplace," he said to me. I cried bitterly and he let me go.

I went where my uncle [her mother's brother] lived and slept there. The next day my uncle said to me, "It is strange that you came and slept with us. Some-thing has happened to you." "My husband treats me very badly. That is why I am unwilling to keep on living with him," I said to him.

"It is known broadly that he abuses you. No one will reproach you if you think of being divorced. I myself will not scold you. It is a rule that a married couple should alike treat each other well. As for me, I treat the one with whom I live [my wife] well and she treats me well. She always cooks for me when I am working. And if I were suddenly to treat her badly while she was still treating me well and, while she was still living morally, were I to become jealous over something without reason, her relatives would not like it. For I surely would be doing wrong. If she cast me off, none of her relatives would scold her. Everyone, all over, would be glad of what happened to me. Certainly I should not find another woman who behaved as well. Surely I should always want back the one who behaved well. But I might have angered her. I alone should be thinking of her. Surely she would not think of me. She would hate me as much as possible," my uncle said to me.

"Well, my niece, now you are of sufficient age to listen attentively," he said to me. "You probably still think of what your mother told you. You may foolishly begin to be immoral. You should look at men quietly [without an immoral purpose]. Whomever you think will treat you well is the one whom you should take for your husband. If he happens to treat you well, you should live quietly with him. That, my niece, is what I want you to do. Because your mother is gone is why I tell you as I understand it. And if you are now divorced, you should stay single for at least one or two years. You should just be working diligently. Then you might marry that one," my uncle said to me.

And so I became divorced. Of course my former husband was always trying to get me but I could not be kind again to him. I hated him tremendously.

And then the wife of the man with whom I had talked when I was still a virgin died. After I had been divorced for one year and he had become a widower free from death-customs, he again began to court me. Of course others courted me but I did not talk to them. And soon I began talking with him, for we were already acquainted with each other while we were young. And soon he asked me why I became divorced. I told him exactly how it was that I became divorced.

"Well! Your husband was entirely wrong in what he thought of us. I ceased seeing you when you were married. Even if I had seen you I should not have been able to screw up my courage to say anything to you. You surely would have reported me. You acted that way when you were married. If I had persuaded you to marry me at the time, I should not have beaten you. Why, how often have you heard of me striking the one with whom I was living [his wife]? I never struck her even once. Nor did I scold her. She also danced vigorously at dances before she became ill. That is how I should treat you too. You might dance vigorously if you felt like dancing vigorously. To dance vigorously is natural. If you are willing we shall do that. I want you to consent very much. I have always thought, 'I wish I might live with her,'" he said to me. "Well, I might consent in a year, but not now," I said to him. For a long time we were merely talking with each other.

Soon the time came which I had set for us to live together [act as husband and wife]. When we saw each other, he said to me, "Well, at last it is the time you set for your consent. Tonight at night do not latch your door firmly. I shall come to you." That is what I did. He came. And sometimes he would sleep far off in a wickiup where his relatives lived. And at any time I went and visited my relatives. He never spoke crossly to me. So I loved him dearly. The other one, the one with whom I first lived, was sensual. That is why I hated him.

And after I married the other one I was so well. When there was a dance, he said to me, "Go and dance. I should be made ashamed by their talk if you were not seen when something is going on. Clothe yourself in fine apparel," he would also say to me.

And soon when we were talking together, he said to me, "I wish I had been able to persuade you long ago, for we first talked with each other." "Well," I said to him, "I was not master of my own person while my mother was yet living. The fact is that had I been master of myself, I couldn't have married him. Perhaps you might have persuaded me, for I had already become acquainted with you. For I was always thinking of you, especially at first. When I first stopped talking to you I was lonely," I said to him.

"Well, let it be, for we have each other nicely at last," he said to me. My, but he talked so nicely. I had been living with him for two years. I continued to love him more and more as he treated me well.

Soon we had another child, a little girl, but it died after it was four months old. Then they had me drink medicine so that I would not have a child again, as they died when I had them.

I never heard my husband speak crossly. Even when there were Shawnee dances at night, he said to me, "Have a fine time dancing."

"Well, I have surely found a man. If this man were to cast me off today, I should tag after him anyhow," I thought. When he went to any place for a long time, I yearned for him. And I thought, 'He has made me happy by treating me well.' Then I began to make things for him, his finery, his moccasins, his leggings, his shirt, his garters, his cross-belt. After I had made finery of every kind for him, I said, "These are what I have made for you, as you have made me happy as long as I have lived with you. You have never made me angry in any way. That is why I made them for you."

'You must dance vigorously,' I thought.

I had more and more charge over everything. It seems as if he was a good hunter, for he brought in much game when he went hunting. So we never were in want of meat, as he knew how to hunt. I was rightly married to him. I was married to him a good many years. I did not even think of divorce, as I liked his ways so much.

Then he fell ill. I felt very sorry for him. I felt terribly. Soon he became sicker and sicker. I cried in vain, as I felt so badly about him. And he died. It was terrible for me. I undid my hair and loosened it. For several nights I could not sleep as I was sorrowful. On the fourth day I called the men. "You are to divide all these possessions of ours among you," I said to my male relatives. And then the female relatives of my dead husband came to comb my hair. And they brought other garments for me to wear. I wore black clothing. And soon those male relatives of mine to whom I had given our possessions brought food of every kind. The women brought all things which women raise. I went over to those women who had combed my hair and told them to take that food. I was fasting. And I became lazy. I only wanted to lie down. I kept on sleeping. I was lonely.

That uncle [her mother's brother] mentioned before heard about it. He came to me. "I have come to see, my niece, whether you are sick. You are losing much weight. I have come to instruct you as to what you should do. I know that you listened to what I told you when you were divorced. You have made me very happy. Now this is what you are to do, my niece. Do not think so very much of him all the time, for it is dangerous to do that. Something will happen to you if you dream that you are sleeping with him. You will cease to live very soon. Do not talk much, and do not laugh as long as you are bound by death ceremonies. You must be always quietly making something. Nor must you look around much. That is what is done when one's husband or wife dies.

"When they are taken to be buried, those surviving accompany them to the place where the dead are brought. After they are placed on top of the hole, the relatives begin to speak to those ghosts. After they have spoken to them, first the relatives begin to throw tobacco for them, then others throw tobacco afterwards. After all have offered tobacco to the ghosts, then last of all the husbands or wives offer tobacco to them. They walk around in a circle where the dead person is. Then they walk towards the East. They continue to go anyplace in the brush. They go through very thick brush. They are never to look backward. If they were to look backward they would die soon. They are to go far off and then turn to go back. That is what they are supposed to do. Perhaps you did not do that, so I have heard," my uncle said to me.

"I did not know that was the way. For I did not hear my mother, when she was alive, speak of how those unreleased from death-ceremonies should act. That is why I did not know what should be done. I did not go there when my husband was buried. I stayed here in the wickiup," I told my uncle.

"This is why they do that, why they wander around in thick bush, so they may run and hide from that soul," he said to me. "So that is why you feel so badly. If you had done as I now tell you, you would not be that way. And when you eat, always put some on the fire for him. Do not forget to do this as long as an adoption-feast has not been held and as long as you are not freed from death-ceremonies. That is what you must do," my uncle said to me. And he departed.

And then always when I ate I put food on the fire for my husband. And I tried to cease to think of him all the time, as I was afraid to die early.

Later on I heard that an adoption feast was about to take place. Sure enough they soon came to summon me. When I went in there, the ones who were adopted were eating there. When they fed me, it was as if we were eating with my husband for the last time, in order that he might be released.

After I had eaten, I was told, "Take off your clothing." Then they began to clothe me in fresh clothes, and my hair was combed and my face was washed. And then I was told, "Do not take off your clothing. For now you are to be clad like this. You may begin to wear finery. You may go and do whatever you please. If you are desirous of marrying anyone, you may marry him. Someone who will take care of you if you marry him. Do not be afraid of us. You have pleased us by treating our relative well while he was alive. So you must believe what we say to you this day." And then I departed.[3]

For the first time I began to wear fresh clothing. I began to be careful. And that uncle of mine came again. "At last I have come to give you instructions again, my niece. This day you have ceased to be restricted by death-ceremonies. You know how hard it was to find a good man who treated you well. A good man is hard to find. So you must feel very badly. You know how your first husband treated you in the past. He abused you badly. So you should not forget your last husband for a long time. The men will begin to court you. Do not think of beginning to respond to them right away. For you are still young. It will be nothing if you do not marry anyone for a long time, at least four years. Your next husband will not be as good. And I am very proud that you believed me when I told you to do what was right. Some women become immoral when their mothers die, they cease to be guided by anyone. Well, my niece, I have finished instructing you. If you do that, you will lead a straight life."

I did as he told me. None of the men who were courting me was able to get my consent. I sharply scolded anyone who courted me. For four years I remained single, showing how sorry I was for my husband. If I had had a child I should have never married again. As it was, I was too much alone all the time. "That is why," I thought, "I am always lonely." When more than four years were up, I again began to be kind to one man. Soon he asked that we should marry.

"Now I began to be kind to you so that we should be married. Your husband was my friend. We used to talk together a great deal. He said to me, 'If I die first, you must court the one with whom I live, so as to marry her. She behaves very well. She is your sister-in-law, as we are friends. I do not want other men to marry her, as she is too good. That really is why I say it to you. It might happen that I should die first, for we do not know when we are to die. And you must treat her nicely, as I love her dearly because she is good,' he said to me. So I am trying to get you to agree for us to marry. As I was told, 'you must treat her well,' I could not begin to treat you meanly. I should try to treat you as my friend treated you," he said to me. Then I consented.

Oh, he never became angry, but he was rather lazy. He was slow in making anything. And he was a gambler. I did not love him as much as I did the one who was dead.

And I began to wish to have a child again. "If I had a child I should have it do things for me. Surely they will not all die," I thought. Soon I asked an old woman who knew about medicine. "Is there perhaps a medicine whereby one might be able to have a child if one drank it?" I said to her. "Surely I know one," she said to me, "you might have a child if you drink it, for you already have had children," she said to me. "It was because I drank a medicine that I ceased having children," I said to her. "That is nothing. You might easily have a child," she said to me. So she gave me medicine to drink. Sure enough, I began to have children.

After we had many children, then my husband died. "Well, I shall never marry again," I thought, "for now these children of mine will help me get a living."

Dancing Vigorously: Conclusions

This story sounds truthful to us on a number of levels. What Anonymous tells about her life accords easily with independent records of many kinds. We have historical, ethnographic, and biographical writings from this place, period, and these people. In addition, the characters and situations she describes feel familiar to contemporary readers. Getting a first period, having a baby, or managing a husband — these are universal experiences for women.

Here Michelson as a person becomes queasy. He says not a word about her babies, birth control, or her poignant tale of happiness lost, found, and lost again. Instead, he adds voluminous footnotes about "good moral character" for Fox women. He seems to think that women should act only in ways that make them marriageable, and that all females are merely wives or wives-to-be. Here are some footnotes from "The Autobiography of a Fox Indian Woman" that indicate his concern. They throw more light on the collector's craft than on the lives of women.

#5 Lazy girls are disliked.

#8 Girls should learn to cook, make matting, sacks, beadwork, and moccasins. In this way after marrying they will have an easy time.

#19 It is considered improper for a boy and a girl, unless very young, to be seen talking together. A young man cannot meet his inamorata openly; it must be in the brush or at night when the old people are asleep.

#21 A girl is not supposed to go off by herself unless she has some good reason. If a girl gads about and does no housework, she soon acquires an unenviable reputation . . . Young men rarely but occasionally marry girls of bad reputations.

#28 It is a fact that Fox women who have good reputations do exactly as the mother advised her daughter.

#33 Today divorcées are very apt to be immoral. Hence the man's word of caution.

Incidentally, there is no evidence that Native Americans actually shared Michelson's rigid ideas of the relationships between women and men. To the contrary, there is considerable evidence that his male Fox assistants were bemoaning the changes in behavior they had witnessed since foreigners (European-Americans) came into their lives and destroyed their cultural autonomy. They may have also agreed, as men sometimes do, that young women need to be controlled, or cannot do the right things without guidance from their elders.

It does not matter, however, that the translator and compilers missed the major points of Anonymous's story. It still speaks to us about a woman's life, regardless of time or place. For example, Michelson makes a special point of the second husband's generosity in allowing Anonymous to attend dances:

Formerly dancing was pretty likely to be rough; and girls and their lovers would meet on such occasions. The husband's confidence in his wife could not be shown to greater advantage than by permitting, or rather urging, his wife to be present. ("The Autobiography of a Fox Indian Woman," P. 343).

However, the man who brought us her story does not comment on the spirited reciprocity Anonymous brings to her narrative. As she learns to love this husband and to number his good qualities, she returns the permission and goodwill. And so she says to him, "You must dance vigorously."

"Self-Life-Writing": Books to Read

If we translate the notion of "autobiography" out of its European context and into a Native American perspective, we would have the term "self-life-writing."[4] But there was no tradition of writing one's life story in Native American societies or of telling about one's life from the point of view of being born and moving through adolescence and adulthood. That belongs to the Western notion of being an "individual" — the self or "auto" of autobiography. In fact, writing itself was an alien act to these cultures before Christianity and colonial governments.

University-trained American anthropologists felt a deep sense of urgency during the last part of the nineteenth century and far into the twentieth century. They assumed that Native American cultures were going to "vanish." Like Michelson, they worked from a strong sense of mission to "salvage" the artifacts, knowledge, and languages before everything disappeared. They wanted to document languages, rituals, kinship systems, mythology, healing systems, religions, and material culture. They thought ordinary lives and ordinary activities were just as important as great wars, unusual times, and famous leaders. The U.S. government, many private organizations, and universities sponsored an extraordinary amount of research designed to save as much information as possible. As a result there are a number of classic autobiographies that complement Anonymous's story. I describe some of the most accessible here.

Ruth Underhill's autobiography of Chona, *Papago Woman* (Prospect Heights, IL: Waveland Press, 1989), was originally published in 1936 as a Memoir of the American Anthropological Association. Chona was about 90 years old when she talked with the anthropologist. In fact, both women commonly strike readers as so fascinating that the book has been through a number of reincarnations.

Two of the most important autobiographies in anthropology are about a sister and a brother from the Woodland or Winnebago, a Native American culture similar to the Mesquakie. The first of this set was *The Autobiography of a Winnebago Indian: Crashing Thunder* (New York: Dover Paperback, 1920). Anthropologist Paul Radin brought this story into print. Although the siblings had grown up in the same culture, their experiences are radically different. Crashing Thunder's story is a drama of religious experience, from drunkenness and murder to salvation through peyote. As Radin presents it, this man's life contained high dramas of visions and adversity.

By contrast, Crashing Thunder's younger sister, Mountain Wolf Woman, tells a woman's story: food-gathering, relatives, husbands, children, and the twists of domestic fate. She is a responsible church member who respects the Peyote Way, the fading traditions of the Winnebago tribe, and Pullman trains. Anthropologist Nancy O. Lurie used her privileges as Mountain Wolf Woman's niece to collect, translate, and edit this extremely valuable volume, *Mountain Wolf Woman, Sister of Crashing Thunder: The Autobiography of a Winnebago Indian* (Ann Arbor: University of Michigan Press, 1961). Both of these autobiographies are timeless classics in self-life-writing; they complement Anonymous's story and point to the worth of listening to and helping each other tell our stories.

Other autobiographies in this vein include David Jones, *Sanapia: Comanche Medicine Woman* (New York: Holt, Rinehart and Winston, 1972); Frank Linderman, *Pretty Shield: Medicine Woman of the Crow* (Bison Books, 1932); and Ignatia Broker, *Night Flying Woman: An Ojibwa Narrative* (St. Paul: Minnesota Historical Society Press, 1983).

Although writing a story of one's life might be an alien concept to Native Americans, storytelling certainly was not. In an oral culture, stories and elaborate language are the stuff of life itself. Today, anthropologists no longer have "salvage anxieties," and Native American women and men are writing their own lives in novels and biographies, as well as in autobiographies. There are far too many seriously important works to mention. Two books by the same woman, however, stand out. If you have yet to read about Mary Crow Dog, born Mary Brave Bird, then start here.

Mary gave birth to a baby boy during the siege of Wounded Knee in 1973. Her first book, *Lakota Woman* (New York: HarperCollins, 1990), won the American Book Award in 1991. Here is a compelling life caught up in the Sioux heritage, white lifestyles, tribal patriarchy, feminist philosophy, alcohol, abuse, poverty, politics, freedom, and tradition. Her story continues in *Ohitika Woman* (New York: HarperCollins, 1993). Writer Richard Erdoes helped her. Their collaboration follows a long tradition in Native and European-American contacts and male–female joint endeavors.

Resolving Some Remaining Questions

1. Anonymous certainly seems to receive lots of advice from her kinfolk. Why does she need advice; what does she do with it? Where do people in other groups get advice? Is this the same as wisdom or information? Gossip? Intrusion?

2. Much material about the comparative psychology of child rearing is embedded in this account. This material parallels a large body of literature from

Native American cultures. What are the primary characteristics of being a child or a parent in this culture?

3. Anonymous does not use the language of "romance" or "falling in love" to describe her relationships with her husbands. Different ethics or ideologies are in play here. What are the qualities or attributes that she brings to her marriages and expects from her husbands?

4. Can we or should we judge Michelson's endeavor of "collecting" a life story from a person who seemed to have nothing in common with him? Did he commit a colonial, imperialist act? Did he save something important? Did he know what he was doing?

Endnotes to Chapter 1

1. This selection comes from "The Autobiography of a Fox Indian Woman" published in the 40th Annual Reports of the Bureau of American Ethnology in 1925. The author Truman Michelson was born in 1879 and studied at Harvard and the universities of Leipzig and Bonn in Germany. He worked as an ethnologist for the Bureau of American Ethnology, a division of the national Smithsonian museum system. He also taught at George Washington University. He worked with Arapaho, and Eskimo at James Bay and Hudson Bay, but is mainly credited with classifying Algonquian tribes using linguistics. Other autobiographies collected and edited by Truman Michelson include "Narrative of an Arapaho Woman," *American Anthropologist* 35 (1933): 595–610 and "The Narrative of a Southern Cheyenne Woman," *Smithsonian Miscellaneous Collections* 77: 5 (1932). Michelson's three autobiographies on women are unusual because anthropology, like other social sciences at that time, was seriously "male-bound."

2. Note that getting married in this cultural context involved concern for morality, etiquette, formal gift exchanges, as well as parents' assistance and approval. Divorce was easy and often enhanced family harmony.

3. About Fox funeral customs: In keeping with her ancestors' customs, Anonymous fasts, divides her dead husband's belongings among her male relatives, and wears the mourning clothes her husband's family provides. But because her mother is dead, she does not know all the manners of mourning until her maternal uncle takes her under his guidance as he had done at her divorce. He counsels her to put aside excessive grief and look to the future rather

than dwelling morbidly on the past. Had she followed the tribal custom of walking far into the bush away from her husband's grave without looking back, she could have successfully hidden from his departing soul. In the wick-iup, however, his soul visited her. So her mother's brother helps her establish normal relations with her husband's memory by feeding his soul with food thrown into the fire and by remembering his good qualities for four years. Then his family throws an adoption feast to mark her return to ordinary life. She is released from mourning and eligible to remarry at will.

4. The term "self-life-writing" comes from Arnold Krupat, ed. *Native American Autobiography: An Anthology* (Madison: University of Wisconsin Press, 1994).

This pen and ink drawing by Tekisui Ishii captures
the moment at which Etsu's two lives came together.
It shows a young woman raised in the intricate
codes of the elite Samurai class of Japan meeting
the equally formal Victorian world of her adopted
country. The husband whom she only just met
stands in the background.

From Etsu Sugimoto, A Daughter of the Samurai, 157.

Etsu

"The Eyelids of a Samurai Know Not Moisture."

When Etsu Inagaki Sugimoto wrote her autobiography, *A Daughter of the Samurai,* she added this subtitle: "How a daughter of feudal Japan, living hundreds of years in one generation, became a modern American." So the frame she picked for her story will be ours.

The Samurai were a small but highly visible hereditary class of nobles in Japan. They followed an elaborate code of behavior that demanded feudal loyalty and placed honor above life. Samurai were warriors; they loved the manners, values, ceremonials, and costumes of a rich military culture. As a class the Samurai lost their power after a series of reforms in 1868; in the text these historic events are called the Restoration. However, the legends and traditions of the Samurai are still alive in contemporary Japanese consciousness just as pioneers, cowboys, Pilgrims, or the Kennedy clan are alive to many Americans.

As often happens with elite classes in complex societies, women's lives were completely subjected to dynastic control, whether their fathers, sons, or husbands. They were expected to face marriage, childbirth, and the task of training their children to leave home with the same standards of bravery, good manners, and appropriate clothing in which warriors greeted battle. Here are a few of the active duties of a Samurai wife: supply the army from stores produced at home, conduct the financial business of their large estates, ride horseback, carry a special dagger or sword to use in hand-to-hand combat against an enemy, and use it against herself if necessary to avoid disgrace. Indeed, Samurai children learned to sleep on wooden pillows in stiff and disciplined positions.

Etsu was raised in the code of the warrior, under the rigid ceremonial regime of a Samurai household in a remote and very cold region of Japan. The Inagaki family, in common with other Samurai nobles in that period, had lost most of their property and power. But the force of their traditions remained strong. Etsu's large family had decided their daughter's destiny: She was to become a Buddhist priestess. So they despaired of a daughter with curly hair, not straight hair. They also feared that her mind ran away with her like the mind of a boy is allowed to do. If she acted wild or boyish, she could never be suited for the life of a priestess, much less for the duties of a proper wife.

Readers will notice the threads of rebellion, independence, and amazing self-esteem that blossom in such unlikely soil. Etsu fights against the fate that makes women inferior. Yet her autobiography is in no sense feminist, politically astute, or even intended as a model for others to follow. Nonetheless, beneath its charming simplicity, we see the Samurai warrior emerging. I take from it a sense of a woman skilled in courtesies, who finds deep meaning in duty done and in surprising ways of living her life with independence and integrity. Always obedient, graceful, and loving, Etsu finds some astonishing avenues of resistance and achievement.

We notice also the delicacy and tact she uses in describing her feelings; she treats her thoughts gently, like butterflies or peach blossoms. She is infallibly reticent, courteous under pressure. She has no concern for current events; she offers no statistics or analysis, and she argues no points. Even more telling, she never attributes motives to anyone. One is always left to fill in, to complete her stories with an act of imagination. As she said in one magazine interview,

> Centuries of training have made the Japanese an undemonstrative people, but the repression of the appearance of deep feeling deceives no one, even on the stage. The expressiveness of repression is an art in Japan. . . . The writer does not insult the imagination of his readers by explaining the motive. [1]

Furthermore, a daughter of the Samurai does not cry, complain, or criticize.

Etsu wrote in English, a language she learned only for the purpose of being a better wife. Something about her phrasing, her choice of words, or the images she plants slowly compel our attention. I have the feeling that she would not, could not, have written her autobiography in the Japanese language. Somehow it is English that propels her into revealing the texture of her life. She clearly wants to communicate with people of her adopted country. She also wants to talk about women and men in ways that only her experiences in another land and another language have made open to her.

Apparently, through contacts in New York, Mrs. Sugimoto was encouraged by a newspaper columnist to publish some short stories about her girlhood in

Japan. The first stories she wrote were about her dog whose immortal soul she put in danger, about her childish sadness over her curly hair, and her naive responses to the strange customs of Americans. Later she put them together for the book. I suspect that her publishers patronized her; they thought her quaint, exotic, and utterly charming — a tiny, formal woman in a silk kimono with loose sleeves. Reviewers and readers saw the book as a charming story about the differences between Japanese and American cultures. They saw it as a bridge between two worlds or as revelations about Japanese life rarely viewed. I see a woman's story.

Etsu loved Japan and Japanese traditions. At the same time she quite clearly fell in love with her new country. Vast changes were occurring in both nations at that time. In fact, Japan and the United States were at war with each other during the period in which the book enjoyed its greatest popularity. But Etsu makes no effort to reconcile conflicting emotions, much less warring nations, in her story. She expresses no opinion, engages no controversies, although she was certainly aware of them. Instead, she recounts only what she has seen, heard, and felt in the two countries she loves.

As Etsu's story opens, her older brother has just returned from America where he had been living since he left Japan in disgrace. He had refused at the last minute to marry the bride selected for him. The occasion of his return is his father's death and his reluctant decision to assume family leadership. The family is poor but proud. The palace in which they once lived has burned down. They are forced to sell off land and precious art — even their Samurai swords.

Etsu's mother and grandmother, with the help of all the servants and other relatives, are carefully molding her character and training her in the elaborate standards of etiquette appropriate for a Samurai woman. They are preparing her to live, marry, and die in the codes of courage and courtesy the Samurai followed for so long. Whether as priestess or as wife, she will be sent from her natal home forever. Here is her story.

The Day of the Bird

Brother had been at home a year when the letters from his friend in America began coming more frequently. After each one Grandmother, Brother, and Mother would have long talks, and not all of them were happy ones. In a vague way I sometimes thought these discussions had something to do with me; and one day was a little troubled when a long conference ended by Brother's abruptly coming out of the room with only a short bow that was almost rude. He started swiftly toward the door, then turning, came back and stood by my side, looking steadily at me for a moment. But he went on without saying a word.

Several weeks later a thick, heavy letter came, one with many stamps; and after another talk in Grandmother's room, Brother sent Jiya out with the long lacquer box tied with a cord which I knew held a "rounding letter" for all the relatives. Jiya would wait at each place for it to be read before carrying it on to the next place. That afternoon I noticed Mother was very thoughtful and quiet; and Grandmother sat by her fire-box, silent and stern, with her long, slender pipe in her hand. The tiny bowl held only three puffs, and, after refilling it twice, she always put it away, but she seemed to have forgotten it that day and sat holding it a long time.

The next day there was a meeting of the family council.

It has always been a Japanese custom to decide important family problems by calling an assembly of the older relatives. There had been family councils ever since I could remember, but, being the youngest of the family, and a girl, I was not concerned in them, and I never gave more than a passing thought as to whether this time it would mean the selling of another piece of land or of one of our roll pictures. We had been selling things all my life. Sister and I were so accustomed to seeing the second-hand man go into the big plaster storehouse with old Jiya that we made a practice of playing a guessing game as to whether he would come out with a small package in his hand or a big bundle on his shoulders. Mother used to look troubled when a group of men came to look at things, but Father would laugh and say, "Useless beauty had a place in the old life, but the new asks only for ugly usefulness."

But one thing Father never laughed about. Whenever negotiations were pending in regard to land he was always watchful. The outside limits of our once large estate had gradually been withdrawn within the wall, and year by year they were closing in nearer to the house; but Father would never part with any portion of the garden overlooked by Grandmother's room. After his death, Brother was equally considerate; so as long as she lived, Grandmother could gaze out upon the garden, the stream, and the little slope of azaleas against the background of feathery bamboo just as she had done for years.

This family council was the largest that had been held since Father's death. Two gray-haired uncles were there with the aunts, besides two other aunts, and a young uncle who had come all the way from Tokyo on purpose for this meeting. They had been in the room a long time, and I was busy writing at my desk when I heard a soft "Allow me to speak!" behind me, and there was Toshi at the door, looking rather excited.

"Little Mistress," she said with an unusually deep bow, "your honourable mother asks you to go to the room where the guests are."

I entered the big room. Brother was sitting by the *tokonoma* [the sacred space in the formal living room], and next to him were two gray-haired uncles and the young uncle from Tokyo. Opposite sat Honourable Grandmother, the four aunts, and Mother. Tea had been served and all had cups before them or in their hands. As I pushed back the door they looked up and gazed at me as if they had never seen me before. I was a little startled, but of course I made a low, ceremonious bow. Mother motioned to me, and I slipped over beside her on the mat.

"Etsu-ko," Mother said very gently, "the gods have been kind to you, and your destiny as a bride has been decided. Your honourable brother and your venerable kindred have given much thought to your future. It is proper that you should express your gratitude to the Honourable All."

I made a long, low bow, touching my forehead to the floor. Then I went out and returned to my desk and my writing. I had no thought of asking, "Who is it?" I did not think of my engagement as a personal matter at all. It was a family affair. Like every Japanese girl, I had known from babyhood that sometime, as a matter of course, I should marry, but that was a faraway necessity to be considered when the time came. I did not look forward to it. I did not dread it. I did not think of it at all. The fact that I was not quite thirteen had nothing to do with it. That was the attitude of all girls.

The formal ceremony of the betrothal took place some months later. It was not an elaborate affair, like a wedding, but was very important; for in old-fashioned families the betrothal was considered as sacred as the marriage itself, and indeed it could not be nearly so easily broken as might be the marriage tie.

There was an air of quiet excitement in the whole house that day. The servants, who always felt a personal interest in everything that happened in the family, had hung weather dolls of folded paper on the *nanten* bush near the porch, to insure sunshine, and were jubilant over the result; and even Mother, who always seemed more calm when she was excited, went around giving unnecessary directions to various maids. "Be careful in powdering Etsu-ko Sama's face," I heard her say to Ishi. "Get the paint smooth." And when the hairdresser arrived Mother made a second trip to the room to give a special order that Etsu-ko Sama's hair must be pulled *straight*.

As soon as I was dressed, I went to Grandmother's room for morning greetings. Her kindly smile was more gentle than usual, and we had a pleasant talk before breakfast was announced. As we were leaving the room, she reminded me that it was the Day of the Bird.

"Yes, I know," I said. "A betrothal ceremony always takes place on the Day of the Bird. Honourable Grandmother, why is it?"

"Be not ambitious to be vain!" she said, smiling and resting her arm on my shoulder as we walked down the porch. "This day was chosen by your relatives with the kind wish that good fortune will bless your life with silks and brocades as plentiful as are the feathers of the birds."

Matsuo's aged uncle, Mr. Omori, had arrived from Kyoto a few days before and had been entertained at the home of the go-between. The ceremony had to take place in the waxing rather than the waning of the day; so about the middle of the forenoon, when I went into the best room, I found the others already assembled. Matsuo's uncle was seated on a cushion near the tokonoma. He sat very straight and had a pleasant face. I liked him. Grandmother, Brother, Mother, and the two go-betweens were there, and I sat beside Mother. The woman go-between brought me a small white table with a square of crepe over it, on which was Matsuo's crest. It was the engagement gift from his family, and I was looking for the first time upon the crest that I should have to wear all my life; but I did not seriously realize it. Another tray held other gifts, the most important of which was a pair of folding fans, signifying a wish for constantly widening happiness.

Then Toshi brought into the room two trays and set them before Mr. Omori. It was my family's gift to Matsuo.

Of course, I had been told exactly what to do; so I lifted the square of crepe from my table, displaying a roll of magnificent brocade for a sash. On Mr. Omori's tables were the essential pair of fans and a wide-pleated silk skirt call *hakama* — the regulation dress for a Japanese gentleman. These have been the betrothal gifts from time immemorial.

I bowed most formal thanks, and Mr. Omori did the same. Then the gifts were placed on the tokonoma and everybody, even Grandmother, made a slight bow and murmured, "Congratulations!"

Soon after, the maids brought the small tables for our dinner, placing those for the gentlemen on one side of the room and those for the ladies on the other. Then Toshi, with her tray, took her place in the open space at the end of the two lines, each person made a slight bow, and the dinner commenced. The conversation was general and the guests seemed to have a pleasant time, but, of course, I was very quiet and dignified.

The most interesting part of the day to me came after everyone had gone and Ishi was taking off my dress. She eyed my head very closely. "*Maa! Maa!* Etsu-bo Sama," she said. "It was such luck that today was cold and dry. Your hair has not one bit of a crinkle!"

For once my unruly hair had not disgraced my family, and giving a sigh of relief, I placed my head carefully upon my little wooden pillow and went contentedly to sleep.

After my betrothal my life was a sort of make-believe game, for my education as a wife began that very day. I had already received the usual training in cooking, sewing, and various household duties, as well as flower arranging, tea serving, and other womanly accomplishments; but now I had to put these things into practice as if I were already in my husband's home. I was expected to select without assistance the proper flowers, the suitable roll picture and tokonoma ornament, and see that the house was always arranged according to certain established rules.

Every moment my life was filled with training and preparation. The object was not explained to me, for this education was a taken-for-granted part of every betrothal; and it happened in my case that no special explanation was necessary other than that I had to be careful not in any way to show disrespect to wood-sorrel since Matsuo's crest was conventionalized wood-sorrel. Except that I had to learn to like tuna, which was a favourite dish of Matsuo's and which I never cared for, my diet was not affected at all by my betrothal. Sister had a long training, for she had been betrothed five years, including the year of postponement on account of Father's death. As her expected husband's crest was conventionalized plum, she never, during the five years, tasted plum, even in jelly. It would have been disrespectful.

The hardest thing I did that year was to learn how to make a sleeping cushion. I loved to sew and was rather skillful with the needle, but I had never made anything by myself. Ishi or Toshi had always helped me. But every Japanese housewife had to know how to make cushions, for they were our chairs and our beds; so Mother said that I must make a sleeping-cushion entirely alone. This was a difficult thing for anyone to do, and my sleeves were wet with foolish tears when for the fourth time I pulled out the threads and turned the immense cushions inside out, in order to refit the corners, which, in spite of my persistent efforts, *would* stay twisted.

Another of my duties was the preparation, on anniversaries and at festival times, of a shadow table for my absent fiance. On these days I myself cooked the food which Brother told us Matsuo especially liked. His table was placed next to mine and I arranged for it to be always served before my own. Thus I learned to be watchful for the comfort of my prospective husband. Grandmother and Mother always spoke as if Matsuo were present, and I was as careful of my dress and conduct as if he had really been in the room. Thus I grew to respect him and to respect my own position as his wife.

During these months Mother and I came closer to each other than we had ever been before. She did not confide in me — that was not Mother's way — but it seemed that an invisible cord of sympathy was drawing our hearts together. I had always greatly admired my mother, but there was a little awe mixed with my admiration. Father had been my comrade and my friend as well as my wise adviser; and my whole heart was filled with tender love for my dear, patient, unselfish Ishi. But Mother was aloft, like the sun, flawless and steady, filling the home with life-giving warmth, yet too far away to be treated familiarly. So I was surprised one day, when she came quietly to my room and told me there was something she wanted to speak to me about before she told Grandmother. Our house had received word from the go-between that Matsuo had removed to a city in the eastern part of America, and had gone into business for himself. On this account he had decided not to return to Japan for several years, and asked that I be sent to him there.

Mother always accepted inevitable circumstances with calm resignation, but this was a very unusual and puzzling situation. For generations Japanese mothers, believing that the destined home for every girl is settled by the gods, have sent their daughters as brides to distant provinces; so my going to America was not a matter of deep concern. But for a bride to go into a home where there was neither mother-in-law nor an elder sister of wisdom-age to train her in the ways of the new household, was a serious problem. And this was not a case that could be referred to the family council; for I was as much bound to Matsuo as if I were already married, and in his affairs the Inagaki family had no authority. In this strange situation Mother turned to me, and for the first time in my life I was consulted in a family matter. I think I changed from girl to woman in the hour of conversation with my mother.

We decided that, at least for the present, there was but one problem for us to face. That was how to prepare for an unknown life in a strange land. In this my relatives could take no part. Of course, all were excited and each one volunteered advice; but the only practical suggestion came from Brother. He said that I must have an English education. That meant that I should have to be sent to school in Tokyo.

All that winter the household was busy getting me ready for school. The pathos of these preparations I did not realize; nor, I think, did any of us. Mother spent evening after evening bending her stately head over wonderful embroidered garments, ripping out, stitch by stitch, the exquisite work of hands folded in rest generations ago. Then Ishi would dye the silk and make it into plain garments suitable for my school life.

And many things were sold. Grandmother and Mother consented to any sacrifice, though sometimes their faces were sad; but Brother seemed to have lost all feeling for the precious old belongings and would part with them without one expression of regret.

"Treasures are a useless care," he often said. "In a poor house like ours there is no need to keep dozens of chests of retainers' armor. They had their place in the past, but hereafter the sons of our ancestors must fight on the battlefield of commerce. Business is the key to wealth, and in this new world wealth is the only power."

I thought little of it then, but now it aches me to remember the sword-hilt ornaments of exquisite workmanship in gold and silver and bronze that were sold for almost nothing; and I can see, even now, how the great scales of the dealer in old iron tipped heavily with the weight of swords that once were the pride of our humblest retainers.

One cold evening I went into Grandmother's room and snuggled down beside her cushion, close to the fire-box, just as I used to do in the days which were beginning to seem to me far in the past. We had grown somewhat apart that year. I was no longer the little child she could make happy with sweets, could train in politeness and teach useful lessons by means of airy lore; and I felt that, much as she loved me, the new conditions that my future faced were beyond her old-fashioned comprehension. But I learned that night, while I talked with her, that samurai training will prepare one for any future.

As we sat in the quiet room, lighted only by the soft glow of the charcoal fire, she told me how, that very day sixty years before, she, as a bride, had left her home in a distant province to come to her husband in Nagaoka. Most brides of her rank visited their homes each year in long processions of grandeur, but, though messengers were sent with inquiries and gifts every New Year and summer-festival season, Grandmother never, after she entered the marriage palanquin, saw her home or her people again. In those days of slow travel, distance was counted by time rather than miles, and hers was a long trip. She left home on the night of a full moon, and another full moon was in the sky when she was carried through the entrance gate of her husband's home.

"I was just your age — fourteen," she said, "and sometimes as the procession passed through strange provinces, climbing over mountains and crossing wide rivers, I wondered many things. It was farther than Kyoto that I came, and at the gateway of each province there were long waits while the officials of the procession exchanged papers and received permission for us to pass. At these times my nurse always came and remained beside my palanquin, and the spear-retainers and 'six-shoulders' of coolie carriers were with us; so I did not fear. But the world seemed very strange and large to me. And the people I came to live among were very different from my own. The customs were new; even the language had an accent and idioms that seemed peculiar. It was like a foreign land. And so, of late, I have thought much of you and the unknown country to which your fate is taking you. Remember, Etsu-bo," and her voice was strangely tender, "where you live is a small matter. The life of a samurai, man or woman, is just the same: loyalty to the overlord; bravery in defence of his honour. In your distant, destined home, remember Grandmother's words: loyalty to your husband; bravery in defence of his honour. It will bring you peace."

How I Became a Christian

In my Nagaoka home, notwithstanding the love and care that surrounded me, my mind was always filled with unanswered questions. My education as a priestess had developed my mind, but it had grown in cramped silence; for, liberal as was my father in his views regarding my training, I was influenced by the home atmosphere of conservatism, and rarely spoke, even to him, of my inmost thoughts.

But occasionally this reserve was broken. Once, just after I had made many bows of farewell to the departing guests of the three-hundredth death celebration of an investor, I asked:

"Honourable Father, who is the first, the away-back, the very beginning of our ancestors?"

"Little Daughter," Father gravely answered, "that is a presumptuous question for a well-bred girl to ask; but I will be honest and tell you that I do not know. Our great Confucius replied to his disciple concerning that very question, 'We know not life.'"

I was very young, but I well understood that I must in the future be more demure and womanly in my inquiries, and not ask questions with the freedom of a boy.

The influence of my school life in Tokyo had been subtle. Unconsciously I had expanded, until gradually I became convinced that asking questions was only a part of normal development. Then, for the first time in my life, I attempted to put into words some of the secret thoughts of my heart. This was gently encouraged by my tactful teachers; and, as time passed on, I realized more and more that they were wonderfully wise for women, and my confidence in them grew. Not only this, but their effortless influence to inspire happiness changed my entire outlook on life. My childhood had been happy, but it had never known one throb of what may be called joyousness. I used to gaze at the full moon sailing in the deep sky, with all the poetic ecstasy of the Japanese heart, but always, like a shadow, came the thought, "It will grow less from tonight." Our flower viewings were a delight to me, but invariably, as I travelled homeward, I sighed to myself: "The lovely blossoms will fall before the winds of tomorrow." So it was with everything. In the midst of gladness I unconsciously sent out a heart search for a thread of sadness. I ascribe this morbid tendency to the Buddhist teaching of my childhood; for there is a strain of hopeless sadness in all Buddhist thought.

But my life at school blew into my heart a breath of healthful cheerfulness. As the restraint which had held me like a vise began to relax, so also there melted within me the tendency to melancholy. It could not be otherwise; for the teachers, whether working, playing, laughing, or even reproving, were a continual surprise.

In my home, surprises had been infrequent. People bowed, walked, talked, and smiled exactly as they had bowed, walked, talked, and smiled yesterday, and the day before, and in all past time. But these astonishing teachers were never the same. They changed me so unexpectedly in voice and manner with each person to whom they spoke, that their very changeableness was a refreshing attraction. They reminded me of cherry blossoms.

Japanese people love flowers for what they mean. I was taught from baby-hood that the plum, bravely pushing its blossoms through the snows of early spring, is our bridal flower because it is an emblem of duty through hardship. The cherry is beautiful and it never fades, for the lightest breeze scatters the still fresh and fragrant petals into another beauty of tinted, floating clouds; which again changes to a carpet of delicate, white-and-pink shells — like my teachers, always changing and always beautiful.

Although I now know that my first impressions of American womanhood were exaggerated, I have never regretted this idealization; for through it I came to realize the tragic truth that the Japanese woman — like the plum blossom, mod-est, gentle, and bearing unjust hardship without complaint — is often little else than a useless sacrifice; while the American woman — self-respecting, untram-melled, changing with quick adaptability to new conditions — carries inspiration to every heart, because her life, like the blossom of the cherry, blooms in freedom and naturalness.

This realization was of slow growth, and it brought with it much silent questioning.

From childhood I had known, as did all Japanese people, that woman is greatly inferior to man. This I never questioned. It was fate. But as I grew older I so constantly saw that fate brings inconveniences and humiliation to blameless people that I fell into a habit of puzzling, in a crude, childish way, over this great unkind Power. At last a day came when my heart broke into open rebellion.

Ever since the hard days before the Restoration, my mother had been subject to occasional attacks of asthma, which we all were sincere in believing was due to some unknown wrong committed by her in a previous existence. Once when, after a breathless struggle, I heard her gasp, "It is fate and must be borne," I ran to Ishi and asked indignantly why fate made my mother suffer.

"It cannot be helped," she replied, with pitying tears in her eyes. "It is because of the unworthiness of woman. But you must be calm, Etsu-bo Sama. The Hon-ourable Mistress does not complain. She is proud to bear silently."

I was too young to understand, but with my heart pounding in hot rebellion against the powerful, mysterious injustice, I pulled myself into Ishi's lap and, con-vulsively clinging to her, begged her to tell me a story — quick — of clashing swords, and flying arrows, and heroes who fought and won.

Japanese children were not taught that rebellious thoughts, if unexpressed, are a wrong to the gods, so the resentment in my heart grew. But as it grew, there slowly drifted into, and curiously blended with it, a blind wonder why my mother and Ishi, when hardship came for which they were not to blame, should submit to it, not only dutifully and patiently — that, of course, it was their place, as women, to do — but with pride. Something within me cried out that, however dutiful they might be in act, their *hearts* ought to rebel; yet I had known both unnecessarily to accept a humiliating blame that they knew was not theirs! That those two noble women should encourage self-humiliation I resented more bitterly than I did the hard decrees of fate.

Of course, this thought was not clear in my mind at that time. Then and for years after, my idea of fate — for in fate I firmly believed — was of a vague, floating, stupendous power, for which I felt only resentful wonder.

Beyond the wall on the one side of our school was a rough path leading past several small villages, with ricefields and patches of clover scattered between. One day, when a teacher was taking a group of us girls for a walk, we came upon a ricefield dotted with wild flowers. We were gathering them with merry chattering and laughter when two village farmers passed by, walking slowly and watching us curiously.

"What is the world coming to," said one, "when workable-age young misses waste time wandering about through bushes and wild grass!"

"They are grasshoppers trying to climb the mountain," the other replied, "but the sun will scorch them with scorn. There can be only pity for the young man who takes one of those for his bride."

The men were rough and ignorant, but they were *men*; and though we all laughed, not one of the girls was far enough from the shackles of her mother's day not to feel a shadow of discomfort as we walked homeward.

The teacher paused as we came to the moss-covered stone wall of an old shrine and pointed to a nearby cherry tree, young and thrifty, growing out of the hollow of another tree whose fallen trunk was so old and twisted that it looked like a rough-scaled dragon. Beside it was one of the wooden standards so often seen in an artistic or noted spot. On the tablet was inscribed the poem:

The blossoms of to-day draw strength
from the roots of a thousand years ago.

"This tree is like you girls," said the teacher, with a smile. "Japan's beautiful old civilization has given its strength to you young women of today. Now it is your duty to grow bravely and give to new Japan, in return, a greater strength and beauty than even the old possessed. Do not forget!"

We walked on homeward. Just as we reached our gate in the hedge wall one of the girls, who had been rather quiet, turned to me.

"Nevertheless," she said, defiantly, "the grasshoppers *are* climbing the mountain into the sunlight."

As I learned to value womanhood, I realized more and more that my love of freedom and my belief in my right to grow toward it meant more than freedom to act, to talk, to think. Freedom also claimed a *spiritual* right to grow.

I do not know exactly how I became a Christian. It was not a sudden thing. It seems to have been a natural spiritual development — so natural that only a few puzzles stand out clearly as I look back along the path. As I read, and thought, and felt, my soul reached out into the unknown; and gradually, easily, almost unconsciously, I drifted out of a faith of philosophy, mysticism, and resignation into one of high ideals, freedom, cheerfulness, and hope.

Of the wonder and glory of what I consider the greatest faith of the world I do not speak. Of that many know. And the selfish gain to me is beyond all words of languages.

When I was sent to the mission school, the fact that the teachers were of another religion was not considered at all. They were thought of only as teachers of the language and manners of America; so when I wrote to Mother, asking her consent to my becoming a Christian, I know she was greatly surprised. But she was a wise woman. She replied, "My daughter, this is an important thing. I think it will be best for you to wait until vacation. Then we will talk of it."

So I postponed being baptized, and when vacations came, I went to Nagaoka. The people there knew little of Christianity. The only impression most of them had was that it was a curious belief lacking in ceremony, whose converts were required to trample upon sacred things. The people of Nagaoka looked upon the stories of Japan's Christian martyrs as a distant and pitiful thing; but they had none of the shuddering horror felt in some communities of southern Japan, whose memories of the tragedies of four centuries ago had reason to live.

My mother, who had learned from Father to be tolerant of the opinions of others, had no prejudice against the new religion; but she believed that the great duty in life for sons and daughters consisted in rigid observance of the ritual for ancestor-worship and the ceremonies in memory of the dead. When I first reached home her heart was heavy with dread, but when she learned that my new faith did not require disrespect to ancestors, her relief and gratitude were pathetic, and she readily gave her consent.

But Honourable Grandmother! My proud, loyal grandmother! It was impossible for her to understand, and I think my becoming a heretic was to her a lifelong sorrow. Her grief was my heaviest cross.

It was hard, too, to visit my relatives and friends. They looked upon me as a curiosity, and my mother was in a continual state of explanation and apology. One old aunt closed the doors of her shrine and pasted white paper over them that the ancestors might be spared the knowledge of my "peculiarity."

Another aunt, who invited me out to dinner, served no fish, feeling that, since I was so puzzlingly removed from ordinary life, I could not be feasted in the usual way. After discarding one plan after another, she finally concluded it would be both harmless and respectful for her to treat me as a priest.

All these things among the friends I had known from babyhood hurt me. I could bravely have borne persecution, but to be set apart as something strange almost broke my heart. How I longed for my father! He would have understood, but I was alone in the midst of kindly ignorance. Everybody loved me, but they all looked at me in helpless pity.

At first I was unhappy, but my three months at home changed everything, both for my friends and for myself. When I returned to school I carried with me all the respect and love of the home friends that had always been mine, and which — thank God — I have kept until now.

I think I am a true Christian. At least my belief has given me untold comfort and a perfect heart-satisfaction, but it has never separated me from by Buddhist friends. They have respect for this strange belief of mine; for they feel that, although I am loyal to the Christian God, I still keep the utmost reverence for my fathers and respect for the faith that was the highest and holiest thing they knew.

[For six years, Etsu prepares for her marriage to a man she has not yet met. Meanwhile, she is linked to networks of American Christians who help at each stage as she makes her way across the world. A woman named Mrs. Wilson had written to Etsu's mother: Never worry about your daughter in a distant land. We will care for her. Etsu's mother kept this tear-marked letter on the family shrine for years. In fact, Mrs. Wilson introduced the couple to another American woman, a widow, who offered to take Etsu and Matsuo into her home. This woman, never named, becomes Etsu's adopted mother and American sponsor. The newlyweds move into her home and treat her with the respect owed to their mothers still in Japan. It is clear from the text which of her mothers Etsu refers to. So here we pick up the story as she meets and marries Matsuo. Please note, her autobiography makes no more comments about any of their private moments or personal feelings than those included here.]

Sailing Unknown Seas

When I was whirled into the dusky station of the city of my destination, I peered rather curiously from the car window. I was not anxious. I had always been taken care of, and it did not trouble me that I was to meet one I had never known before. On the crowded platform I saw a young Japanese man, erect, alert, watching eagerly each person who stepped from the train. It was Matsuo. He wore a gray suit and a straw hat, and to me looked modern, progressive, foreign in everything except his face. Of course, he knew who I was at once, but to my astonishment, his first words were, "Why did you wear Japanese dress?" There flashed into my mind a picture of the grave faces of the family council and my grandmother's words regarding pipe-sleeves. Yet here was I in a land of pipe-sleeves, gazing on my future husband, a pipe-sleeved man. I laugh about it now, but then I was only a lonely, loose-sleeved, reproved little girl. . . .

For ten restful days I was made welcome in that beautiful home [the Wilson's]; then came the second of *"The Three Inevitables"* — for, in Old Japan, marriage held its place equally with birth and death. My wedding took place on a beautiful day in June. The sun shone, the soft wind murmured through the branches of the grand old trees on the lawn, the reception room, with its treasures of art gathered from all lands, was fragrant with blossoms, and before a wonderful inlaid console table were two crossed flags — American and Japanese. There Matsuo and Etsu stood while the Christian words were spoken which made them one. By Matsuo's side was his business partner, a good kind man, and beside me stood one who ever since has proved my best and truest friend. So we were married. Everyone said it was a beautiful wedding. To me the room was filled with a blur of strange things and people, all throbbing with the spirit of a great kindness; and vaguely, mistily, I realized that there had been fulfilled a sacred vow that the gods had made long before I was born.

Strange Customs

One thing in America, to which I could not grow accustomed, was the joking attitude in regard to women and money. From men and women of all classes, from newspapers, novels, lecturers, and once even from the pulpit, I heard allusions to amusing stories of women secreting money in odd places, coaxing it from their husbands, borrowing it from a friend, or saving it secretly for some private purpose. There was never anything dishonourable implied in this. Perhaps the money was saved to get new curtains for the parlour, or even a birthday present for the husband. These jokes were a puzzle to me — and a constantly growing one; for as time passed on, I myself saw things which made me realize that probably a foundation of serious truth might lie beneath some of the amusing stories.

Our suburb was small and we were all interested in each other's affairs, so I was acquainted with almost everybody. I knew the ladies to be women of education and culture, yet there seemed to be among them a universal and openly confessed lack of responsibility about money. They all dressed well and seemed to have money for specific purposes, but no open purse to use with free and responsible judgment. Once, at a church fair, where I had a table, several ladies, after walking around the hall and examining the various booths, had bought some small, cheap articles, but left the expensive ones, saying, "My husband will be here later on and I'll get him to buy it," or "When the gentlemen come those high-priced things will sell." I had never known a Japanese man to buy anything for his home, or be expected to.

Once, when I was shopping with a friend, she stopped at her husband's office to ask him for money. I thought that was strange enough, but a still more curious thing happened when I went with Mother to a meeting of the church ladies where they were raising a certain amount for some unusual purpose. The Ladies' Aid had recently made a great many calls on the husbands' purses, and so this time each member had pledged herself to bring five dollars which she must obtain without asking her husband for it. The meeting I attended was the one where the money was handed in, each lady telling, as she gave it, how she had succeeded in getting her five dollars. Most had saved it in various ways, a little at a time. One said that she had made a real sacrifice and returned to her milliner a new hat — paid for, but not worn — receiving in exchange one that was five dollars less in price. Another had sold two theatre tickets which had been given her. Still another told, in very witty rhyme, how she, a poor Ladies' Aid lady, had spent most of her leisure time for a week and had pledged herself for a week longer, in darning stockings for the children of her neighbor, a rich non-Ladies' Aid lady.

The meeting was intensely interesting. It reminded me of our poem-making parties, only of course this was gayer and these stories were on an undignified subject. I enjoyed it all until a pretty, bright, and beautifully dressed woman rose and said that she didn't know how to save money and she didn't know how to earn it. She had promised not to cheat in her charge account at the store, and she had promised not to ask her husband for the five dollars, so she had done the only thing that was left for her to do: She had stolen it from her husband's pocket when he was asleep.

This report caused a great deal of merriment, but I was saddened. All the reports seemed tragic after she said, "That was the only thing left to do." It seemed incredible, here in America, where women are free and commanding, that a woman of dignity and culture, the mistress of a home, the mother of children, should be forced to either ask her husband for money, or be placed in a humiliating position.

When I left home, Japan, at large, was still following the old custom of educating a girl to be responsible for the well-being of her entire family — husband included. The husband was the lord of the family; but the wife was mistress of the home and, according to her own judgment, controlled all its expenses — the house, the food, the children's clothing and education; all social and charitable responsibilities, and her own dress, the material and style of which were expected to conform to her husband's position.

Where did she get the money? The husband's income was for his family, and his wife was the banker. When he wanted money for himself he asked her for it, and it was her pride to manage so that she could allow him the amount suitable for a man of his standing. As to what the requirements of his position might be, there was little question, for to know this was part of the wife's education. The husband might shrug his shoulders and say, "It's very inconvenient," but the entire house and its standing were his pride, and any disarrangement that would mar the whole was his loss. Therefore the needs of the home came first. A man married, primarily, as a duty to the gods and to his ancestors; secondarily, to obtain a mistress for his home who would guide it in such a manner that it and his family might be a credit to him. If she managed well, he was complimented by his friends. If she failed, he was pitied.

This was true of all classes except lords of large estates or financial kings of business. In these cases there was a home treasurer, but he was at the call of the mistress, and her judgment as to her needs was supreme. The treasurer's only power of protest lay in the right to say, with many apologies, "The Honourable Mistress is about to overdraw her account." The hint was generally sufficient, for a Japanese woman, like everyone in a responsible position, desired to do her duty creditably.

The standards of my own and my adopted country differed so widely in some ways, and my love for both lands was so sincere, that sometimes I had an odd feeling of standing upon a cloud in space, and gazing with measuring eyes upon two separate worlds. At first I was continually trying to explain, by Japanese standards, all the queer things that came every day before my surprised eyes; for no one seemed to know the origin or significance of even the most familiar customs, nor why they existed and were followed. To me, coming from a land where there is an unforgotten reason for every fashion of dress, for every motion in etiquette — indeed, for almost every trivial act of life — this indifference of Americans seemed very singular.

Mother's furniture, which was of beautiful wood and some of it carved, at first made me feel as if I were in a museum; but when I went into other homes, I found that none were simple and plain. Many reminded me of *godowns* [storage houses], so crowded were they with, not only chairs, tables, and pictures, but numbers of little things — small statues, empty vases, shells, and framed photographs, as well as really rare and costly ornaments; all scattered about with utter disregard, according to Japanese standards, of order or appropriateness. It was several months before I could overcome the impression that the disarranged profusion of articles was a temporary convenience, and that very soon they would be returned to the godown. Most of these objects were beautiful, but some of them were the shape of a shoe or of the sole of the foot. This seemed to be a favourite design, or else my unwilling eyes always spied it out, for in almost every house I entered I would see it in a paperweight, a vase, or some other small article. Once I even saw a little wooden shoe used as a holder for toothpicks.

Generations of prejudice made this very objectionable to me, for in Japan the feet are the least honoured part of the body; and the most beautiful or costly gift would lose all value if it had the shape of footwear.

And Japanese curios! They were everywhere, and in the most astonishingly inappropriate surroundings. Lunch boxes and rice-bowls on parlour tables, cheap roll pictures hanging on elegant walls, shrine gongs used for dining-room table bells; sword-guards for paperweights; ink-boxes for handkerchiefs and letter-boxes for gloves; marriage-cups for pin-trays, and even little bamboo spittoons I have seen used to hold flowers.

In time my stubborn mind learned, to some extent, to separate an article from its surroundings; and then I began to see its artistic worth with the eyes of an American. Also I acquired the habit, whenever I saw absurd things here which evidently arose from little knowledge of Japan, of trying to recall similar absurdity in Japan regarding foreign things. And I never failed to find more than one to offset each single instance here. One time a recollection was forced upon me by an innocent question from a young lady who told me, in a tone of disbelief, that she had heard in a lecture on Japan that elegantly dressed Japanese ladies sometimes wore ordinary, cheap chenille table covers around their shoulders in place of scarfs. I could only laugh and acknowledge that, a few years before, that had been a popular fashion. Imported articles were rare and expensive, and since we never used table covers ourselves, we had no thought of their being anything but beautiful shawls.

New Experiences

January brought to Matsuo and me a quiet celebration of our own. For weeks before, the letters from Japan had been coming more frequently, and occasionally the postman would hand in a package wrapped in oil-paper and sealed with the oval stamp of Uncle Otani's house, or the big square one of Inagaki.

One of these packages contained a thin sash of soft white cotton, each end of which had been dipped in rouge, and also two emblems of congratulation — baby storks of rice-dough, one white and one red.

These were Mother's gifts for the "Five-month ceremony," a special celebration observed by expectant parents on that date. My thoughtful, loving, faraway mother! The tears came to my eyes as I explained it all to my dear American mother, who in sweet understanding of the sacred ceremony asked how to prepare everything according to Japanese custom.

At this celebration, besides the husband and wife, only women members of the two families are present. The young father-to-be sits beside his wife and the sash is passed through the sleeves of his garment from left to right. Then it is properly adjusted around the wife. From then on, she is called "a lady of retirement," and her food, exercise, amusements, and reading are all of a character called "education of Coming." The gay, light balls of many-coloured silk thread which are seen in American shops belong to this time.

In the package with the sash was a charm-card from my good Ishi. To obtain it she had made a pilgrimage of two days to the temple of Kishibo-jin — "Demon of the Mother-heart" — believing sincerely that the bit of paper with its mysterious symbols would protect me from every evil.

These recollections flooded my mind as I sat stitching on dainty, wee garments into every one of which I breathed a prayer that my baby might be a boy. I wanted a son, not only because every Japanese family believes it most desirable that the name should be carried on without adoption, but also for the selfish reason that both Matsuo's family and my own would look upon me with more pride were I the mother of a son. Neither Matsuo nor I had, to any great extent, the feeling that woman is inferior to man, which has been so common a belief among all classes in Japan; but law and custom being what they were, it was such a serious inconvenience — yes, calamity — to have *no* son, that congratulations always fell more readily from the lips when the first-born was a boy.

Little girls were always welcome in Japanese homes. Indeed, it was a great sorrow to have all sons and no daughter — a calamity second only to having all daughters and no son.

And then the baby came — well and sweet and strong — upholding in her perfect babyhood the traditions of both America and Japan. I forgot that I had ever wanted a son, and Matsuo, after his first glimpse of his little daughter, remembered that he had always liked girls better than boys.

Whether the paper charm of Kishibo-jin was of value or not, my good Ishi's loving thought for me was a boon to my heart during those first weeks when I so longed for her wisdom and her love. And yet it was well that she was not with me, for she could never have fitted into our American life. The gentle, time-taking ways of a Japanese nurse crooning to a little bundle of crepe and brocade swinging in a hammock on her back would never have done for my active baby, who so soon learned to crow with delight and clutch disrespectfully at her father's head as he tossed her aloft in his strong arms.

We decided to bring the baby up with all the healthful freedom given to an American child, but we wanted her to have a Japanese name. The meaning of Matsuo's name was "pine" — the emblem of strength; mine was "ricefield" — the emblem of usefulness. "Therefore," said Matsuo, "the baby is already a combination of strength and usefulness, but she must have beauty also. So, let us give her the name of our kind American mother, which translated, means 'flower.'"

"And if we use the old-fashioned termination [word ending]," I cried with delight, "it will mean 'foreign fields' or 'strange land.'"

"Hanano — Flower in a Strange Land!" cried Matsuo, clapping his hands. "Nothing could be better."

Mother consented, and thus it was decided.

Flower in a Strange Land

There is a saying in Japan, "Only the fingers of a babe can tie a uniting knot that will pull two families together." As the Japanese marriage is not an affair of individuals I had never applied the saying to Matsuo and myself, but one day some Mysterious Power twisted this bit of truth into an incident that played an unsuspected and important part in my life and in that of my husband. Matsuo was a man who had always been vitally interested in his business. I think that, before the baby came, there had been nothing in his life to which it was second. He and I were very good friends, but we seldom talked freely to each other except in the presence of others. Indeed, we had no common topic of conversation; for he was interested in his own plans, and my mind was taken up with my home and with my new friends. But from the day the baby came, everything changed. Now we had many things to talk about, and for the first time I began to feel acquainted with my husband.

But always, deep in my heart, was the feeling that the baby was *mine*. I did not trace any likeness to Matsuo; nor did I want to. I do not mean that I objected to her resembling him, but that I never thought of her as really *belonging* to anyone but myself and my own family.

One day when I was in the city I stopped for a few moments at my husband's store. He happened to be busy and I waited in the office. His desk looked to me in great disorder, and right in front, in a wide pigeon-hole, was an odd thing to be in a cluttered-up office. It was a little lacquer box of exquisite workmanship and bearing a crest that is rarely seen outside a museum. I lifted the lid, and there, before my startled eyes, were three strange objects — a green paper whirligig, some little pieces of clay the baby's fingers had pressed into crude shapes, and a collapsed balloon.

I stood still, my heart beating quickly; then I turned away, feeling as if I had taken an unbidden glance into the heart of a stranger. In that moment came the realization that there was another claim on my baby as tender and strong as my own, and with a throb of remorse my heart turned toward my husband with a strange new feeling.

Matsuo was more demonstrative to me than would have been polite had we been living in Japan, but we both respected formality, and it was years before I realized how deep were his feelings for his family.

Chiyo

"Mamma, may I say to God just what I please?" Hanano asked.

"Yes, dear," I replied, but I was startled when, from the little bowed figure with clasped hands, came a sudden, "Hello, God!"

I reached out my hand to check her. Then I remembered that I had always taught her to respect her father next to God, and that was the greeting she used to him when he was too far away to be seen. I softly withdrew my hand. Then again I was startled by the solemn little voice, whispering, "Please give me a little sister like Susan's."

I was too much surprised to speak, and she went on with "Now I lay me," to the end.

As I tucked her into bed, I said, "How did you happen to ask God for a little sister, Hanano?"

"That's how Susan got her sister, " she replied. "She prayed for her a long time, and now she's here."

I went away a little awed, for I knew her prayer would be answered.

The March festival was long past, and May almost gone, when one morning Hanano's father told her that she had a little sister and led her into the room where the baby was. Hanano gazed with wide-open, astonished eyes upon a black-haired, pink-faced little Chiyo. She said not a word but walked straight down the stairs to Grandma.

"I didn't pray for *that*," she told Mother, with a troubled look. "I wanted a baby with yellow hair like Susan's little sister."

Clara happened to be in the room, and with the freedom of an American servant, said, "Yellow hair on a Japanese baby *would* be a funny sight!" and burst out laughing.

"It's *not* a Japanese baby!" Hanano indignantly cried. "I didn't *ask* for a Japanese baby! I *don't* want a Japanese baby!"

Mother took the child on her lap and told her how proud we were to have two little Japanese girls in our home, and so brought a slow comfort to the disappointed little heart.

That afternoon Mother saw Hanano sitting a long time very quietly in front of the big mirror that stood between the two front windows of the parlour.

"What is it you see, dear?" Mother asked.

"I s'pose I'm a Japanese girl, too," Hanano answered slowly. "I don't look like Susan or Alice."

She winked several times very fast then, with a choking gulp, her loyalty to blue eyes and yellow hair succumbed to loyalty to love, and she added, "But Mamma is pretty! I'm going to be like her!" and climbed down from the chair.

No one can sound the depths of a child's thoughts, but from that day Hanano developed an interest in Japanese things. Matsuo was fond of listening to her prattle and of playing with her, but she depended on me for stories; and so, night after night, I would talk of our heroes and repeat to her the songs and fairy lore which had been part of my child life. Best of all she liked to have me talk of the pretty black-haired children — I always said they were pretty — who made chains of cherry blossoms or played games in a garden with a stone lantern and a curving bridge that spanned a pond set in the midst of flowers and tiny trees. I almost grew homesick as I painted these word pictures for her, or sat in the twilight singing a plaintive Japanese lullaby to the baby, while Hanano stood beside me, humming softly beneath her breath.

Was this sudden love for the land she had never seen an inheritance, or — for children sometimes seem to be uncannily endowed with insight — was it premonition?

One day the old familiar world ended for me, leaving me with memories — comforting ones and regretful ones — all closely wrapped in a whirl of anxious, frightened questioning, for no longer had I a husband or my children a father. Matsuo, with a last merry word and a sleepy smile, had quickly and painlessly slipped over the border into the old-new country beyond our ken.

And now, for my children and myself, nothing was left but farewells, and a long, lonely journey. The country that had reached out so pleasant a welcome to me, that had so willingly pardoned my ignorance and my mistakes, the country where my children were born and where I had received kindness greater than words can express — this wonderful, busy, practical country had no need of, nor did it want, anything that I could give. It had been a broad, kindly, loving home for me and mine, but a place for the present only. It held no promise of usefulness for my growing children and had not need of my old age. And what is life if one can only learn, and of what one learns gives nothing?

The past years were like a dream. From a land of misty, poetic ideas I had drifted through a puzzling tangle of practical deeds, gathering valuable thoughts as I floated easily along, and now — back to the land of mist and poesy. What was ahead of me? I wondered.

In Japan Again

When the weary sight of tumbling and tossing waves was past and I was once again in Japan, I found myself in the midst of surroundings almost as strange as those I had met when I landed in America.

The provinces and classes in Japan had for so many centuries held steadfast, each to its own customs, that even yet there were only occasional evidences to be seen of their slow yielding to the equalizing influences of modern life; and I had gone at once to Matsuo's home in western Japan, where standards of dress and etiquette, ideas, and even idioms of speech were entirely different from those of either Nagaoka or Tokyo.

We were met on our arrival by a crowd of Matsuo's relatives, all in ceremonial dress, for we had brought the sacred ashes with us; and from then until the forty-nine days of ceremonies for the dead were over, I was treated as an honoured messenger-guest. After that my position was very humble, for a son's widow is an unimportant person in Japan, and, virtually, that is what I was, Matsuo having been, until he decided to remain in America, the adopted son of Uncle Otani.

I was very anxious about my girls; for in Japan children belong to the family — not to the parents. Hanano, on the death of her father, had become the head of our little family, but we were only a branch of the main family of which Uncle Otani was the head. So it had been taken for granted by all relatives, my own as well as Matsuo's, that the children and I would make our home with Uncle Otani. He would have made room for me in his handsome house and would have supplied me with beautiful clothes, but I should have had no authority, even over my own children. This might not have been so bad under some circumstances; for Uncle Otani would have been generous in giving the children every advantage that he considered proper for them to have. But with all his kindness — and a kinder man never lived — I could not forget that he belonged to the old-fashioned merchant class that considered education beyond the grammar school undesirable for girls.

The situation was difficult; for, from my humble position, I could not say a word. But I had one hope. Hanano, although legal head of our family, was a minor; and her mother, as present regent, held a certain power. Exerting this, I asked for consultation with Uncle Otani. I explained to him that Matsuo had expressed in his will a desire that, since he had no son, his daughters should receive the liberal education that had been planned for them in America. Then I boldly asked, in Hanano's name and by the power of her father's request, that I should be allowed the privilege of guiding their studies.

Uncle Otani was astonished at such an unheard-of request, but the situation was unusual and a family council was summoned at once. In the case of a consultation concerning a widow, it is customary for her family to be represented; and Brother being unable to be present, Mother sent in his place my progressive Tokyo uncle — the one who had taken so vigorous a part in our council meetings before my marriage. It was necessary for Hanano, as official head of her family, to be present, but of course she was to speak only through me.

Since she had not yet learned to wear Japanese dress properly, I put on her best white dress, trimmed with lace and ruffles. I arranged everything so that it would be very loose; for it is difficult to sit quietly in Japanese fashion while wearing American clothing, and yet it is inexcusably rude at a ceremonial gathering to move — however slightly — the lower part of the body. I explained this to Hanano, and told her how her grandfather, when two years younger than she, had held the seat of state in the formidable political meetings before the Restoration. "Honourable Grandmother told me he always sat very straight and dignified," I said, "and you must be like him." Then we went in to the meeting.

I could not help being uneasy about the way my bold request might be received. To most of the council I was nothing but a widowed dependent of my daughter — a woman with advanced and peculiar notions — and they had the power, if three voices of the council disapproved of me and my ideas, not only to refuse my request, but to separate me from my children entirely. I should be well provided for, in my present home, if I chose, or elsewhere, but the children would remain with their father's people and no law of Heaven or earth was powerful enough in Japan to prevent it. Matsuo's family had no desire to do any unjust thing; nor did I suspect that they had, but — they held the power.

The conference, which was long, consisted of a series of polite suggestions and earnest, but never excited, arguments. I listened with my head bowed, occasionally — but not too often — glancing toward my little anxious-eyed daughter, sitting erect and motionless in the midst of the dignified row of elders. For two hours she did not move. Then one poor, cramped little leg jerked, her fluffy dress spread out, and with a quick catching at her knee, she gasped, "Oh!"

Not a face turned toward her, but with an anguished clutch at my throat I bowed to the floor, saying "I humbly pray the honourable council to pardon the rudeness of my foreign-trained child and permit her to retire with me from the august assembly."

Uncle Otani, without moving, gave a grunt of assent.

As I made my last bow at the sliding door and slipped it back in place, my Tokyo uncle tapped his pipe carefully against the rim of the tobacco box by his side.

"It is fortunate for O Etsu San seems a reliable woman," he said slowly; "for surely it would be a puzzling venture for any of us to take into our family two rough American children with their untrained feet, their flouncing garments, and their abrupt speech."

Whether that remark was intended to be kind or cruel, I never knew; and whether or not it had influence, I never knew; but after another hour of slow, careful, earnest, and perfectly fair discussion, the council decided that on account of Matsuo's request, combined with the fact that his widow appeared to be a trustworthy person, consent was given to a temporary trial of the experiment.

That night I pulled my cushions in between my children's beds — close, close — and crept beneath the covers, faint with relief and gratitude.

[With the approval of the family council, Etsu moved to Tokyo, into a house of her own with relatives and servants from her childhood home. She had to make complicated and unusual arrangements for schooling her children who were Japanese, but raised in America and who spoke English as their first language. The girls were homesick for America; and Etsu says of herself, "I was chained — but I was content."]

Tragic Trifles

Hanano always had been brave about bearing silently little troubles that could not be helped, and she seemed so busy and interested in her new life that I did not realize that deep in her heart was a longing for the old home. Our garden had two entrances, one through the house and one through a little brushwood wicket on the path that led from a wooden gate to the kitchen door. One day, just as I reached home, a sudden shower threatened to drench me. So, instead of going around to the big gateway, I slipped through the wooden gate, and ran across the stones of the garden to the porch. Leaving my shoes on the step I was hurrying to my room when I heard the voices of the children.

"This shady place," said Hanano, "is where Grandma's chair always was, on the porch. And under this tree is where the hammock was where you took your nap and where Papa almost sat down on you that time. And this is the big stone steps where we always had firecrackers on Fourth of July. And this is the well. And this is the drawbridge. And this is the place where Clara went to feed the chickens. It's all exactly right, Chiyo, for I drew it myself, and you must not forget again. Don't tell Mamma, for she would be sorry, and she is our only treasure that we have left. All the rest are gone, Chiyo, and we can never have them again. So it can't be helped, and we just have to stand it. But you mustn't forget that all this — for ever — is where our love is. And now, let us sing."

They stood up, holding hands, and the childish voices rose in a clear, steady "My Country, 'tis of Thee!"

I cried softly as I moved about in the next room and thought of the transplanted morning glories. "Is it right," I wondered, "to plant a little unasked flower in a garden of love and happiness, from which it must soon be wrenched away, only for another, and a dwarfed, start in strange, new surroundings? The garden had much to give of strength and inspiration, but is it worth the cost? Oh, is it worth the cost?" . . .

When Hanano was fifteen, the family council brought up the subject I had been most dreading. According to Japanese custom, when there are only daughters in a family, a son is adopted, who takes the family name and marries the eldest daughter. Thus the name is perpetuated. The question of the selection of a son for me, I had dealt with in as tactful a manner as possible, but after having refused two or three offers, I saw that I was expected to give a positive decision soon.

It is never wise for a Japanese woman, if she wishes to retain a position of influence and dignity, to say much on any subject. Actions, not words, are her most successful means of expression; but the time came when I saw that I must speak. With a letter of wise suggestions from my ever-faithful American mother in my hand, I went before the council and asked to be allowed to take the children back to my former home for a few years more of study. This request caused excited discussions; but I now had friends in the council, both Matsuo's family and of my own, and my past faithful adherence to their wishes brought a glorious reward. Again my petition was granted, and, with my heart weighted with gratitude and my soul singing in joy, I began my preparations to return to America.

❖

Afterword

And there the book ends. As you can see from the sections included here, Etsu's account has a certain timelessness. She is extremely vague about names, times, places, or relationships to external or historical events. So let's put her narrative into a broader perspective. She came to America in 1901 to be married. She returned when her first-born daughter was fifteen years old. She wrote no more about her personal life beyond this point.

In 1920, the post of instructor in Japanese language and history at Columbia University fell vacant when the man who was teaching failed to return. So Etsu began teaching there. She used her own teaching methods and was easily recognized on campus in her Japanese traditional dress. She taught at Columbia University until 1927. At some point she also became a U.S. citizen.

In 1926 *A Daughter of the Samurai* was published. It was widely reviewed both in Asia and in the United States. Immensely popular, it came out in a new edition in 1947. The book was one of the most continuously successful nonfiction books of that entire period. For many American readers, this autobiography was their introduction to Japan as a country and to Japanese as people one could talk to and relate to. Etsu published three other books; all of them are tales of Japanese life, remembered in love, but no longer lived. These books never achieved the extraordinary reach of her autobiography.

I found and read Etsu Sugimoto's book sometime in the 1950s, a schoolgirl in rural Oklahoma. There she was, having adventures, and all the while a dutiful daughter, wife, mother, friend, and patriot. Then, as now, I want to know about her daughters, what caused her husband's death, how she responded to the book's publication, how she lived in two such different cultures simultaneously, and what happened to her family during World War II.

At that time I took many things in her autobiography for granted. Of course she wrote so well in English; what else. Of course she loved America; so did I. Of course, she would somehow have money and resources. Now I see her conversion to Christianity less as inevitable and more as a "coming out" story. I also see that her life may well have been a Japanese equivalent to Victorian England, which has been such a formative influence on our contemporary consciousness. Now I read her beautiful prose, written in her second language, not her first, and marvel at the beauty and the bravery. Each time I hear subtleties, like wind chimes, that I did not hear before. Writing an autobiography is not about answering all the questions we might have; it is about telling entirely different kinds of truth.

Etsu Inagaki Sugimoto died June 20, 1950, at the age of 76. She was at her home in Tokyo, Japan.

For Love of Books

Why does *A Daughter of the Samurai* remind me of *Gone with the Wind*? Perhaps I know deep down that women's lives are often as improbable and compelling as good fiction is. Perhaps I also know that fiction tells its own reality. Once again, there are thousands of great books you could read. Here are only a few suggestions of books that complement Etsu's story and may lead you into writing and reading women's lives.

Not every Japanese woman who moves to America falls in love with her adopted country. Not every Japanese woman who moves to America is kindly treated. So Akemi Kikumura tells her life's story to her daughter; it provides a sharp and necessary contrast to Etsu's. In *Through Harsh Winters: The Story of a Japanese Immigrant Woman* (Novato, CA: Chandler and Sharp, 1981), the themes are suffering and deprivation. This book is extremely useful as a model for any of us who want to write the lives of our friends and relatives.

Maxine Hong Kingston has written an unusual and wonderfully popular auto-biographical novel, allegorical autobiography, or fictionalized personal account (how we describe such an imaginative work is very fluid). In *The Woman Warrior: Memories of a Girlhood Among Ghosts* (New York: Random House, 1976), she writes about women's rights and her own socialization as a Chinese-American or American Chinese — again the terms are flexible. Notice again how powerful and un-expected the image of a woman warrior is.

The Baroness Shizue Ishimoto was also raised in an ultra-traditional family and betrothed to a man she had never met. She too came to America and returned to Japan with many radical ideas, including a plan to form women's associations and information about using birth control. Naturally, she calls her book, *Facing Two Ways: The Story of My Life* (Stanford, CA: Stanford University Press). First published in 1935, it is the perfect complement to Etsu's story.

A Chinese woman, Ning Tai-t'ai, paints her helplessness in the face of her "fate." She sounds like a loyal follower of the Chinese philosopher, Confucius. But steadily, firmly, she goes about creating her life according to her own require-ments. American readers have a great deal to learn about freedom from these women! Ida Pruitt edited this work, called *A Daughter of Han: The Autobiography of Chinese Working Woman* (Stanford, CA: Stanford University Press, first published in 1945).

Jung Chang wrote *Wild Swan: Three Daughters of China* (New York: Anchor, 1991) about her grandmother, her mother, and herself. Here is a century of women swept up in tragic, shocking, revolutionary, and altogether harrowing times. This book is an amazing and extraordinary achievement. So are these women's lives.

Questions Worth Answering

1. How and why does Etsu's conversion to Christianity resemble what feminists call "conscious-raising"? Do her relationships to her late husband's family resemble any of the techniques or approaches we associate with the women's movement? How is what she did rebellion or resistance? Samurai courage? Necessity as the mother of invention?

2. Okay, so what kind of a marriage did she have? All we know about Etsu's husband is included here. What was he really like? Is this how arranged marriages work?

3. Loving two countries the way Etsu loved Japan and America is a singularly old-fashioned notion. Today we talk about "constructing our ethnic, sexual, and cultural identities." How did Etsu build or construct hers? Did she have what we call an "identity"?

4. Was Etsu the kind of mother her mother was? Does the kind of mother we are depend on our circumstances, our beliefs, our feelings, or the actions of others around us? Or something else?

Endnote to Chapter 2

1. Etsu Sugimoto, "Japanese Love Stories," *Bookmaster* 63 (June 1926): 416.

Scholar Mary de Rachewiltz stands in front of a poster announcing the opening of an art exhibit dedicated to her father, poet Ezra Pound. The quote, "Beauty is difficult" is a line from one of his poems.

Mary

"You Can't Get Through Hell in a Hurry"

Mary de Rachewiltz was born Maria Rudge. She was the daughter of Ezra Pound and his lifetime lover and companion, Olga Rudge. He was a poet and she a concert violinist. Both were expatriate Americans, engrossed in the heady, glamorous intellectual and artistic life of Europe between the great world wars. They had met each other in Paris and, to all appearances, fallen in love.

Ezra was, however, already married to an Englishwoman, Dorothy Shakespear Pound. Olga was an artist, a performer; she knew little about babies. So the parents-to-be were traveling between Paris, Olga's little house in Venice, the village of Rapallo on the Italian seacoast, and various concert engagements. As the birth approached, Olga and Ezra stopped in the small Alpine town of Bruneck in the historic region of Tirol (sometimes written Tyrol). The baby, born on July 9, 1925, was premature and delicate. A peasant woman from the village of Gais was also giving birth, but her infant did not live. She had milk and understood babies. So these improbable parents fostered their newborn daughter with a German-speaking, very Catholic, and very Tirolean peasant family high in an Alpine valley which had just become a part of the nation of Italy.

So little Maria, Mary, had two sets of parents, each with radically different lives. As she grew up, she moved between the peasant farmhouse of Joanna and Jakob Marcher in Gais and the Rudge-Pound town house in Venice. No greater contrasts can be imagined. Mary called her foster parents *Mamme* and *Tatte*. Her other parents had many names, depending on circumstances and the gradual clearing of Mary's confusion. First she called them *the strangers.* Then they were known as the *Herr* and the *Frau,* German for the *Lord* and the *Lady.* Then her foster mother told her to call them *Tattile* and *Mamile,* Puster Valley dialect for *little father* and *little mother.* Later, Olga will tell her daughter to speak Italian and address her father as *Babbo.*

The baby grew up in a hard-working peasant household that held only two books: *The Life of Christ* and *The Lives of the Saints.* Mary's foster family spoke a local dialect of German because this area, Tirol, had belonged to Austria and the Habsburg Empire until 1919 when an international treaty ceded it to Italy. But school officials taught only in Italian and punished students for speaking German or following their much-loved Tirolean customs. By contrast, Mary's parents wanted her to learn English; at the same time they steeped her in the language of poetry and music. Thus her narrative, like Pound's poetry, is full of these languages and the unusual circumstances under which she learned them.

Mary de Rachewiltz deliberately centers her autobiography on her famous parent; so it is called *Ezra Pound, Father and Teacher: Discretions.* The subtitle is meant to contrast with writings Pound called "Indiscretions." Pound scholars and poets all over the world treasure Mary's autobiography — it is the most intimate glimpse they will ever have of Ezra Pound. Her book also illuminates some of the key passages of the *Cantos,* Pound's long and extraordinary epic poems.[1]

Mary sprinkles quotes from the *Cantos* throughout her autobiography. For her, Pound's poems are the shaping force of her life. Her conversations as well as her autobiography contain fragments, references, and quotes from them. In fact, she would rather talk about the *Cantos* than about her own life. She tells American students who visit her home in northern Italy:

> Now the *Cantos* are difficult. Yes. Difficult and long. But they are worth it. I'm one of the few lucky people who has had fifty years time to live with them, who has had the fortune to hear them read to me before I understood what they were all about. As long as you read the *Cantos* believing there is something in them that's worth following, they're not difficult. But "You can't get through hell in a hurry." This is a line in the *Cantos.* It means that we all start in a dark forest like Dante's *Purgutorio.* "And it can't be all in one language." That's also a line from the *Cantos.* In fact most things that I say are quotations from the *Cantos.* Because, you see, Pound has said it so well, once and for all. That is, in fact, what great poets do. That's what poetry is — something alive and charged with meaning.

Mary was not only the child of a famous father; she was the offspring of a very talented and high-spirited mother. It may be said that her parents had a lifelong love affair of the kind usually found in legends. As you will see from the narrative, it cannot be simple to have such parents.

Mary's mother, Olga Rudge, appears in many guises throughout the *Cantos*. To Pound she appears as his muse, a trim-coiffed goddess, a Circe or Aphrodite to his Odysseus. For fifty years she inspired him, cared for him, believed in his genius, and collected every scrap of paper he wrote. Before he died Pound penned some pieces as possible endings to the *Cantos*. In one of these fragments, he asked that Olga's acts of beauty be remembered. He said her name was courage.

In the United States many people have heard about Ezra Pound's imprisonment in St. Elizabeth's Home for the Criminally Insane on charges of treason. They may also have heard of his anti-Semitic remarks and judge him as a fascist or a racist. Olga and Mary worked with Pound's wife, the Italian government, the government of the United States, and many prominent poets and writers to secure Pound's release. They lived within the shadow of his imprisonment for the twelve years he spent at St. Elizabeth's and for the years that followed.

Mary's narrative is more personal than political; it centers on the unconventional circumstances of her early years, World War II, her father's fame and infamy, the renovation of a very old castle, and how she built her own unusual life. Although Mary may sometimes claim that her life is otherwise unremarkable, she herself is an accomplished writer, translator, and scholar.

You will notice in the following selections how she frames the circumstances of her birth, the events over which she has no control, and the temperaments of her parents. I cherish the delicacy of Mary's account — the tact, the nuances; it is no wonder she calls it "Discretions."

The first part of Mary's narrative centers on the abrupt cultural contrasts of her childhood. Periodically she goes to visit Tattile (Babbo) and Mamile in Venice. But she is homesick for her adopted family, her animals, and the mountain home of her foster parents. Part of the discretions of which Mary speaks concerns her own status or identities. As you will see, for example, Mary does not know about Pound's wife and her son until much later in the story. Until her late teens, in fact, Mary remains an inhabitant of one of the sealed compartments in Pound's life. Before that, there were only occasional leaks between his worlds. On one such rare occasion, her paternal grandfather visits her. His advice, recounted here, makes her special and somehow grounds her.

The second part of her narrative records the short periods in which she lived with both parents and her eccentric education with her father as mentor, colleague, and teacher. At the height of World War II and the beginning of her own adulthood, her father brings her revelations, then is arrested and imprisoned. In the last part of her story, Mary marries, builds a family in a ruined castle, and grows into the Pound legacy. She becomes an extraordinary woman; here is her extraordinary story.

❖

At the end of the summer, without warning, the strangers returned. A busy harvest time, with the cold pressing down from the mountains. And they hit baking today, the most hectic of all days. Bread is baked every two or three months on farms in the Pustertal. Houses have bread rooms, with long wooden racks to keep the loaves dry and ventilated. Our black vaulted kitchen, with its two chicken coops serving as tables to eat on and the cement swill trough, was dominated by an enormous bread oven, the heating of which took a good seven hours. Tatte started to pile up logs in the middle of the night. In the early morning when Mamme lifted the lid off the wooden yeasting tub, the whole house heaved with the smell of fermented dough. The making of bread is difficult; it requires practice and training. Mamme's hands tossed the loaves like butterflies, light, swift, expert; and Tatte with a long wooden oar shoved them into the oven. It was a great day for children who could pitch in and make themselves useful. But the smaller ones were pushed aside and babies neglected.

So they found me unkempt and wet in the wicker carriage. The lady frowned. Mamme blushed. "Until that day I had you spotless!" Tatte shrugged: *"Man muss essen a."* [One must eat.] And the Herr understood: *"Gut, gut."* [Good, good.]

The strangers left and it was agreed that next day I would be brought to them at their hotel in town. Mamme had seldom been in Bruneck. The idea that she would have to cross the threshold of the awe-inspiring Hotel Post worried her greatly. With what care she dressed up! It is a good hour's walk from Gais to Bruneck. She must have hurried and talked and sung to me all the way, as she pushed the pram, talked and sung out her excitement, her fears, her pride, her hopes. My earliest memories are of Mamme singing and talking and confiding in me as though I were a little Lord Jesus.

How did she get the pram up Herr Photograph Kofler's dark and narrow stairs? Or was he summoned with his equipment to the hotel? Details are not available, but a picture testifies that I was a healthy, happy baby. The Frau was appeased and satisfied and Mamme was allowed to take her gift-from-heaven back home in the late afternoon. Again a big bill tucked away in her bosom and a great weight off her chest.

The strangers were leaving next day for unknown places. . .

How is it far, if you think of it?

Paris is how far? Ages in understanding. Venice, Rapallo, Rome? A bit nearer. And she shall have music wherever she goes . . . In the style of the twenties. Their style: *"M. et Mme. vous invitent . . ."*

things have ends and beginning

And feigning? Ah, it will take generations to put an end to things started in feigning — to the despair of it.

Our dynasty came in because of a great sensibility.

Ours? For the sake of Art? . . . we seek to fulfill. . . Over the chaos hovers one certainty: I, the child, was wanted. The rest is music and poetry.

And from now on whenever the scrupulous biographer will report a concert in Budapest, a performance in Vienna, a trip to Frankfurt, Wörgl, Salzburg, it may be assumed that the journey was interrupted, for a few hours or for a few days in Bruneck.

On a balcony of the Hotel Post, the Herr and the Frau, enthroned in wicker chairs. I pastured a flock of thin, caoutchouc, flat-bellied geese precariously floating in a bowl of water at their feet. And I wanted to stroke the shoes dangling in front of my eyes, so smooth and shiny. *"Net!"* Mamme warned watching over me from the doorway. *Net.* I must not touch the Lord and Lady's shoes and I must call them Tattile and Mamile.

My curiosity was insatiable and Mamme's natural gift for making up stories during the day was supplemented in the evening by the talk of men. Tatte simply had to go out, to rest and smoke his pipe in company. Mamme's protests were to no avail. She too liked company, would have liked visitors. But when they came, she dominated the conversation and Tatte twitched nervously, spitting more often than was necessary. He was interested in politics, wanted the latest news. Mamme was interested in miracles and old legends. Tatte's sister, by all referred to as Töite because she was godmother to twenty-two nieces and nephews, in due course, including Margit and myself, was married to a tobacco-chewer and heavy drinker, a one-cow farmer, Leo. He subscribed to the weekly paper and she earned the money for it by her skill at turning old rags into slippers. She kept late hours and had to have a well-heated room for her fingers to remain supple and for the flour-and-water glue not to get hard. Moreover, she had to give all her attention to the sewing and keep tight lips.

I watched them from behind the table, next to Töite, cutting miniature slippers out of snippets thrown under the table or shoved over to me. The stoves in the Tyrol are vaulted, in white plaster, surrounded by benches. Four uprights hold a broad bench over the stove, the crossbars around the middle of the stove serve to lean against and to hang up socks and diapers. Leo always lay on the plank over the stove and at regular intervals from that height would let fly over the heads of the men seated on the bench below, a dark clot, . . . *hittin' the gob at 25 feet. Every time, ping* . . . , in the middle of the square wooden box by the door into which the others emptied their pipes and spat from a short distance with lesser skill.

Needless to say, the only language heard, known, and mastered was Tyrolese. *Puschtrerisch,* more precisely. Thus when grandfather Homer [Pound's father] was brought to Gais, we could not communicate. He had been informed of my existence and his advice was being sought. Should the nature-child be brought into civilization? His verdict: "It would kill her. The plant is too tender to be uprooted." He added that one could try acclimatization — slowly, short visits — but at no cost must I be separated from Mamme yet. We all loved him for his wisdom.

Grandfather's visit conferred a sense of stability. The Herr and the Frau were difficult to figure out, but a Grossvater you do not conjure up out of nowhere. It means there is a background. His first visit left a landmark. He gave me a beautiful doll, and I called it Rosile, for she had pink porcelain cheeks. The black eyes that snapped open and shut became an exotic ideal. Everyone I knew had green, gray, or blue eyes. The picture of three generations was taken by Photographer Mariner in Bruneck.

Mamme and Tatte tossed questions, intrigued, intriguing: "The house in Venice belongs to the Frau, if I got it right, she said her father bought it for her. The outside is nothing much; I don't know why she does not get it painted. But inside she has it beautiful on three floors — though such open fires as we wouldn't have any more . . ."

I was placed on a high dark-blue armchair, on a pile of cushions over which was spread a leopard skin. Facing me, over a monumental dark table, on a high dark-blue armchair, sat Mamile, majestic and beautiful like a queen towards me; soft and willowy, smiling like a fairy towards Tattile.

Tattile occupied a dark-blue broad bench against the wall. The wall was bright yellow with painted ocher columns, and a bright glass star hung over us. This was the dining room on the ground floor. I liked Mamile's room upstairs the best; it had no open fire and the most beautiful dress hung on the door. The door was a looking glass, facing the king-size, pearl-gray velvet couch. On the long, low bookcase stood two pairs of strange shoes, one of straw and one of black wood. Later, I learnt that these were Japanese shoes and the dress a kimono, and the jewel-studded silver bird on the same shelf a gift from d'Annunzio. To me all these things were objects of great veneration, like the brocade mantle, the tiara, and the rings covering the bones and the skull of a saint in our village church.

The wall along the stairs leading to the top room was taken up completely by gray opaque canvas into which I read nothingness; chaos, the universe or the torso of a giant, crucified. Tami Koume's Super-artificial-growing-creation, whispering: "We are now standing at the critical moment of humanity. We must be saved by something."

To this house of elegance, tense symbols, charged with learning, wisdom, and harmony, I was first brought I think at the age of four, following Homer's advice of gradual weaning from the soil.

By now I was able to communicate somewhat in Italian. Mamile said in Venice I must speak Italian all the time and call Tattile *Babbo.* Her stern attitude handicapped me more than the language barrier had done. For fear of lapsing into German or saying the wrong thing, I turned poker face. If Tattile now and again resorted to German she knitted her brows. *"Caro!"* So I did not tell her then that twice a week, with the slate hidden under my apron, I went to our neighbors for German lessons. A very exciting secret. The Tyroleans, deprived of instruction in German, had formed an underground movement which, among other things, trained voluntary teachers and provided textbooks. And we were to read and write in the Gothic alphabet. The political motives were obvious; parents and children had to pledge utter secrecy. We took knitting and sewing with us, and the boys carpentry tools. In case anyone entered, we were to wipe the slates and pretend we were working, and the book would disappear among the teacher's clothes. The house in which the lessons were held had been carefully chosen, off the road; since the owners were notoriously unfriendly to strangers, peddlers and carabinieri were not likely to drop by.

Between themselves, Babbo and Mamile continued to speak English. All I could do was watch their eyes and facial expressions. For some obscure reason, I was afraid of Mamile. Perhaps I disliked her. An incomprehensible entity with a grudge, a dark resentment as though I were permanently doing her wrong. Mamme's early tears and her complaints that the Frau was *murre,* a *muddo Sock,* exacting, nagging had probably left its mark on me. I stood as though forever waiting for mercy. One day at the Lido, I cut my toe, and went up to them sitting at a table in the open, waiting for lunch. I saw Babbo's dark face and thought: I should not have cut myself, should not have held up the bleeding toe, a breach in manners; I have ruined their appetite.

Babbo rushed me down to the sea and had me wash my toe, tied his hand-kerchief around it and carried me back to the table. But throughout lunch he sat furious and ate almost nothing, his face propped up between his fists. It seemed to me that after a while Mamile's tone became coaxing. I thought she might be inter-ceding for me. Years later, when I understood English, the incident was recalled by: "the time he wouldn't eat his lunch and the sprig had cut her toe. Such a rude thing to say to poor Alice." While I was playing on the beach a group of friends led by Giorgio and Alice Levi had turned up, and one of the ladies asked for an autograph. She got an E. P. signature. She insisted for a few lines from the poet, and received:

> a lesson that no school book teaches:
> some women's b . . . are too big for their breeches.

And it applied to the visitors. Fawning and insistence put in their place, but Mamile must have given him a severe talking-to for him to get into such a fury. It was the first time I had seen him angry. It seemed as though he were visibly fight-ing a wasp nest in his brain. Quite different from when he was merely pensive. That occurred often, and I knew immediately that he wanted me to refrain from talking. Inherent in his silence was suspense, a joyous sense of expectation, until he broke into a kind of chant that sometimes went on for hours, interrupted and picked up again, no matter whether he was sitting at a table or walking in the streets. Hard as I tried to imitate this humming, I never could. No words: sounds bordering on ventriloquism, as though some alien power were rumbling in the cave of his chest in a language other than human; then it moved up to his head and the tone became nasal, metallic. Athena banging in her glistening helmet inside Jupiter's skull, clamoring for release. A hasty scribbling on a piece of paper, a tearing off of newspaper clippings, a frantic annotation in a book. Something had clicked, some truth revealed, a new thought, a new line, a new melody.

Le Paradis.
For a flash,
    for an hour.

Babbo used to leave the house right after breakfast and briskly cross over the bridge to the other side of the Canal where, at Signora Scarpa's, he had a room to work in, a typewriter, and an address. I listened for his return. The tapping of his black malacca cane up the cul-de-sac Calle Querini. A rattle downstairs and a loud, prolonged *MIAO*. From the first floor; *Miao* — Mamile answered, and my tedium was over. I rushed down the two flights of stairs ready to go out. Shop-ping, a blissful ritual.

The end of another September. Another visit to Venice. I went reluctantly. It seemed to me I was too busy, full of responsibilities and needed. This playing at being a *hearrische* in Venice was a waste of time. Who did I think I was when I came back? The more spiteful made fun of me, if in my dress or manner they detected something foreign. And it vexed me to be dragged out of my world, made to wear clothes and assume manners that in real life were of no use to me. Time I was taking care of myself. The Herr had said everyone must work, be self-sufficient, either by one's brain or one's hands. I decided I preferred working in the fields with Tatte to studying. I was following the general trend; propaganda against Italy was infiltrating every plane, and what they taught us at school was at home considered nonsense because the teacher was Italian, hence a fool.

And so, once again, I felt I had disappointed Mamile. My Italian had improved very little, why did I not study it more? The clothes I had brought with me were all too long. I was grown-up; in Gais I could not possibly wear short skirts! Nonsense — Frau Marcher had bad taste. And I was given two dresses — in retrospect very pretty — that made me feel like a doll, and an indecent one at that: too short. And I was told not to go skipping on the Zattere. I was too heavy and clumsy and must practice being light and graceful. Nonsense! — *tumma Tanz* — at home weight was the thing to have, weight behind the work. So, I was growing into a problem: a clumsy, pig-headed peasant instead of a graceful bright sprig. Not, at any rate, definitely not,

"... a victim — beautiful perhaps, but a victim; expiring of aromatic pain from the jasmine, lacking in impulse, a mere bundle of discriminations."

One afternoon Babbo and I went alone to the Lido for a swim. He smiled and blinked, and I was happy and off guard. At this stage it was always he who put questions to me. When I grew up he insisted I put questions to him. He must have inspired me to prate about Gais, for suddenly he asked: And when do you want to go home? He said *casa*. I was not sure whether he meant Calle Querini or Gais; I did not think I had a say in such matters. I replied, *Presto*. So he knew I meant Gais. "Why?" I must take care of Loisl [her foster brother], I miss him. There is so much work this time of the year, they'll miss me. *Heimweh* [German: homesick]. When we got back, Babbo and Mamile talked for what seemed an interminable time. Finally she turned to me: So you want to go back soon? "*Si.*" And this was all I managed to say. The room filled with repulsion and hostility. A solid blackness. She started to cry. Babbo took her on his knees and tried to soothe her. It was pitiful to see a great goddess cry in her anger and hurt pride. Or was she a mortal woman hankering after her child's love? I sat on the floor feeling miserable as the cause of all this misery and began crying too, like a grown-up at first, silently. Then, loud sobs, clamoring for attention. Babbo told me to come over to them, and sat me on his other knee and patted us both until the sobbing ended. Then he handed me his big handkerchief and dashed out of the house; he found out about trains, bought me a ticket, and sent a telegram to Mamme asking her to meet me in Bruneck next evening.

[In the next section fourteen year-old Mary leaves school in Florence and goes to the beautiful Italian village of Rapallo; she does not yet know that her father's wife, Dorothy, also lives there. In fact, she doesn't know a wife (or her son Omar in England) even exists. Mary knows that her father's parents live there, but she does not see them. Olga, her mother, keeps an apartment at Sant' Ambrogio, a steep walk up the hill; Ezra splits his time between the women. He is his daughter's teacher and intellectual mentor — in a tutorial situation she called the "Ezuversity." In this section, Pound is leaving for America to plead with President Roosevelt to keep the United States out of the war then building in Europe. Devastated by the carnage of World War I, he passionately desired peace and social justice; he believed that poets must speak out for the truth of their visions. Roosevelt declined to meet with him. Pound returned and began a series of radio broadcasts over Italian radio. But as the United States entered the war, he was not only on enemy soil, but seemed to some to be speaking out about or against his own country. The authorities were not pleased. His words landed him in serious trouble.]

In April 1939 I saw Rapallo for the first time. Since I had spent most of the previous summer studying, the school granted me a few days off, to say goodbye to Babbo. He was going to America. Mamile was at the station to meet me. We drove in a *carrozza* to the bottom of the hill. Then we climbed for almost an hour on a broad cobbled path, on narrow stone steps flanked by gray holding walls, upwards under olives, past eucalyptus and lemon trees. The sea so different from the Venice sea, colors sharp and clear. It was a sunny, scented spring day, the terraces full of daffodils.

Casa 60 was then orange-colored, with Ionic columns painted on the outside walls, a flight of smooth black lavagna steps leading up to the green front door half hidden by Virginia creepers and honeysuckle. *Thk thk thk GRR:* the sound of the olive press on the ground floor. *Ploff, chhu:* the bucket hitting the water in the well.

The ingle of Circe . . . in the timeless air.

The house inside: light. White and empty. Polished red brick-tile floors. A square entrance, and four doors open on rooms with a view to the sea, olives and a blossoming cherry tree. Pale blue and pink vaulted ceilings with painted morning glory convoluting into bouquets and wreaths.

The furniture, unpainted, was all made by Babbo. A long bookcase and a mirror in the entrance; a table in the dining room and four plain straw-bottomed chairs along the walls; a desk, a high broad shelf for music and violin, and a narrow bookcase fitted in under the window in Mamile's room. The only spot of color was given by the orange damask couch; the only ease was suggested by two armchairs, a broad one and a normal-size one, twins to the ones in Venice. A Babbo-made desk stood also in "my" room, where the rest of the furniture was an iron bed, a night table with a marble top, and a chair. This was referred to as the Yeats furniture. It came from the flat my grandparents took over from the Yeatses. The only items in the house with a touch of hardness.

There was nothing else in the house. Sheer beauty and scent of — honeysuckle? lemon or orange blossoms? One painting: blue sea, white shell. In the kitchen: an iron funnel over the charcoal and a row of dark-brown clay pots on the board mantelpiece. No junk, no clutter. Only candlelight.

"*MIAO*" — and the rattle of Babbo's stick on the front door. He was laden with parcels, papers and envelopes sticking out of his pocket. We relieved him of the encumbrances while being kissed and gently buffeted on the cheeks. He went into his room to change and then threw himself on the orange couch. There was nothing in "his" room except two of his stools, a change of clothes and a packing-case dresser ingeniously disguised by chintz.

Mamile in the meantime prepared tea; I laid out the cakes and was told to carry everything into her room on a low tray-table. Her room was the center of the house. After the tea ritual and some chitchat, Babbo: "She feel up to the *Chaconne*?"

And I heard Bach's *Chaconne,* probably for the first time. It registered for good. Mamile had placed the iron music stand in the center of the room and herself in front of the window. In Venice I had heard her practice for hours and had been oppressed by the sounds. I had never watched her. At concerts in other people's houses I would glance at her now and again, but never really saw her. Now a new person stood in front of me. Was I looking at her through Babbo's eyes? Some mix-up, exchange of perception, or fusion of vision? Or was it because she was playing exclusively for Babbo going on a long journey? Love flowing into the groove *dove sta memora*. "The birds answering fiddle and her between me and wisdom and view of the bay" — called to my mind, years later. For the duration of her playing I saw no shade of darkness, no resentment. The violet-blue eyes clear and luminous. Finally I had a glimpse of their true world *nel terzo cielo.* But as soon as the music stopped the vision came to an end. Mamile resumed her authoritarian ways and the switch to their third-person language:

"He take the child for a walk and show her." "Yes ma'am." "You go and talk to Babbo." We obeyed.

Babbo left Sant' Ambrogio early next morning. Except for repeated bear hugs, it was as though he were merely going across the canal in Venice to his work-room. Mamile was once more distant and impenetrable, but I had a glimpse of her great beauty, and my fear of her changed into a kind of veneration. There was no way or reason to express this change of feelings. Besides, the thought of Babbo going to America was very exciting and kept me busy, especially this new fantasy that we might soon go and live there.

The usual "Hurry up or we won't see the boat pull out." My fascination with the Ligurian landscape, lunch at a restaurant, some place high up from where one could see the harbor; in the afternoon, the exploring of the narrow streets behind the harbor and the shop windows in the center of Genoa; the return to Rapallo and the lit-up coastline — all seemed a prelude to my own great voyage and made me forget the disappointment about not seeing my grandparents.

The walk up to Sant' Ambrogio in the dark had something unfathomable, something fluid, almost eerie. Mamile seemed familiar with each stone, but she flashed a torch for me in spots where the sky and the sea were hidden and fireflies provided the only specks of light. In high open spaces the darkness was attenu-ated by the reflection from the lights in the bay and the stars above.

We had hidden a pair of old espadrilles at the bottom of the *salita* [mule path]. "That's what all the peasant women on the hills do when they go to town. One can't walk on these stones with proper shoes. After concerts I sling the fiddle over my shoulder; I need both hands free to carry my music and the shoes and hold up my evening gown. . . . Tomorrow we'll have tea with some friends, they have a delightful garden, Else is very kind, she usually asks me to dinner before a con-cert, that gives me a chance to powder my nose . . ." Mamile was in a talking mood. After the last flight of stone stairs, under the church, we sat down for a while on the narrow bench in front of the long gray stone house at the top. "I always have to sit down here. Gee, I am tired sometimes."

The image clung to me: Mamile, alone on the hill path in the middle of the night, climbing with the violin strapped over her back, carrying high-heeled golden or satin shoes and a music case in one hand and holding up the long eve-ning gown with the other. In an old pair of espadrilles. And "Gee" was all she said, after endless practicing and the walk down and the climb back, alone. "It's awful when it rains, the violin is so sensitive."

I knew exactly what Babbo meant when, later on, he once told me: The real artist in the family is your mother.

How is it far . . . ?

No longer very far — neither in time nor in understanding. Did I at fourteen or fifteen start to understand? Or merely store and believe?

Without character you will be unable to play on that instrument . . .

Babbo spent every second afternoon in Sant' Ambrogio with us; sometimes he came for lunch, sometimes he stayed for dinner, which meant that I had from two to three hours' instruction every day. Evenings Mamile continued her coaching in English, sometimes also a few hours after lunch, so that in those two years of seclusion we read through all Jane Austen, Thackeray, Stevenson, Hardy, and about a dozen volumes of Henry James; and Alice James's diary.

With Father Chute and with Mamile it was learning and reading in an orderly manner, but Babbo provided action, work, in streams and in flashes. He brought me Hardy's *Under the Greenwood Tree* to translate into Italian. I felt flattered and challenged — at being admitted into his workshop. The job of translating was much tougher than I had foreseen, but with the passing of time I listened more and more eagerly for his cane on the cobblestones of the *salita* and then the rattle on the door, for he brought with him a dimension of — no, not stillness, but magnitude, momentum. He made me feel that work, learning, was worthwhile, exciting.

Our life centered around Babbo's visits, and the pattern was much the same as on that afternoon in April 1939, the day before he left for America. Except that now he no longer arrived laden with parcels. Yet never empty-handed: a few roast chestnuts or peanuts, a slice of *farinata* or *castagnaccio,* pancakes made with chicken or chickpea flour, for our tea; and in an old envelope the cat's food, scraps from his lunch.

In place of the bunch of letters he read us his radio speeches. We were his first audience and, in the light of what we read in the papers and heard over the Italian radio, they seemed to me clear and justified.

"Damn it all, if you had a single-minded objection to violence you could have prevented this war." — "Freud is not the answer to violence."

After reading to us what he had written, it was my turn: I had to recite five lines from the *Odyssey* and translate. He then read five new lines as my next assignment. And it seemed as though he possessed two voices: one angry, sardonic, sometimes shrill and violent for the radio speeches; one calm, harmonious, heroic for Homer, as though he were taking a deep, refreshing plunge into the wine-colored sea after a scorching battle.

Then I had to read my translation from Hardy, usually one or two pages. The following year it was *Cantos*. Both tasks were really beyond my capacities, but he never lost his patience, just corrected and reconnected: "Take the thing and rewrite it in Italian. If a poem is good in the original you must make a good poem in translation, and it applies to prose too." But discussions were reserved usually for the *salita*. . . .

Yet there was a war going on; Germany and England were destroying each other's towns and people and Babbo wrote speeches in anger and disgust. The artist-antenna sensitive to the fury of the madness pervading the world. At times I felt the urge to *do* something — but what? "What the world will need most when the war is over is someone with an education" — and he tried to expand it as much as he could, dipping back into his own school years: "Now let me see, when I was your age . . ." And up came tidbits of geology, arithmetic, geometry.

And there were dramatic moments and periods of great tension following the news of Pearl Harbor. Babbo went to Rome. When America officially declared war he stopped broadcasting over the Italian radio. Impressive envelopes arrived summoning all American citizens to return to the States, to get in touch with the Swiss legations. Mamile seemed at a loss. And what about me? What, who, was I?

Babbo came back from Rome, indignant and discouraged. They would not allow him on the last clipper out of Rome. It was reserved for American diplomats and press envoys. If he and his family wanted to leave Europe it would have to be by slow boat. Months on a route full of mines and torpedoes. "Is that the way they want to get rid of me?" I think a way out was suggested by train to Portugal. I do not remember details. The words that stick in my mind are: clipper, the last clipper, frozen assets, frozen bank account. Grandfather's U.S. government pension withheld, the old man in the hospital with a broken hip. Mamile's house in Venice sequestered as alien property.

Checkmate?

Babbo resumed his broadcasting. More violent. But what I remember most clearly — and the document obviously exists — is a long letter he wrote to? — perhaps the attorney general — via the Swiss legation, in which he explained the reasons for his broadcasting. American officials had made his return to the States impossible. The Italian government had offered him the freedom of the microphone, assuring him that he would not be asked to say anything contrary to his conscience as an American citizen. And as an American citizen he felt it was his duty to avail himself of the only means open to him to protest against the politics of a president who was exceeding his rights, endangering the Constitution, who had promised American mothers that their sons would not be sacrificed, while actively preparing for war.

The result was indictment for treason. And Babbo's answer: Treason is being committed in the White House and not in Rapallo.

Also:

that free speech without free radio speech is as zero

I would have preferred to stay on in Sant' Ambrogio, not to interrupt my own struggle to grasp, to catch glimmers of his thoughts. I had come to hope that someday, if I followed him closely, I might understand everything he said and wrote, all the references and shades of meaning. The sincerity of his expressions and intentions conferred such dignity upon him that I felt sure he was enunciating eternal truths. The beauty of it was that he believed it too. It never occurred to me at the time that the Axis might not win. But "victory" had become something so abstract that it seemed not to matter which side won. *Il nemico è l'ignoranza* — ignorance was the enemy. And usury [lending money at an exorbitant rate of interest] the cause of all wars.

But there was an inner, metaphysical war going on at the same time, over which he had no power. The usury of time itself was at work inside him.

Time is the evil. Evil.
. . . Geryon twin with usura

He was losing ground, I now see, losing grip on what most specifically he should have been able to control, his own *words*.

lord of his work and master of utterance

— he was that no longer. And perhaps he sensed it and the more strongly clung to the utterances of Confucius, because his own tongue was tricking him, running away with him, leading him into excess, away from his pivot, into blind spots. I know no other explanation for some of his violent expressions — perhaps he felt the exasperation at not being able to get his real meaning across. The long hostility of his country must have weighed heavily upon him, but he remained free from self-pity. I think Babbo was as little eager for me to go back to Gais as I was. On the other hand, Gais still stood for security, the only place where food and a welcome were assured. Besides, underlying his teaching was the belief that one should never be separated from the soil for too long; to grow things should be one's primary concern, especially in times when food was scarce.

And so in July 1943 I went — "for a month or two" — but in a sense it was for good.

[Mary is, at this point, eighteen years old, eccentrically educated, and a stateless person, an American without papers in an enemy country. So she returns to the Gais farmstead. Then one day, a surprise visitor arrives — in the midst of war. It is der Herr, Tattile, Babbo covered with dust and hungry. He must talk to her.]

I ran upstairs. A long silent embrace. Finally I managed to speak: How did you get here, where from? And he pointed to his feet, red, full of blisters, his ankles swollen.

"I walked out of Rome." And slowly he told me of the confusion at the radio offices as soon as it became known that the Allies had landed. All the high officials moving out of Rome, some to the south, some to the north. No one thought of him. He returned to the Albergo Italia to pay his bill and leave the small leather case and the black cane and his wide-brimmed Borsalino hat with the clerk at the desk. Then he went to the degli Ubertis'. They lent him a pair of walking boots — which did not fit him as he thought at first, hence the blisters — a narrow-brimmed, unobtrusive hat and a knapsack. He stopped to say goodbye at Nora Naldi's; he wanted to let Mamile's friend know his whereabouts. He told them he was going to see his daughter in Gais. They tried to dissuade him, offered to put him up until one knew what was going to happen. The war might be over in a few days, things might return to normal. No. He accepted two eggs which Nora prepared for him and walked out of Rome.

He said I should study the map which he pulled out of his knapsack. A very detailed map which the degli Ubertis had given him, full of his own markings and comments written on the margin and on the back. "And only in Verona it dawned upon me that this was a military map and if they caught me with it they might have taken me for a spy." The predicament he was in was almost grotesque, even to his own eyes. During the following days we went over that map very carefully; once his weariness had been conquered he seemed proud of his feat. He had not walked all the way, naturally. Bologna had been the last precarious place. He had slept in an air raid shelter. From Bologna to Verona it was all one stretch by train. In Verona he spent a day trying to come to a decision as to what he should do — keep going north or take a train to Milan; a few trains were running, perhaps as far as Rapallo. The situation seemed under control, under German control. He decided he would stick to his original plan and come and see me first; he had something important to tell me.

And after I had brought him supper and Mamme and Tatte had come in to wish him goodnight, failing utterly to hide their perplexity and curiosity as to what had happened, what would happen, but repressing all questions, so that he should have a good rest — he started to talk. "Sit down and put out the light." His eyes were smarting.

"I don't know how much of this you already suspect, the doors at Sant' Ambrogio are not exactly soundproof." No, those doors did not close very well, but I had never overheard any conversation between him and Mamile. I felt he almost wished I had; it might have made things simpler for him. Not only did I show no curiosity, but I was completely unsuspecting about what was on his mind. He tossed about for a beginning. Where? When? And it was almost three o'clock in the morning when he finally thought he had said everything, "*Mi par d'aver detto ogni cosa*" — though the following days he returned to the subject several times. Now I learned that in Rapallo there was also a wife. His wife, with a son in England. The news was not imparted as a secret, simply as facts that I was only now old enough to understand. Things would be set right — "If this war ever ends . . ." All plain and simple. I felt no resentment, only a vague sense of pity.

Buona notte. Buon riposa. I tiptoed into Margit's room. She groaned and moved over in her bed.

Somewhere between Mamme and Tatte's world on earth and God in Heaven there was an island of demigods not ruled by human laws. Here the range of imagination was wider, feelings more passionate and ruthless. Long before I had been fascinated by oracles, doom, hubris; before I had been made aware of and warned against Freudian trends and the dangers of oversimplification, I had felt uneasy with Mamile. "The impossibility of winning the mother's affection" was a fact now named. She had wanted a son. A torchbearer. Babbo's candor sustained me and his vision:

A little light, like a rushlight
to lead back to splendour.

Splendour, it all coheres. The dark echoes of the threat ". . . Thy truth then be thy dower!" did not reach me in Lear's voice.

Every myth I came to know I believed in, and lived through, giving it new twists. This did not interfere with the plane of daily life, nor with my Catholicism.

Moreover, during the past two years in Sant' Ambrogio I had come to enjoy and be eager to participate in Babbo's work through translation, to understand some of his ideas and theories through study. This meant more to me than being legitimate or illegitimate. Records would have to be set straight, eventually, simply because it was in keeping with the norm. Falsification of history, falsification of records tied up with:

'And if a man have not order within him
'His family will not act with due order. . . .

What carried weight in my life then was Babbo's inner order; everything would forever depend on that. Later remembering:

What thou lovest well is thy true heritage

Many shades of emotion will remain hidden, embedded in the *Cantos* as mythology, since poetry is the true medium for truth. Prose fits facts, but facts carry little weight, they can simply be recorded as part of "the tale of the tribe."

[Ironically, Pound did not tell his daughter then that the U.S. government had issued a warrant for his arrest. He was, in fact, under indictment for treason. He returned to Rapallo and the throes of the painful domesticity he had created. Olga's house in Venice and Dorothy's Rapallo apartment had been taken away. By 1944 Dorothy had moved in with Olga. All Pound's books, correspondence, and papers were carted up the hill. To outside observers, the two women appeared to live in social accord. Olga repeatedly commented, "We were civilized." There were only predictable disagreements about cooking and shopping.[2] But in the following section, Mary disagrees and interprets parts of "Canto 81" as his cry of despair from that period — his attempt, in fact, to understand the feelings of two women he loved. But "Canto 81" and Mary's next meeting with her father both take place at an internment camp in Pisa. The time is 1945; the war has ended. Americans have invaded Italy and arrested Ezra Pound. He is locked in a cage; Olga summons Mary to help.]

I had last seen him in Gais weary and full of dust, with crumpled clothes, so his appearance was not too surprising. He had aged a lot and his eyes were inflamed. It was the dust and the light, he said, but now he was getting treatment. He sounded grateful, he had kept his trait of being most appreciative of small kindnesses, and he made the medical care and the tent that he was allowed to sleep in sound like great blessings. In the *gabbia* he had collapsed. A severe sunstroke, he thought. He used the Italian for *cage,* and since we had not seen the cages we did not have a clear idea of what he meant. It was only years later when I visited him in Saint Elizabeth's Hospital in Washington that he described the gorilla cage in detail and how he had felt threatened by the sharp iron spikes. He had been deprived of belt and shoelaces to ensure that he could do himself no harm; and yet when, for no apparent reason, they reinforced his cage with stronger iron netting, they cut the old netting about ten inches from the ground so as to form a low hedge of spikes all around. He had interpreted it as a not-too-subtle invitation to suicide: the easiest way to slash his wrists. I realized that during certain hours of despair the temptation had been great.

Of his life in the DTC [Disciplinary Training Centre] he himself has left us the best record in the Pisan *Cantos.* Despite his walking tours and his familiarity with the hills and the sea, never had he lived so close to and been so dependent on nature as while in the death cell, and in the drenched tent, under Mount Taishan at Pisa, where the sight of a lizard upheld him; when

> **the loneliness of death came upon me**
> **(at 3 P.M. for an instant) . . .**

and

> **When the mind swings by a grass-blade**
> **an ant's forefoot shall save you . . .**

He told us he was now allowed to go into the infirmary after office hours and use the typewriter. He had not lost his humor: "because of exemplary conduct," and he winked mischievously towards Mamile. He also apologized to her for his untidy appearance, pointing at the unlaced shoes. As ever he tried to express more with his eyes than in words. A guard was standing by the entrance of the tent; he looked embarrassed at having to stand there and made up for it by allowing us to stay almost an hour. When he could concede no more he said: "Time to go, Mr. Pound." And he left us alone in the tent to say goodbye. **'Nothing. Nothing that you can do . . .'** — it was reciprocal.

Aside from the tent and a few guards, I have no memory of the DTC. The image of Babbo, grizzled and red-eyed in a U.S. army blouse and trousers, in unlaced shoes without socks, with his old twinkle and bear hug, stands as on a huge screen in the foreground.

Shortly after our visit the first batch of Pisan *Cantos* arrived. He wanted me to type them up and make several copies. For the Base Censor to allow them out he had written a note to the effect that they contained nothing seditious, no private code or personal message. But for us they contained more than all this. I was overwhelmed by the responsibility of the typing. What if I misspelled? I remember pondering for hours over **Vai soli**; not knowing the origin of the quotation, I felt sure it must be **Mai soli,** but dared not alter it. And fountain pan? — **dust to the fountain pan.** It was only after I had detached myself from the chore and responsibility of the typing that slowly the entire passage crystallized and I could see the rose in the steel dust participating in the poet's vision. . . .

We who have passed over Lethe. For me he had by then entered into the dimension of the Beyond. This feeling had nothing to do with hero worship or morbid attachment. It was respect. Transcendental. I did not go as far as sewing fragments of *Cantos* into my clothes, but I certainly wrapped them tightly around my mind. I suppose it was because of the intense enjoyment and insight certain passages offered that the *Cantos* slowly became the one book I could not do without. My "Bible," as friends have often teased me.

But I was not the only one to have strong feelings about them. Never had I seen Mamile cry so unrestrainedly as when she read "Canto 81":

Pull down thy vanity

And the cry of AOI is an outburst more personal than any other in the *Cantos* and expresses the stress of almost two years when he was pent up with two women who loved him, whom he loved, and who coldly hated each other. Whatever the civilized appearances, the polite behavior, and the facade in front of the world, their hatred and tension had permeated the house.

Les larmes que j'ai crees m'inodent
Tard, tres tard je t'ai connue, la Tristesse,
I have been hard as youth sixty years.

Until then the attitude toward personal feelings had been somewhat Henry Jamesian: feelings are things other people have. One never spoke of them or showed them.

Babbo was gone. There was nothing left. I would return to Gais, to my brothers and sisters there who were not my brothers and sisters at all, but at least there was no pretending. Needless to say, I hated the American officials for not giving us notice: hadn't they known three days before that they were going to fly their prisoner to the U.S.A.? Couldn't they have let us say goodbye to him? It had not been ill will on the part of the guards at the prison camp; they had all been kind. But the anonymous power, because it was anonymous, has no heart.

So I decided to turn my back on a situation I did not accept. At the time I thought I had the freedom of choice. I felt sure of what was right or wrong, true or false, sincere or devious. "Listen to your own heart and then act." How? My confidence in Confucian ethics was unshakable. I could not go far wrong. The world of which I had had a glimpse in Venice, Siena, and Rome had obviously collapsed. The society of great minds in elegant surroundings for which I had fostered vague hopes had been dispersed by the war. America: a big question mark, holding Babbo in its tentacles and me in the dark. It frightened me. But Rapallo too was devious and treacherous. I was bored and unhappy. I wrote bad poetry and grew fat, and was of no help or consolation to Mamile. I hated myself.

Finally I took courage and announced I would go back to Gais. "That may well be the best place for you, but first finish your job. And read this." A typed will. I read it carefully but did not realize its importance and far-reaching effects, nor what literary executor implied.

My job consisted in making an inventory of Babbo's papers and books. As soon as we heard that he had been taken to Washington, Mamile decided we must put all his papers in order and seal them up and sort out and list all the magazines and books, marking those which had items by him, etc. And so for weeks, I tied strings around the Moriondo chocolate boxes where he kept his personal letters and sealed them, and files where he kept his carbons and letters from literary and political correspondents. I assembled and sorted newspapers and magazines and tied them up in parcels, numbered and labeled. Pamphlets, Baedekers, broadsheets, each scrap of paper had assumed vital importance: one stray sentence might help his cause. I liked doing this, for it kept me in touch with Babbo's work. But there was also a feeling of doom in the whole process: a sealing up and saving for eternity every single word he had read or written.

By the beginning of March all Babbo's papers were neatly tied up and sealed, all his belongings listed. His writing table was tidy, pencils and rusty paper clips waiting for his hand to pick them up again. His hat on a hook by the door, the wine-red peignoir on a hook by the bed, worn out slippers and sandals lined up on the cupboard floor, old underwear neatly darned and stacked, strewn with mothballs and eucalyptus. The bassoon, the tennis rackets and walking stick, everything. Embalmed. Deadweight. Unbearable. Light and lightness had fled from the house, hovering, shrouded, and sighing, among the gray olive branches outside. The dark almond tree by the window burst into white tears as I left.

I was eager to start out on a life of my own, free, with clear and high ideals, and, to be sure, an overdose of pride. I thought I was rejecting all the lies and pretensions and compromises, Mamile's dark resentment, Grandmother's stubbornness, Dorothy and Omar, whatever, whoever they were. I was leaving everything behind. All I wanted to keep was something to believe in — the freedom to live the kind of life I had thought Babbo had meant me to live — simple and laborious. I set forth, with no regrets other than Mamile's disappointment. But in reality, far from cutting myself loose neatly, I was setting out to build castles — castles in the air turning into a castle on the rock into which slowly streamed everyone and everything with all the clatter of outlived feelings and discarded belongings and all the papers tied up and sealed for eternity, tossed and torn and disrupted by a horde of disciples and publishers scholars secretaries and collectors — hogs after truffles, greedy widows and fearful wives, chucked from attic to attic from trunk to trunk in a whirlwind . . .

And all because Mercury — for the fun of it? — had withheld a telegram for over a year.

At the bottom of the hill-path, a few days before my departure for Gais, a swift boy from the telegraph office holding a bicycle, handed me an impressive bundle of papers. Half a dozen wrappers from Red Cross stations, German Commandos, post offices, and inside it all simply: *"Buon Natale e Felice Anno Nuovo. Boris."* Happy New Year!

The boy whom I had met at that April picnic outside Rome with Princess Troubetzkoi had no friends or relatives in the North when in 1944 the Italian Red Cross distributed free telegraph-forms for Christmas greetings from the South to the North, so he thought of me.

That April in Rome with Babbo belonged to another era, but the urge to communicate and for some intellectual contact was strong. There was no one in Gais I could talk to. So letters started to fly back and forth: my correspondent was intrigued by a girl who had set out to start on her own, farming of all things. In his surroundings there was nothing so clear cut and solid. He would like to invest 100,000 lire in a cow, he wrote. Could he come and see me?

[So Mary has met a prince, Boris de Rachewiltz. They marry. They move into and renovate Brunnenburg, the castle on the rock she mentions above. Her father is locked away in the United States, but Mary's unusual home gradually becomes the focus of the Pound networks and the hopes for his release. In this last section, she makes the ruined old castle home, and delights in her children's lives.]

On the first of April we left for Meran. Food was still rationed, and I had to go to the doctor for a certificate to get more sugar. I knew the baby was due at Easter, but the doctor said no, earlier. I had felt fine ever since leaving Rome, but he said my muscles were not strong and it would be a difficult delivery; I couldn't have it at home.

Whey did we choose Meran? Probably the doctor's suggestion. It's a mystery to me now, except that the Bruneck hospital was so very dreary and they had no room anyway. The moon was still up as we walked down the mountain for the early train. The landscape still wintry. . . .

It was spring in Meran. The Clinic Martinsbrunn seemed heaven. Tea with cream in tiny silver pitchers and dainty *kipfel* served by smiling white nuns. For two or three days I enjoyed it to the full, then panic over the bill started to loom bigger and bigger. I walked among apple blossoms blessing God for so much beauty. I walked for hours on the Tappainerweg pleading with the baby to please come quick.

On Easter Sunday Boris returned and we went for a long walk. He wanted to visit the castles one saw from Martinsbrunn, especially the nearest, the one right under Schloss Tirol, that looked so strange. All I wanted was to speed up the baby.

We reached Brunnenburg in the late afternoon, having walked around it in a wide circle: Thurnstein, St. Peter, Schloss Tirol, the village and then down a steep path. The outer gate was bolted. A woman came out from the farm and shouted in Italian that we mustn't try to go in, it was forbidden and very dangerous. And then looking at me she added: and you shouldn't be on the road in such a condition. Dangerous? Yes, the roof, the walls may collapse any minute. We thought she was mad and skirted the outside, intrigued and thrilled. The walls seemed very solid to us. The only trouble was: absolutely no way in except through the door. We noticed there was no glass in the windows. Quite clearly the place was abandoned. . . .

The nuns were appalled when they heard how far we had walked, but knew little about Brunnenburg. They thought it belonged to the government, no one had lived in it for over twenty years, people said it was haunted.

That evening the pains started and next day, Easter Monday, as the sirens and bells announced midday, our son arrived with loud yells and I felt happy beyond imagination. Guilty perhaps of thinking more in terms of a grandson for my parents than a son for my husband. But Boris had his reward naming him: Sigifredo Walter Igor Raimondo — after his most glorious ancestors. Only Walter was Father's choice, in honor of Walther von der Vogelweide.

As soon as I could get out of bed I went to the window and saw the big magnolia in the garden underneath had burst into flower, and I rejoiced for beauty and the good omen. The open magnolias looked like lotus flowers, inside me shone the picture of my son, and now in my memory lives a Baby Bodhisattva kneeling full of sweet austerity upon the flower of the lotus.

One has so much courage in spring with a newborn baby at the breast and feeling fine. It seemed to me I could take the whole world on my shoulders, never thinking another winter would come and that I would feel weary.

[Mary and Boris try to buy a castle overlooking her home village of Gais. Isabel Pound, her grandmother, has finally recognized her granddaughter and comes to spend her final days with her. Mary is, of course, exhausted by the time she buries her grandmother. So she visits relatives in England.]

After my two months in England, I did not return to Gais, but to Tirolo. It had become clear that we could never buy Neuhaus. With the castle went a farm, land, and woods. Besides, Boris had liked Brunnenburg much better, despite the fact that it was uninhabitable. Being a ruin, it had one advantage: we could afford it. Juvenile recklessness, of course: little did we suspect how much it would cost us over the years in worry, work, and money. But for the moment we had our tower. A Roman tower of our own. With the most splendid view over two open valleys and endless ranges of mountains. The climate was much milder. One was not driven into hibernation and handicapped by ice and snow.

After a few weeks at the village inn we were able to camp in the highest room in the tower. The village carpenter and his son moved into one of the ground-floor rooms with all their tools and set to work repairing doors, floors, and ceilings. A Neapolitan engineer gave us advice in exchange for a sojourn in good mountain air, and directed the works: he was the right man for us at the moment, an expert in propping up, mending, shifting, making do. The tourist boom had not yet set in. Labor was abundant and cheap. And the spirit moving us was *dos moi pou sto kai kosmon kineso* — give me a place to stand and I will move the universe. Our faith and euphoria spread to the young people in the village. All the girls wanted to look after our son, and the boys were eager to help tidy up the place which in their schooldays they had stormed in imaginary conquests. One old woman with shiny eyes thanked me for having put some light back where it had been dark for so long. I think all the superstitious peasants were relieved that the place was no longer so sinister and haunted. It was reassuring to look down from the village on our lit-up windows.

Boris's appearance and his lack of spoken German were something exotic. Rumors about his connections with the tsars and the kings of Bulgaria took root: the importance of being Boris. As for me, with my dialect, I was easy to understand by peasants and workmen. They liked me and told me of their *Nannerls* — all the Habsburg princes seem to have had a penchant for fair farmers' daughters, and sometimes they even married them as in the love story of the postmaster's daughter in Marling. Because I came from the Pustertal I was perforce the daughter of a *Holzhandler:* for the *Burgrafler* with their vineyards and apples, the Pustertal means lumber and potatoes. Well, the family fortune and money had been founded on lumbering before.

In town they pricked up their ears. Soon the local paper carried the headlines: *L'ombra di Margaretha Maultasch si aggira nella sale di Castel Fontana."* The Ugly Duchess's ghost moves in the halls of Brunnenburg — it also said that we slept on straw, which was slightly exaggerated. And we laughed and kept busy, scrubbing, mixing our paints, looking for door-handles and hinges among scrap iron; calculating glass, wood, and plaster by the square meter, getting acquainted, poking around barns and attics for Tyrolean furniture.

True, towards the end of the first winter I had to run away because the banging on the door had become too loud and insistent: the plumber and the electrician wanted to be paid. We had been, wisely, reckless — had had water and light installed. Having been shown by our deaf and dumb neighbor in his field a spring that by right belonged to the castle, we had proceeded to *Quellenfassen* — to catch the spring — and then built a small reservoir for pressure. Major jobs, undertaken by firms in town.

Boris was in Rome attending classes at the Biblicum and trying to raise money.

This was at the time of the Bollingen award to Ezra Pound in 1948. Mamile too had gone to Rome, to rally old friends. It seemed as though Babbo might be released any moment. I was caught in the flurry. But I remember mainly the pain and the rage over certain ungenerous statements by American literati, and my own worries: what about my home that was to be His *palazzo?* — Pa'-in-law gave me money to return to Brunnenburg. With a seed parcel from UNRRA, I laid out a vegetable garden. There were several patches of ground inside the walls and also a white cherry tree and some plum trees with delicious fruit.

Again the only way to make a living was to take in paying guests, and again it was Babbo who sent them. The first was Mary Barnard, a young poetess who had corresponded with him before the war and had been to see him at Saint

Elizabeth's. She came to Europe on a *Cantos*-itinerary. And then Signora Agresti Rossetti, who had expressed concern for the lungs of her adopted niece. Babbo wrote to her she should bring the girl to me for good mountain air, and paid for it.

We had little comfort to offer as yet, but much beauty, of the kind people respond to and enhance. Signora Agresti, who seemed to me then a very old lady, sitting on a tree stump on our veranda, for lack of chairs, a rosary in her hands, gazing serenely at the Mut [a mountain peak behind the castle] is a sight I shall never forget.

And then Patrizia Barbara Cinzia Flavia was born. This time it was easy. I ran down the mountain to Martinsbrunn and two hours later she was there. The February new moon had brought her, on Ash Wednesday. Next morning we were snowed in: her little hands and feet were as delicate and perfect as the snowflakes that kept falling. Lots of auburn hair and silence, contentment, reserve.

I had always joked: twelve boys is what I want. But the joy of one little girl seemed to make up for eleven boys. Two years later we took on a baby girl without parents — Graziella, gay and good-natured. There was enough space and energy and food and warmth in our home.

"*It's Hard to Stand Firm in the Middle*"

In 1958 Ezra Pound was released from St. Elizabeth's Home for the Criminally Insane in Washington D.C. where he had been held since his arrest. He never came to trial; no one could say if he were sane or insane, traitor or patriot.

Mary visited him in the United States, and had worked for his release when opportunity presented. She wanted to help, but he told her, "All you can do is plant a little decency at Brunnenburg." So she readied the castle for his reception, for a future that would appreciate his greatness.

But Pound returned to a very different Italy than he had left. The postwar years had erased the literary life he knew. Brunnenburg was colder, steeper, and starker than he had imagined. He was despondent, depressed; his moods rose and fell. Apparently, he may have also recognized the problems he had created. Retreating into silence, he often lacked the will to words a poet needs.

For Pound, being a grandfather was a great joy. Eventually, in 1962 the patient and determined Olga swooped down and reclaimed the man she called *EP*. As ever, she was an irresistible force. In any event, his wife Dorothy could no longer manage, and Mary had her own hands full with a husband, children and a run-down castle. Olga and his grandchildren brought love and equilibrium to Pound's last years. He died in her house in Venice in 1972.

At Brunnenburg, Mary had become the center, the keeper of the flame, for Pound's literary inheritance. She who had wanted a farm and flocks now tended the letters, papers, editions of the *Cantos,* and eventually, Olga. In April 1995 poets and Pound scholars from all over the world gathered at Brunnenburg to celebrate Olga's 100th birthday. They gathered in Mary's tower, surrounded by Pound artifacts and memorabilia. Olga died in March of 1996. If Pound saw himself as Homer's Odysseus, then Olga was the wind at the poet's back. He said of her, the truth is in the kindness.

"What Thou Lovest Well Remains"

Since 1948 Mary de Rachewiltz has received hundreds of guests at Brunnenburg Castle, on a hillside above the lovely Italian city of Merano. She graciously opens her castle to American student groups to come, live there, study, work, play, hike, gather grapes, make wine, and listen to Pound's poetry. On the Fourth of July, she hangs an American flag on her tower. A leather-bound copy of the U.S. Constitution resides reverently in the Pound Library. Her son, his wife, and their two sons live there too. Relatives, friends, and fellow scholars or poets come to visit and to stay. Brunnenburg is a working farm and a museum devoted to the lives and work of Tirolean peasant estates. Since 1987 I have had the privilege and pleasure of being a guest there; I take a group of American students to study, live and work at Brunnenburg during the summer.[3] Mary and I talk frequently.

I asked her, "What does it mean — to be the daughter of Ezra Pound?"

She replied, "The daughter doesn't make a difference — much. What happens is this, you find me in the morning sitting here on the balcony with Dante's *Vita Nuova* in front of me, which of course, I had already read when I was fourteen. In school we had to do it. And enjoying it tremendously, being perfectly happy. That's the best I can wish everybody — to find a book. It doesn't have to be Pound — for me it happens to be Pound. You find your own authors.

"Dante wrote *Vita Nuova*; a 'new life' always means the last life, the final life, the real life, the life of the soul. So first we are born in our bodies, then the real earth we have to achieve. No mother gives us the real earth. That is something we have to achieve on our own.

"Again, what do you do? I mean, we are simply born into strange situations, and there's really nothing you can do. So you do it according to your own conscience, and do no evil. In the end Pound did all the terrible things he was against.

That's where the tragedy lies — he says in the *Cantos,* 'When one's friends hate each other, how can there be peace in the world?' That's the horror: 'and of a man seeking good and doing evil.' This is a terrible anguish to be left with at the end of so much work. It's a terribly painful subject, but it is the subject that undid him. But it is also the subject that we must have the openness to face.

"Pound said, free speech without free radio speech is as zero. Now when the Declaration of Independence was written, things like radio were not invented yet — so certain boundaries had to be enlarged. He, of course, achieved this by speaking on the radio. It was because he spoke on the radio that, at the age of sixty, he found himself indicted for treason. And as such, he is known in America. Unfortunately. And as such, he spent many years of his life paying for this so-called transgression. It is a problem that one has to face head on. Otherwise there are always these ambiguous attitudes. Was he a fascist? Was he a traitor? And the answer, very clearly, that he himself gave, and certainly I would always give and would give my life to defend, is that he was neither a fascist nor a traitor. Indeed, he was a real patriot — in the best sense of the word. An American patriot.

"And above all, he realized that there had been blind spots in his ideas. In fact, he was starting to say the problem with me is that I took a binocular and looked at it from the wrong end. This was his terrible dilemma — because he found himself accused by all sides of having been on the wrong side, of having been with the evildoers. So in the end of the *Cantos,* he says, "That I lost my center, fighting the world. The dreams clash and are shattered."

Finally, I asked her, "Do you have any advice to students who consider being poets or writers?"

She answered, "It's very important to meet older people. In fact, there is this wonderful line in the *Cantos,* 'To have gathered from the air a live tradition, or from a fine old eye the unconquered flame, this is not vanity.'

"Meet people who have borne much and who have seen things. Even if it's just to pay homage or to look into their eyes.

"Read Pound. Read him without listening to what teachers say. I'm not a teacher; I'm a reader. In the *Cantos,* there is stuff for everybody. Because this is the thing, you see. We have to fill ourselves with music, with poetry, with philosophy, because in the end — *we are alone.* I remember when a young Yale professor once told me, 'we are all solipsistically encased.' And I got furious and I said, 'you idiot, that's not so, that's just what you professors are, solipsistically encased, because you sit there in your little cubicle and write books which nobody will read.' But, as I grow older, I can see exactly what he meant.

"And my father once wrote to my mother that he thought in the end, 'we all have to sit on our own rock.' Which is another way of saying we are solipsistically encased. In the end, it is only what you have inside that will help you."

"*The Muses of the Daughters of Memory*"

If we can't look such people in the eye, perhaps we have the opportunity to listen to their voices. Here are a few unusual life stories by or about unusual women. In some, women have written their autobiographies (or been written about) because of their kinship links to a famous family member.

Anthropologist Mary Catherine Bateson grew up with two famous parents, Margaret Mead and Gregory Bateson. Her autobiography is a memoir about them called *With a Daughter's Eye: A Memoir of Margaret Mead and Gregory Bateson* (New York: William Morrow, 1984). When you finish it, turn immediately to Mead's own autobiography, *Blackberry Winter: My Earlier Years* (New York: William Morrow, 1972). This book, Mead's only personal account, is at times riveting in its disclosures and at other times, frustrating at what she simply leaves out.

Mary Douglas Leakey, wife of Louis B. Leakey, mother of Richard Leakey, and scientist-archaeologist in her own professional right, is at the center of a prehistoric dynasty. She, her late husband, and sons are international figures in the history of humankind over the last two million years. Her account, *Disclosing the Past: An Autobiography* (New York: Doubleday, 1984) tells of a brilliant archaeological partnership spanning more than thirty years in East Africa.

Love, danger, and freedom in the midst of a revolution makes very adventuresome reading. Sattareh Farman Farmaian wrote *Daughter of Persia: A Woman's Journey from Her Father's Harem Through the Islamic Revolution* (New York: Crown, 1992, with the assistance of Dona Munker). On one level this is a captivating memoir of one woman's incredible life and the value of personal freedom; on another it is an eloquent eyewitness to the struggle of the country of Iran to find its place in a world of nations.

For a very different, comparative perspective on one woman's life mirrored in Iranian history, read Ashraf Pahlavi, *Faces in the Mirror* (New York: Prentice-Hall, 1980). Pahlavi is the sister of the late Shah or ruler of Iran. She grew up in elite and highly privileged circumstances and witnessed the revolution there after her brother's death. She and Farmaian help us make sense of lived history and dramatic events not of one's own choosing.

Stina Katchadourian grew up speaking Finnish and Swedish as her native tongues. Then she married a man whose mother grew up speaking Armenian and Turkish. At the end of the mother/mother-in-law's life she composed a memoir, a compelling love story bounded by massacres and genocide, migrations and family machinations. Her son translated her story into English, and her daughter-in-law edited and expanded the narrative for English-speaking audiences. Their book is *Efronia: An Armenian Love Story* (based on a memoir by Efronia Katchadourian.

Translated by Herant Katchadourian. Boston: Northeastern University Press, 1993). This memoir is the first in a new series called "Women's Life Writings from Around the World" (edited by Marilyn Yalom).

Worth Discussing

1. Mary's autobiography contains a strong sense of physical spaces, the personality or character of houses, and local environments. Yet there is very little of what anthropologists call "social space" or cultural definitions of social interactions, roles, and appropriate behaviors; that is, who may do what with whom and when. How does architecture or physical spaces as well as social spaces define women's lives differently?

2. Olga Rudge and Ezra Pound may be said to have had an unusual "relationship" as well as unusual "parenting" skills. (These are American terms and I can just hear Mary saying, "You Americans, you have such strange ideas.") What are some ways to discuss Mary's life without bringing contemporary and culturally limited ideas or social judgments to bear?

3. There are several places in Mary's autobiography where she deliberately chooses **how** and **what** to feel, for example, when her father tells her about her birth and his unconventional domestic arrangements. She treats her responses and reactions as options or as outdated trivia, the "clatter of out-lived feelings." How is this possible? Are "feelings" predictable reactions? Or are they under our cognitive control?

4. Fostering is an important and often overlooked custom for raising children. If we can suspend our own cultural notions about how child rearing is "supposed" to be or "should" be, what did these experiences contribute to Mary's life?

Endnotes to Chapter 3

1. To learn more about Ezra Pound, you might check out an excellent literary biography by Noel Stock called *The Life of Ezra Pound* (New York: Random House, 1970). A long account of his complex and fascinating life is found in *A Serious Character: The Life of Ezra Pound* by Humphrey Carpenter (Boston: Houghton Mifflin, 1988). Or do as his daughter suggests, read Pound.

2. See Humphrey Carpenter, *A Serious Character: The Life of Ezra Pound.* (Boston: Houghton-Mifflin, 1988), 636.

3. The University of New Orleans administers a number of major academic programs in Tirol. The largest is in Innsbruck, Austria. The anthropology field school at Brunnenburg Castle has been a smaller part of that program since 1987. As part of these programs, I had the opportunity to conduct field research in Italy and Austria. The resulting ethnography of Tirol (including a history of Brunnenburg) is called *The Hidden Life of Tirol* (Prospect Heights, IL: Waveland Press, 1993).

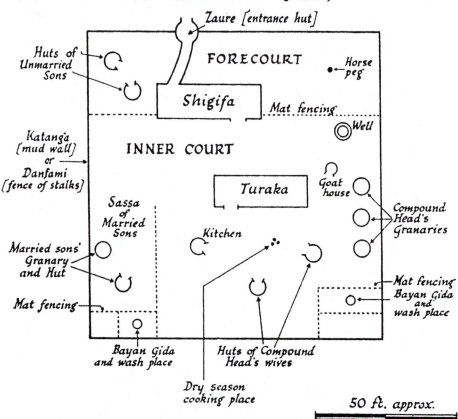

HAUSA COMPOUND (GIDA)

Zaure [entrance hut]

FORECOURT

Huts of Unmarried Sons

Horse peg

Shigifa

Mat fencing

Well

Katanga [mud wall] or Danfami [fence of stalks]

INNER COURT

Turaka

Goat house

Compound Head's Granaries

Sassa of Married Sons

Kitchen

Married sons' Granary and Hut

Mat fencing

Mat fencing Bayan Gida and wash place

Bayan Gida and wash place

Huts of Compound Head's wives

Dry season cooking place

50 ft. approx.

Architecture and the use of shared social spaces shaped Baba's life with various husbands, co-wives, and adopted children. Here is a drawing of one of the Hausa compounds she lived in. Note the separations by marital status, gender, and age.

From Mary F. Smith, Baba of Karo: A Woman of the Muslim Hausa, 36.

Baba

"There Together, I, My Co-Wife, and Our Children"

If you ever had fantasies about living in sprawling extended family compounds or sharing your life with many friends and a few enemies, this is the story for you. If you wondered what happens when one's husbands are married to other women, you will like Baba's account.

Her narrative has the captivating quality of gossip. The intrigues, marriages, separations, and general goings-on reveal the untidy but delicious qualities of lived experience. Baba weaves together ordinary happenings — for her. To us, these details seem wondrously exotic. She talks about kinship, friendship, spirit-worship, the rituals of childbirth and marriage, widowhood, singing or drumming, and the pleasures of giving and receiving gifts.

Baba's autobiography takes place against the backdrop of what is, to Westerners, a distant and exotic place. She lived in northern Nigeria, in the beautiful savannah country on the southern fringes of the Sahara desert of Africa. The scene is often described as orchard bush or open park land. The climate is hot and dry. From November to February, a hot, dry wind (called the *harmattan*) blows from the desert, leaving March and April with intense midday heat, cold nights, dry rivers, and parched vegetation. But rains fall from May to October; everything blossoms. Then people can work their farms.

In Baba's time the staple foods were grains, such as millet, maize, and rice, and the root crops of sweet potatoes, yams, and cassava. Farm products such as groundnuts yielded oil and tasty cakes. Cotton was grown for spinning and weaving. Agricultural products and fabrics were sold locally as well as exported. Farmers also grew sugarcane and onions for local markets and made dyes like indigo and henna for export.

Baba was one of five million Moslem, Hausa-speaking peoples grouped into a series of very large, complex political units under the control of powerful chiefs. Largely followers of Islam, these cultures were then little known outside a small circle of British administrators. You will not need to know the complicated history of this region or the myriad technicalities of Hausa social organizations to enjoy Baba's story. But you will need to know that she lived in a brilliant, dynamic, and ancient culture little known or appreciated here in the West.

The smiths and How They Came to Write Baba's Story

Baba agreed to dictate her life story to Mary Smith (her true name) in 1949 when she was about seventy years old. Mary had accompanied her anthropologist husband, Michael Smith, on an eighteen-month fieldwork trip to northern Nigeria. He wanted to do systematic research on farming, trading, and the elaborate social hierarchies of the Hausa world. This was a time in which European colonial administration and overseas trade had displaced the dynastic politics of the very large, multilayered, and complex chieftainships so characteristic of this area of Africa. Michael Smith and his wife were British citizens and had a grant from the Colonial Social Science Research Council.

In those days many male anthropologists took their wives "into the field" and put them to work there. Mrs. Smith was able to visit the large compounds and talk to women. Her husband could not do this. She learned to speak Hausa, to make friends locally, and to conduct serious research. These are no small achievements; they qualify her as an anthropologist in her own right.

Although the book is listed under her name, nowhere in it does Mary Smith speak about her own unusual experiences in befriending Baba, translating the materials, or coordinating so much information for publication. Instead, her anthropologist-husband speaks about her in his introduction to their book:

> Interviews with Baba occurred daily, for an average period of three hours, and questions were frequently asked to clarify various points. Prior to the start of the work on this autobiography, we had been living in Baba's community for four months, and my wife had collected more than a dozen case-histories from Hausa women in the village, some of whom were related to Baba. My wife undertook these case-studies to supplement my inquiries into Hausa life, since the practices of purdah marriage and the exclusion of men from compounds prohibited me from studying domestic units myself. In Hausa society,

with its custom of secluding wives, it would have been extremely difficult, if not impossible, for a man anthropologist to have interviewed Baba daily and to have received such a complete and unreserved account. In the course of these studies, a friendship grew up between Baba and my wife, and when it appeared more valuable to obtain one detailed life-history from a woman of advanced years than to continue recording the shorter life-spans of younger wives, Baba was an obvious choice, for her intelligence, forthrightness, and faith in our good intentions. It may be worth pointing out that even where adults of opposite sex are not segregated as they are among the Moslem Hausa, a document of this character can only be obtained from a woman by a woman field worker.[1]

With all due respect to Dr. Smith and other colleagues in anthropology, the tedious introduction, footnotes, and the annotations within the text itself may interest specialists. But they hamper readers. This book has meaning today mostly because of the personal details, the lively descriptions, and the obvious intimacy between Mary and Baba. In this age of self-referential, reflexive writings, in which researchers, writers, or translators put themselves and their responses or feelings into the work, we feel strange reading about Baba and finding so little of Mary Smith.

Baba grew up with old and extremely sophisticated storytelling traditions. She liked to circle around a topic several times before she sat down on it. She obviously had no intention of restricting herself to chronological sequences and irrelevant questions. In fact, she had her own categories for what is vital. One can almost hear the interview at times. Mary asks Baba about childbirth or marriage customs. Baba illustrates with a story; after all, she is bored with the technicalities that delight an anthropologist's heart. But Mary Smith wants to (or needs to) fulfill her husband's mission. Ultimately, Baba cooperates and there are very long descriptions of ceremonies, festivals, and customs. But Baba the woman never lets herself be buried.

A Different Kind of Life

Many points in Baba's account challenge our ideas of how the world works. But modern readers cannot write our own cultural assumptions onto the kind of complex society in which Baba lived.

First, you will notice that the wealth of Baba's family partly depended on keeping slaves and that several members of her family had been on slave-raiding expeditions. In fact, her favorite aunt Rabi (whom she treated as her mother) was captured by slave-raiders. Rabi's son ransomed her at a very high cost. Baba's family had lost much of their wealth when the British banned slave trading. This form of slavery, however, appears to be considerably milder than anything that Europeans practiced in the last 300 years. Given how destructive and ugly the customs of slavery were in the United States, it may be difficult to acknowledge the relatively mild forms we see operating here.

Moreover, women were frequently secluded, both spatially and socially. Such practices of seclusion or *purdah* are often part of Islamic religious practices. Contemporary Western women have strong feelings about such practices. As you will see, however, seclusion or semi-seclusion was not the only characteristic of women's lives. Women often initiated their own marriages and divorces and controlled the greater part of personal finances. The frequency of divorce did not make the culture unstable, because kinship ties were more binding, more consequential, than were marital ties. As you shall see, women like Baba often found love and power in unexpected places or in unexpected ways.

Baba and all the kinfolk she stayed with at various times lived in *compounds* such as the one shown in the drawing in this chapter. These were rectangular enclosures surrounded by mud walls, entered through a round hut with a conical thatched roof. They could be quite elaborate in their architecture. A fenced or walled forecourt contained sleeping-quarters for teenagers, unmarried sons, and male guests. Typically, each wife had her own hut or house. Children could be found throughout the compound.

If a man wished his wives to live in complete seclusion, he himself had to fetch the water and wood the household required. Or he had to assign these chores to others. Fortunate households had a well inside the compound. This is why you will find a number of seemingly casual references to who carries water or wood. These are actually references to degrees of seclusion in which Baba lived at various times.

Generally each wife had her own house within her husband's larger compound. There she kept her own possessions; there her young children slept. Typically her husband had his own sleeping quarters and each wife took turns visiting him on the days she was responsible for preparing the household food. Co-wives helped each other out in economic and child-rearing tasks. When not occupied in preparing food for the common household, co-wives did spinning, weaving, or preparing foods or other agricultural materials for sale in the markets. What each made and sold belonged to her, not her husband. A woman was more likely to share economic activities with a co-wife, even a friend, than with a husband.

Baba's life story revolves around certain constant themes. Kinship is first. Friendship, including other women married to her husbands and special friends called *bond-friends,* seems to be second. Marriage runs a distant third.

In Hausaland, a woman was expected to marry young, to remarry soon after divorce or widowhood, and to develop some strategic advantages from being married. A woman's first marriage was the most telling one — not because of romance, sex, or novelty. It mattered because it was the most crucial *rite of passage* in a woman's life. She exchanged the status of a maiden or girl for that of adult woman. To be an adult was to be married. Period.

Although getting married was predictable, staying married was not. Women felt strong attachments to their kinfolk; this fondness might override any attachment they felt to a husband. Men might have as many as four wives; they might be more attached to each other than to their husband. Wives often arranged additional marriages for their husbands and used the situation to further friendships with other women. Alternatively, there was little point in staying with a man who already had a bitchy wife.

A woman's relationships to her co-wives were *as important,* if not more important, than her relationship to her husband. As you will see, divorces were common; this is probably an indication of the strength of the kinship networks, not the fragility of families. Anthropologists say that blood is thicker than water. Kinship is blood; marriage is water.

Notice how Baba talks about the "other women" in her life, her co-wives and her bond-friends. One bond-friend is called *kawa,* several are *kawaye.* Formal bond-friendship between women is a relationship of equals; they share status and age. Women-friends exchange gifts on ceremonial occasions; the gifts become progressively more valuable at each exchange. Mary Smith retained the Hausa word for bond-friends because no equivalent word exists in English. In fact, no equivalent concept exists in English. The formal and informal friendships between women appear to be more emotionally fulfilling than those between husbands and wives.

Having a child was the second most important event in a Hausa woman's life. At this point she became a completed adult. But many women in such groups never conceived a child. No one is certain why this high incidence of infertility existed. Whatever the reason, adopting a baby had become an important feature of Hausa kinship. If a woman like Baba didn't give birth, her relatives arranged for her to adopt a baby. The adoption usually occurred after a baby was weaned, when he or she was about two years old. The child was often a relative, the child of a sister, a bond-friend or a co-wife. More often than not, the child was already living in the compound.

One of the most striking features of Baba's autobiography is the range and flexibility of kinship. For example, look at the number of alternatives children had for finding parents and siblings. Concepts like illegitimacy, orphans, unwanted or neglected children are foreign to Baba's world. Children move in and out, back and forth, between places and people who care for them. They call many relatives, "brother" or "sister." As you will see, they have many "mothers" or "fathers." "Parents" means mothers, fathers, aunts, uncles, co-wives, and most of the senior generation of people related by blood or marriage.

A woman in such a culture can expect to divorce several times during her life and generally will have more marital freedom as she ages. Her large extended family typically "managed," if not actually arranged, a girl's first wedding. Later marriages may be left to a woman's own wishes. This means that the domestic ranking of co-wives is not permanent; no woman suffers a position of subordination or enjoys permanent dominance throughout her life. Nor do women assume the status of their husbands. They don't become Mrs. So-and-So, as Westerners are used to. Husbands and co-wives come and go — as you shall see rather dramatically in Baba's story. Be prepared.

First Memories

In our own compound there was no disagreement, nothing of that kind. My father's wives joked and laughed together. They had nothing to do with quarrelling. They made food, they used to give me nice things, they would say "Let's do this," or "Let's do that," and they did not bicker.

In the morning when the sun got up, our mothers would rise and start making bean-cakes; we would get up and wash our faces and put on our clothes and they would give us the bean-cakes and we would go round the village selling them. When we had sold them we came back and Mother gave us some grain to grind. She did a lot and we did a little. We sang our songs at the door of her hut, we were grinding away. One of us would start the song and the others would answer.

When we had finished grinding we gave our mothers the flour. They cooked a big pot of porridge and a pot of stew; then they would put out the porridge and pour the stew over it, "Take this to so-and-so," "Take this to so-and-so." We picked it up and took it to the men, and then we came back and ate ours with the other children; if we weren't full we got some more. When we were satisfied we put down our wooden bowls and calabashes (there were no enamel bowls then). Then we ran off and played. At nightfall we came back and spread our mats in Mother's hut; the wife who was cooking that day went to the husband's hut. The maker of porridge took fire to the husband's hut, she drew water and she lit the lamp and took it. He would be at the house-door talking to his friends, when he came in he shut the door and went to his hut. The children filled up their mother's hut. In the morning she would wake us up and we all washed our faces.

We brothers and sisters all lived in our mother's hut and at night we would tell stories and talk, then we would go to sleep. When day came we got up and washed our faces, we made porridge and we made millet-balls. When we were able to make porridge and pound grain in the mortar and grind it on the stone, we used to tell Mother to sit down and we would do it for her. When we had slaves they did the house-work, ours was only play. My mother and her co-wife spun thread for sale, they made millet-balls for sale, they made bean-cakes, groundnut cake, roasted salted groundnuts, fried groundnuts, and groundnut oil — they sold them all. At that time our mothers did not know how to weave as we do now, on broadlooms. The wives used to make porridge and stew for their husband, they made it very tasty, with meat. The slaves made their own food separately, and we made a little bit of porridge and a little bit of stew in a very small pot. Boys follow their fathers, they learn to farm and recite the Koran [the Holy Book of Islam]; girls follow their mothers, they spin and cook.

Father was dark, short like his father, with long thin hands and feet. When we got up in the morning we used to go to his hut and greet him. "How did you sleep? Have you rested?" "I am quite well, I am quite rested." When he had dressed he went out to the entrance-hut and ate his food with his brothers, they would all come, one would spread his mat here, one would spread his there. His son would bring him food, millet-balls or porridge. Malam Buhari would come, Andu would come, they would sit down and eat. When they had finished we brought them water to wash their hands, and picked up the things and ate up the remains until we were quite full. We had already had our food inside the compound, then we came and ate what they had left, we picked it all up and took it away. If they were going out to the farm and it was the work season, then they would get up and go. If it was not the farming season they would go to the market, until the afternoon when everyone went home.

My father farmed and he was a Koranic student, a *malam* [also used here as an honorary title for literate men]. He taught the boys to recite from the Book. When we went to Karo, the slaves would sweep the compound and the grain would be distributed, they would come and say, "Greetings, blessings on you! The people from the town have come back." Then there would be games and rejoicing and we would play together. They used to have double names, if you called the first part of the name they answered and completed it, like this: if there was a "Gift of Allah," you would call "Gift!" and she would answer "of Allah!" There was "Wealth belongs to" — "Allah," "Life in this world" — "Patience," "The Lord of all slaves" — "Allah," those were all women slaves. The men were called "May Allah prolong" — "our father's life," "Gift of Allah," and many others. The slaves called us daughters of the house "Yaya," as we call our elder brothers and sisters; they called my brother "Yaya" too, or "Kawu" as we call our mother's brothers.

I played with my ten "sisters," and when the dry season came round we went to live inside the town and left the slaves there in the hamlet. Sarkin [Chief] Gandu was in charge of them, he and his wives and children always lived at Karo. When he went to the farm he gathered them all together to work, when they had finished they went to their homes and did their own work, each one had his own farmland. When we went in to Zarewa in the dry season, the season of marriage feasts, we found everyone making marriage porridge, killing chickens and goats, and taking food to the men to eat, and taking food to the drummers so that they should eat and we should enjoy their drumming.

At the New Year festival, the Feast of the Full Stomach, we eat chickens and meat until we are quite full. When we were young, the boys would go out that night and draw water from twelve wells, then we took the water home and drank it and washed in it. Then we would put on our best clothes and lie down in them and go to sleep. You feel how good the world is.

When I was a maiden the Europeans first arrived. Ever since we were quite small the *malams* had been saying that the Europeans would come with a thing called a train, they would come with a thing called a motor-car, in them you would go and come back in a trice. They would stop wars, they would repair the world, they would stop oppression and lawlessness, we should live at peace with them. We used to go and sit quietly and listen to the prophecies. They would come, fine handsome people, they would not kill anyone, they would not oppress anyone, they would bring all their strange things. We were young girls when a European came with his attendants. "See, there's a white man, what has brought him?" He was asking the way to some town. We ran away and shut the door and he passed by and went on his way.

Not long after all this my own mother was killed by lightning; there was a storm on the fourteenth day of the month of the Great Feast. She came hurrying back from the river with water and went into her hut with her two younger children. Then lightning struck the hut and it blazed up, *pa-a-a-a-a*. The people of the house came rushing in from the entrance-hut, but they found them dead. I was playing with the other children when the storm came; the rain poured down and we went into the house of Makadi the drummer. The market was empty, everyone was sheltering and watching the storm. When I was in the drummer's house they brought the bodies out and took them behind the hut. At that time if someone died they were buried behind their hut. The malams were called, we children hid; the wife of our "father" Sa'i came and took us to her hut in the compound nearby, she stayed with us. When they brought us some food I said, "I can't eat."

After my mother had done my hair and washed me and looked after me, after she had done all that for me, she died in the fire. When they brought her out, quite still, I fell down and cried, when I rose up I threw myself on the ground again, I cried and cried. My younger brother Tango died with her. She was a beautiful woman with lovely hair and light skin. One day at Azahar she went to the well to draw water, then the storm came and her hut caught fire and she could not get out, she died. I was about ten years old and my brother Kadiri was about seven.

I Marry My Cousin Duma

When I was about fourteen years old it was time for me to be married; I had grown up with our six "fathers," the sons of Ibrahim Dara and his younger brother Maidamishi, and when the time came they arranged my marriage within the family, a marriage of kinsfolk. I was married to Duma the son of Sidi; Sidi was the son of my grandfather Mai Yana, Mai Yana and Ibrahim Dara being the sons of two brothers. I called Sidi "father" and his son Duma was my elder brother; I called him "Yaya." Duma's father Sidi and my father put their heads together, the elder brother said to my father, "We will marry them to one another," and his younger brother replied "Very well." They were always arranging marriages between kinsfolk in our family, everyone married his kinswoman and took her to his compound. My mother was dead at that time, and my father's sister Rabi was like my mother, but she had been kidnapped [by slave traders]. My father sent for me and I went to him and curtsied. "Your kinsman desires you," he said; "I also desire him," I replied.

Dabo, the son of Sarkin Zarewa, our town chief, loved me and I wanted him, but my family would not agree to our marrying. They did not like titles and title-holders; they were farmers, they liked their daughters to marry farmers. We often married into the families of blacksmiths, too; blacksmiths are the farmers' friends, they make our tools. Blacksmiths and farmers like to join their children in marriage. That was why I could not marry Sarkin Zarewa's son. There was also a Malam Maigari who wished to marry me, I promised him I would come to him later.

When it was time for me to be married the elders of our family met for the betrothal ceremony. A month later they "set the day"; and two months after that was the wedding feast. That is three months altogether. At the *Salla* [betrothal] feast before our marriage Duma came to visit me. He could come inside our compound and he brought me money and kolanuts and perfume, and told me to go and buy cloth. I went to the market and bought cloth. He came and we conversed together. I bought bowls and some flat baskets and a few plates. Then on the marriage day my father's family and my mother's family all came. They brought sacks of guineacorn, sacks of rice, baskets of salt, of onions and of locust-bean cakes, and oil. They decorated my new hut with all my things, and they set out my plates and bowls and spread mats on the bed and the floor.

If you were going to be taken to your hut today, there is drumming and drumming. Tomorrow your kinsfolk will bring you all sorts of lovely things. The men load their donkeys with sacks of corn and rice, and the women put on their best cloths and carry the plates and bowls. They bring it all to you and put your dowry in your hut. Yesterday evening you were in your hut, you covered your head and wept — no more going to play with the young girls. You would hear their drumming. You would hear it but you wouldn't be able to go out and dance. You feel very angry. Then your mother comes and talks to you, "Be quite, be calm, stop crying!" One of my aunts came (my mother was dead and Aunt Rabi was lost), she sent away the children, "Run away!" Then she talked to me and I was quiet.

Then my husband's wife, my co-wife, came and took me to my new hut. She gave me some food and said to me, "Take out your spinning." We sat there spinning, and she coaxed me, and I felt better. Her name was Ture and when I married Duma she had a daughter Marka — that means steady rain, she was born in the raining season — and a son called Ciwake, which means "Eat-beans"; they were eating beans when he was born. She was a very good-tempered woman. Duma was tall and handsome and sensible. We lived together in peace with no quarrelling or anything of that kind.

At that time I had been married for three years to my kinsman. His chief wife had two children when I married him, she was carrying one on her back and the other could walk. When father's sister Rabi (we called her "Baba's mother") was brought home from Abuja I was very happy. Everyone came to say, "Blessings on your fortune, Baba's mother!" Everyone praised her resourceful son. We heard that the mother of Baba had come home, so we went to her compound, we were all over her — you couldn't see her! She was staying in her son's compound, he had two wives; there were kinsfolk and friends and kawaye, like a whole town.

When she came home I no longer wanted to live in the hamlet. I preferred the town. My "'parents" told me to go back to him, but I refused. Then my husband's "parents" came and said I must go back. When I still said I would not go, then all the elders, men and women, came to Aunt Rabi's compound and assembled in the entrance hut. The old women sat with the men in the entrance hut. Some of them said, "She must have patience and return," others said, "Since she dislikes the marriage it is better that they part." Then they sent for me. I came in and they said, "You must put up with it, you must have patience. Your husband is our kinsman, you must go on with your marriage." I said, "No."

Duma was there. He said, "I want her to calm down and come home; send for her." I came and knelt down, and he asked me, "What have I done to you? Be sensible and come back. You know I want you, stop being angry and come home." I said, "No." He wanted me very much, but I didn't want him. I desired a son of the blacksmiths, Maigari of the South Gate. When I was a girl he used to give me money on market-days. He had wanted to marry me, but I refused so that my parents should not be angry with me and beat me. I had promised him I would come. I said, "Be patient, I will not remain there."

When Aunt Rabi came home I knew she would help me. Before she was taken away, Maigari had begun to court me. Then when she was not there they had married me to someone else. When she came back I felt good. I told her that I didn't like the marriage and she said, "Very well, go and break it up. You didn't want him" she said, "and they did that to you. Go and get divorced, I am back."

Aunt Rabi was there in the entrance hut where they were discussing my marriage; she said to them, "Baba said she did not wish to marry Duma. Very well, you forced her. Now I have come back and she is not going to stay married to him." That was that. All the fathers had come to Aunt Rabi's compound and she had told them off soundly. We all went to Sarkin Zarewa's compound.

But before that I had paid a visit to the chief's house. I went to see his head wife, I knew his wives. She said, "What brings you?" I said, "I have come to break off my marriage." She explained the matter to Sarki. When I went to his house officially, to start the divorce proceedings, I went inside the compound to his own hut, I knelt down and greeted him.

"Allah preserve your life."

"Good woman of Karo, what brings you here?"

"I want to break off my marriage."

"Indeed! Be patient and go back. What is his fault?"

"He hasn't done anything. But I don't like the hamlet, I prefer the town."

Then he looked at me. Then he said, "Very well."

I did not mention the matter of Maigari. Sarki gave me a document and my marriage with Duma was over. Duma and I remained friends. Our kinship did not die.

Second Marriage

I stayed for three months, ninety days, during my *Iddah* [ritual seclusion after divorce — to make sure an ex-wife is not pregnant], in Aunt Rabi's home. Then the one who desired me came forward, a son of the blacksmiths, whom I also desired. He had known me when I was a maiden and he was a young man. Aunt

Rabi didn't like him, she preferred Musa, but I did not like Musa. Then the day I had finished Iddah she said Musa was to be my husband. I said, "No."

Then she was angry so I left her compound and went to Haleru's, to his wife's hut. Haleru was my grandmother Anja's youngest son. Malam Maigari sought me there, he came with his friend Mentari. I received them alone, I bowed down and welcomed them. He said, "We desire you, but your mother Rabi does not want us. We have come to hear from your own mouth what you wish." I said, "Yes, I wish it."

On the day of the marriage I was taken to my new hut. After seven days the dowry was brought. Seven days after Malam Maigari had asked my family for my hand, we were married; and after seven more days they brought my dowry.

I didn't cry because I liked him. I did not love Duma, but my fathers said they would beat me. They would tie my legs and beat me again and again, so I said nothing more. I agreed. Your mothers never beat you, but fathers do. Your own father wouldn't do it. He would call his younger brother and say, "Beat her." His younger brother ties you up tightly like a thief; your father calls him, so that no one shall say that he who begot you did it. But he is there, looking on. Duma never beat me at all. Husbands aren't supposed to do it, only fathers. But some husbands do, if you do something wrong.

For seven days the bridegroom's kin collected the gifts, then the old women and children of Malam Maigari's compound carried them to Ubangida. On the marriage day they brought a calabash of salt, the "salt of seeking," a calabash of kolanuts, the "meat of seeking," and three cloths. These were divided between my father's and my mother's kin. Then they brought ten thousand cowries *sadaki,* this was mine. There was money for greeting the kin, eighty thousand cowries, half for my father's and half for my mother's kin. When my representatives and Malam Maigari's had solemnized the marriage they came back from Karo. All these things are divided up amongst the kinsfolk and friends. They all have a very little so that they may "feel the marriage." I was not present at the marriage cere-mony, neither was Maigari. Our parents went to Malam Buhari's house at Karo, and when they returned they said, "We have performed the ceremony." For this ceremony at Malam Buhari's compound there were the five fathers and my father's and my mother's kinsmen, and about thirty of Malam Maigari's.

That was that, until the day of the feast came. Everyone took up a full cal-abash, and plates, some with rice, some with guineacorn. The bridegroom also sent food for the bride. I remained in Haleru's compound for seven nights.

That night Malam Maigari brought one thousand cowries and twenty kolanuts and some perfume when he came to my hut. The children were teasing him. Then when everyone was asleep and I had put out the lamp and lain down, he came in. He said, "Light the lamp so that I can see your eyes." I hid my eyes, I felt shy. When he had lit the lamp he said, "I thank you, I thank you. You have kept your promise. I thank you, I am happy."

Then we made our marriage for fifteen years, but we had no children. Then I left him. I loved him very much, I left him because I had to — I had no children. There was his head wife, she had two children when I married him. When I left she had eight. Then the youngest of his wives came, she was given to him as alms [marriage without payments]. She brought forth six children, all before my eyes. She was Uwa, her father was a wealthy man in the town who gave her to Malam Maigari as a gift. Her father liked Malam Maigari. They were not kinsfolk, it was just that he admired our husband. So there were three of us.

His head wife, the mother of his household, was a good-tempered woman. We were fourteen years together. Each one of us made food in turn and we all ate. Then when she was not cooking for the household, each one made cakes to sell, or other food. The maker of millet-balls made them, the maker of groundnut-cakes made them, and so on. I spun cotton; I made groundnut-cakes and bean-cakes and other sorts of cakes. I made roasted and salted ground nuts. I also wove cloth, then I made locust-bean cakes. I made a sweetmeat of rice and honey and another of sugar and groundnuts, which was very good to eat.

About four years after I married Malam Maigari my aunt Rabi cooled; that day she sent me her gifts for my marriage — corn, locust-bean cakes, salt, oil, and rice; she sent me all those, when her anger had cooled. That is what people do.

Tales About Other People's Marriages

Here we women have a special custom: if your husband gives you kolanuts and tobacco-flowers, you know that he desires you. You sit in your hut in the evening, eating kolanuts and rubbing the tobacco-flowers on your teeth. You feel good. As you finish with the tobacco-flowers you put them in a flat basket and hand it up on your wall. You do this for seven days; you collect them. On the following Friday you send a young girl to your kawa with the used tobacco-flowers. If your kawa's husband has also been giving her tobacco-flowers and kolanuts, she hangs your little basket on the wall. And for seven days she collects her used flowers. Then when the Friday comes she puts them all together, yours and hers, and sends them back to you. Then you both know that your marriages are going well.

After dark the kawaye will go to visit each other, they laugh and are glad because each one knows her husband desires her. But if the husband of one of them does not give her kolanuts and tobacco-flowers, and the other one sends her a little basket full of used flowers, then the neglected one will break up her marriage. That is, it is her kawa who has caused the marriage to break up. One wants to be treated as well as one's friend.

If a husband is not wealthy and cannot give her presents, then the wife's family will say, "Leave him, leave him! It isn't a good marriage. No gifts, no marriage." The things which make a good marriage are these: a man desires you, you desire him. He marries you. He keeps giving you gifts, he buys you cloth and kolanuts. If he is earning money, he takes out a little of it at the festival and buys you a cloth. A townswoman prefers money, a countrywoman prefers grain — give a countrywoman a hoe and she will do her own farming and eat her corn. But a wealthy man who is quarrelsome — no woman will settle — what is the use of quarrelling? A good-tempered man is better. Yet one desires money . . . You see?

We have a fable about the madness caused by jealousy between a man's wives. There was a wife who went to a malam. She asked him to give her medicine so that her co-wife would go mad and leave her in the compound alone. He said "Here it is. If you call her and she doesn't answer, you will go mad. If she answers, she will go mad. Do you understand?" She said she understood. The next day she returned to him and he gave her the medicine. He said, "It is not my responsibility." She said, "I will find her." She returned home and called her co-wife. Silence. Then she began to dance in the open space of the compound. The madness seized her.

The co-wife's father was a malam also, and he had told her, "Don't take anything she gives you, don't reply if she calls you." When she heard the other wife calling her name she remained quite quiet. When the jealous wife went mad she went off into the bush. That is a tale of long ago; they still do that sort of thing, but not in the same way as they did in the past; nowadays women get charms, but only to drive out their co-wives. They don't use medicine for madness now. They are afraid of you [the British]. They don't want to be caught and taken before the Christians and killed. It is the same with all the bad things of the past — they are finished. People are afraid to do them. Now life is peaceful.

Sometimes a wife, if her husband is away, will steal her own body and go off to other men. Whoever sees her going along the road and desires her, he sends a message by an old woman:

"I have come to greet you. How is the master of the house?"

"He is very well thank you. He has gone away to work."

"When will he return?"

"Tomorrow."

"See, here are some kolanuts, here is some money; so-and-so sent them to you."

"I'll come tonight."

Then quickly, quickly, the wife pays her visit and returns. In the compound of his bond-friend the man will borrow a hut and take her in his compound! If the faithless wife has a co-wife she will say to her, "I am going to visit my family." The co-wife will keep her secret. A married woman may have ten lovers, or even twenty — then or nowadays. She will go and tell her kawa about it. They desire men and they desire money. I never behaved like that.

I remember they used to call Malam Maigari's house "The house of the beautiful women at the South Gate."

Aunt Rabi Breaks Up My Marriage

For fifteen years I was in Malam Maigari's compound. Then my father's sister Rabi came and said, "Look at everyone bearing children, look at everyone else bearing children. Leave that compound and you will bear children too." I said, "I will not leave him, I am not going anywhere else." My kawa Tine had been married five times. Then when she married the Chief of Kilu, she had her first child, a son. My mother Rabi knew this. Yarbala had been married three times. Then when she went to Garaje and married, at last she had a daughter. My father's sister said, "Leave him and you will have children." I refused and said I would not leave his compound. From the very first time she had not liked this marriage.

Malam came into my hut, he talked to me and asked me to be patient. I said, "It's my mother, she wants me to leave you." Malam's elder brother said, "They must not be separated. Ask her where is the fault, no one has ever annoyed her, neither child nor man." I said, "My mother says I must leave, she says I must leave him, she does not want me to remain here in this compound." We were there for some time. Then Malam Maigari said, "I am in love." I said, "It is not anyone's fault, my mother wants me to leave." The chief gave me my divorce paper, he gave Malam his. Malam said he did not wish me to return the sadaki. I was to keep it, he would prefer it so. I went to Aunt Rabi's compound and stayed there. Malam Maigari sent a message to say that if I ceased being angry would I please come back and we would re-make the marriage. Aunt Rabi was rejoicing over me. She was happy, so I said I would not go back.

Even now I love him Malam Maigari and he loves me. When I go to Zarewa to see my kin, I stay for three months in his house; he and his wives are always asking me to come back.

A Third Husband, Malam Hasan, and Many More Friends

Malam Hasan did not build a sleeping-hut for himself. He said he didn't like it. He came to our huts; in mine there were two beds, his and mine. If there are a lot of children, one makes a separate hut for the husband. He eats his food there and then there is a different hut for the children. If it is like our compound was, with no husband's hut, when the children get sense — about three or four years old — then you turn them out and they go and sleep somewhere else when the husband comes to your hut. When they get older and go out playing in the evening, they go to the hut of some old lady and sleep. And in the morning they come home. The boys too sleep in the hut in the forecourt of someone's compound. They gather together and spend the night. Old people are the friends of children.

Yelwa, my adopted daughter, and the girls with whom she is playing often come into my hut. They fill up the hut and sleep; they bring their boys with them. When the old woman is tired of them she drives them out, "Run off to the boys' hut, run off to the boys' hut!" Then they all go off to the hut at the front of some compound. The boys and girls all go and they light a lamp, they talk and tell stories and laugh. When the girls get older, some of them become pregnant, but not many. They laugh and joke but they don't lie together a great deal. Also, when they are thirteen or fourteen years old, you marry them at once and they get a husband. Some of them conceive after five months. Some of them wait five years and are not pregnant. If the girl has been with men, her husband will be angry when he marries her. Some will drive her out; some will put up with it. If she should become pregnant before she is married, her lover, if he is a good man, will say he wishes to marry her. There is a feast and everyone rejoices.

If it is not like that, she will say, "The child is his" and he will say, "No." Some men even run away and go out into the world. Then the girl's family marry her off quickly. If her husband sees that she is pregnant he may go to the judge and say the child is not his. Then there is quarrelling and arguing. Sometimes he will divorce the girl, sometimes he will stay with her. If he divorces her, her family wail. Some girls like that run away and live on their own. Some even kill the child; they say they don't want it. But some put their own thing on their back [take responsibility]. They wash their child and carry him about so that he shall be strong.

There was a girl in our town who had a child before she was married. She said, "It belongs to so-and-so," and he said it was not his. When the child grew up, she was lovely. Then the man said it was his; he married the mother and accepted his own child. "A child born before the beginning" we call it, a child born before his mother is married, that is a bastard. There were not many in Old Giwa, and I have only heard of three since we came here to New Giwa six years ago. They were people from the hamlets, not living in the town. If that happens the kawaye of the girl make songs and the girl feels very ashamed.

What have you been eating, you're swelling up like an okra!
Perhaps it's sweet potatoes you've been eating.

Allah preserve us till harvest
And let us see how the okra swells up!

After nine months, indeed she'll bring it forth. You'll see the okra emerge! They sing songs at her everywhere — where's the pleasure of it? The parents of girls forbid them to go with young men, but some do it.

Those sort of girls sleep in an old woman's hut. Then when the old woman is asleep they slip out quietly, no one knows. A clever one may go off and pay money and get a charm, then she goes to ruin. If they get pregnant some of them drink henna. They vomit and they get diarrhea and they usually miscarry. If they take indigo, they get very ill indeed. Some tie a kolanut round their waist so that they can sleep with a man and not become pregnant. Then there is writing-medicine, the ink of a text; if a malam wants money, then won't he give it to you? Of course he will. But not all malams do it. Some old women don't care, they say the girls can go and do what they like, they let them go and sleep with the young men. Others scold the girls.

I have two kawaye here at Giwa, you remember there were five of us at Zarewa when we were young girls. These are different. One woman says to the other, "My desire" and the other answers, "Good faith." I have had my kawa Yargoggo, the wife of Tanko, for about ten years. Laraba has been my kawa for fifteen years; we have exchanged gifts together. Laraba sent a message to say she liked me, then I bought gifts of friendship and sent them to her — a bottle of perfume, twenty kolanuts, and powder. When I had been living in Giwa for about four years she sent the wife of her younger brother, who came to our compound and said, "I am to tell you that Laraba likes you." I said, "Yes, I like her." I bought gifts of liking, I gave them to my co-wife Adama to take to Laraba.

On the Friday Laraba came. I spread mats, I spread more mats on the floor of my hut. We greeted one another, we rejoiced and gave thanks. A friendship had been made. Laraba divided the kolanuts of friendship among the people of her compound. She sent some to a great many other compounds, to the men and women of her kin and anyone who knew us. You distribute the kolanuts of friendship and everyone who receives one says, "May Allah increase friendship and agreement!" We were there thus until seven days before the feast when Laraba bought two chickens, a calabash full of rice, salt, onions, locust-bean cakes, a calabash of kolanuts, a bottle of oil. She sent it all to me so that I should eat good food. The day before the feast I got about four shillings and I sent her money for hairdressing so that she could buy some henna and stain her arms and legs and have her hairdresser to do her hair.

The following festival she bought a young she-goat and chickens and two calabashes of kolanuts, salt, locust-bean cakes, and oil, and sent it all to me. Then her co-wife had a child, so I bought a big cloth. I put a one-pound note with it and a huge bowl full of guineacorn. The cloth was for her to tie her co-wife's child on her back. The guineacorn was so that she could make gruel, and the money so that she could pay the barber-doctor. That is, I completed the ceremony. There would be no further gifts to cement the friendship.

Thenceforth we would exchange ceremonial gifts with one another. If she had a ceremony in her compound or among her kinsfolk, I would take her a little florin. If I had a ceremony, she would bring me four shillings. Next time she had one I would take her eight shillings — ceremony after ceremony, at each one you do that. When the money reaches ten or twelve shillings we divide. If I am due to give her twelve shillings and we are going to divide, I bring the twelve shillings and give it to her. She keeps six shillings and returns six to me. Then I take out threepence and give it to her in addition. I say, "We will start again." Next time one of us has a ceremony we start again at sixpence. We consult one another and discuss our affairs. Her daughter is my daughter, her son is my son.

When we had lived together, Hasan and I, for about seven years, Danfangi, the chief of Giwa town, died, leaving his wife Adama pregnant. She and I put our heads together — she used to visit our compound — and I said, "Won't you marry my husband? We can have a son and live happily together." Four months after she had her child, we started to seek her in marriage. An old man was also courting her. But she was young and did not want him, so Malam Hasan repaid him his gifts. I said to Malam, "Look at Adama, she wants to marry you." Malam said, "Oh, you! She doesn't want me. Look at her mother, she doesn't agree."

Then I took Malam's gifts to Adama. She and I used to discuss our affairs together. She used to come to our compound and we would have a talk. I would go to their hamlet and gossip to her. After five months, on the day she finished her ablutions [ritual washing after childbirth], Malam gave his friend thirty shillings to take to her, so that her family should divide it. Her mother forbade the marriage; she said she would not agree. The daughter said she did agree. That was that, they accepted our gift.

The Day of Coming Together was a Friday. We were all ready. Then at dawn Chief Fagaci sent Malam Hasan away suddenly on official business. In those days we had no bicycles, so he went on foot. Adama came; but her bridegroom wasn't there. We had a great feast, there was porridge and chickens, rice and sweetmeats from all the kin in the hamlets round about. At night we took food to the bride's compound and everybody ate it. At night, too, we filled up the compound with visitors, and then the bride was brought. The drummers of the big and small drums, the players of stringed instruments and Fagaci's pipeplayers, they all came to the front of our compound. But the bridegroom wasn't at home! We spent the night enjoying ourselves. The *bori* [possessing spirits] came; Giwa, Dangaladiman Busa's mother, was possessed. The menfolk were throwing away their money, the womenfolk were throwing away their money, but still the bridegroom wasn't there.

When he had been four days in Birnin Gwari he returned. We had set out her dowry in rows in the bride's hut, like the ridges on a farm. The bride had her baby on her back. Her kinsfolk all crowded to the wedding, my kinsfolk from Zarewa came too. We swept the house clean.

I took Adama's child, Audi. I carried him on my back. Until she weaned him she only lived with us, we were her guardians. Then when she had weaned Audi she had her first daughter by Malam Hasan. They gave her to me and I carried her about on my back — Hawwa became my daughter. I carried her about on my back, I washed her, I carried her and I washed her and Allah preserved her.

Later there was some dispute about her. Our husband said he would not agree to her being taken away, she must remain with me. He knew I loved her, he did not want my heart to be broken. Just before he died he called us and he said to Adama, "I shall not get up again. Do not cause her sorrow on account of that daughter; Baba is to keep her." I loved Hawwa, my husband gave her to me in that way.

Adama had seven children in our compound; the girls Hawwa, Safia, A'i, Goma and the boys, Wada, Garba, and Audi. I took Hawwa and Wada when they were weaned; they are mine. If they went into Adama's hut she would say, "Run away to your own hut!" and they would run off. Garba and Safia died. Goma died last year. Four of Adama's children are alive now. Ten days after our husband died she brought forth Audu [a baby girl]; it is six years now since Malam Hasan died. Our husband died leaving Adama pregnant, and her first husband had done the same thing.

We lived happily in Malam Hasan's compound. If I asked Adama to do something she said, "Yes, certainly." If she asked me to do something I agreed. There was no jealousy over the children. Our husband gave us sufficient food; we were happy. Even now I visit Adama's compound — she is married to Ibrahim the praise-singer — and we talk.

When our husband became ill we were no longer confined to the compound, we went out. When he had been well, he paid boys to fetch us wood and water. But when we saw that he was in pain we went and fetched the wood and water ourselves. When Malam Hasan told Chief Fagaci that he wasn't well, Fagaci sent away for some herbs. Hasan drank the medicine; he felt better. But then his head started to ache and his body ached. Then one day he lay down and said, "I shan't get up from this illness." We said, "Be patient and bear it. May Allah heal you." Two days later he died. He hadn't been strong for some time, he couldn't eat, he only drank a little gruel.

We were there together, I and my co-wife and our children. She had been pregnant for a long time and ten days later she bore Audu. We wailed, we threw ourselves down on the ground. We wailed and wept.

We remained in the mourning for 130 days. Adama couldn't carry it out, because Audu was born so soon after Malam died. You say your five daily prayers and you pray for your husband. Adama had her child in our compound. I went into her hut but I could not be the midwife because I was in mourning. I went into her hut and I sat down there and I took the child. Adama's own mother looked after the little girl and was midwife.

After 130 days a widow comes out of mourning. That night she does not sleep; there is drumming on calabashes until the morning. The morning comes and she bathes herself; she dresses in a new blouse, a new cloth, a new head-kerchief. She takes off her old clothes and gives them as alms to an old woman. Everyone in your kin and in your husband's kin comes with alms — guineacorn, rice, millet, money. You prepare porridge and *cuge* [a special food made from uncooked grain flour and given away after a death]. The malams come and recite the prayers, and you distribute food to them and send it round the compounds.

If the woman is young, not an old lady like me, that same day that the malams have recited the last prayers, they also recite the marriage verses and she is married again. As I was old I went to the compound of my younger brother Kadiri, taking Yelwa and Haawa with me; I left Adama there in our compound with her baby and Wada and Goma and Lawal.

When your husband dies, you must wail. If you love him, then you are sad at heart also, he isn't there. If you didn't particularly like him, you wail because of compassion. You had got used to him and now he isn't here. Ah, Allah preserve us in health!

I Marry My Present Husband

When my last husband, Malam Hasan, died, Malam Maigari and his wives wanted me to go back. But my younger brother Kadiri married me off here to Ibrahim. Ai, my younger brother is here, I am living in his house, I eat his porridge, I don't have to do any work; his wife Gwamma makes porridge for me. At Malam Maigari's house they said they would like me to go back and just live there. They would do the work for me.

But, you see, I can always lecture Kadiri and he has to listen; this month I was annoyed with him, I told him off and he listened and did what I said. I like my younger brother. There are kinsfolk here. In every compound there are kinsfolk of mine, more than a hundred of my grandchildren and grandchildren's children.

Perhaps later in the dry season I will visit our town. The mother of our house-hold, Malam Maigari's head wife, died last year, and also his eldest son Dogara. He sent to say he wanted me to return — but here I am with my husband Ibrahim. I go and greet him, I take him some kolanuts, he brings me kolanuts. He has no hut in his compound. I say I will not live in the hut of his wife who has gone wan-dering off, because she may return. Also I prefer my brother's house. Also there are my adopted children here, there are kinsfolk here. I said that just now I will not go back.

If Kadiri should bring back the second Gwamma [another one of his wives], then I should leave her hut, in which I am living at the moment. I should get rid of the goats that are in my own hut and sell them. I should return to my own hut. Then there would be quarrelling. If I got tired of it I should go to the home of my children here in Giwa, or I should go to the compound of my children in Zarewa — there are plenty of them. Or I could go to the house of my husband Ibrahim, I married him last year.

Ever since I finished my mourning for Malam Hasan he had been seeking me, they said to me, "Marry him, it is better than living alone." Last year I said, "Very well, I will." We performed the marriage, but I did not join him. His wife went to visit her kin last dry season. She went to a naming-feast, but she hasn't returned yet and he hasn't followed her. It is eight months since she left. True, she may never come back, but the marriage is still there. He said to me, "Come and live in her hut, " but I refused. I am afraid she may come back and drive me out. I said that if he wished me to come he should build a hut for me and I would come in. He hasn't done it yet.

In the mornings I go and greet him and enquire how he has slept. When I don't go he comes to our compound and I meet him in the entrance hut and we greet one another. A few days ago he said, "I hear you are working with your European woman." I said, "Yes, we are busy with our work." He said, "You didn't tell me? I, the master of the house?" So on market-day I gave him sixpence. I said, "'Enjoy the market, buy kolanuts and meat and things for stew." I said, "We are working." He was very pleased.

When Malam Hasan died, Malam Maigari sent to ask me to come back to his compound, but I refused to go back. I like Kadiri, my younger brother, and I wanted to live near him. I have lived in his compound for five years now, I haven't been away at all. I look after my goats, I make a little money, I sell a little firewood, I get a little money to buy marriage cloths for my adopted children. I rear the goats, then when there are five I sell one and buy a little cloth. I sell a goat for fifteen shillings, but if they are small they won't fetch more than seven or eight shillings. Last year I sold one. This year I shan't sell any because there are none big enough. Next year, if Allah preserves them alive, I shall sell two and buy a cloth.

I have never been pregnant with a child. Kadiri only has one, yet my younger sister has lots of children. Her hut is full. I drank malams' medicine, I drank *bori* [spirit] medicine, but I never had one. You can only have that which Allah gives you — isn't that so? That is your destiny.

Giwa School
Zaria Province
3 June 1951

Very many greetings to Mrs. Mary Smith. I hope you are all as well as we are here at Giwa. After greetings, I wish to inform you that Baba received your letter of the 14th of May 1951. She received it on the 18th of May 1951. I read her the news of your son Daniel's birth, also the news of his cot and sucking and great sleeping, and his lack of patience when hungry. She laughed a great deal. Also that he has a lot of hair on his head. She says he got all that hair from his mother, his father has not got much hair on his head.

Baba became ill on the 28th of May 1951, she died on the 3rd of June 1951. She was 74 years old, that is to say she was born in 1877. Before she died she was saying, "I shall die without seeing my son Daniel." I hope you will write down this story for him, so that he can read it one day when he grows up. I gave 1 Pound 2 shillings so that they could buy her a shroud. . . .

Malam Abdu
Arabic Teacher,
Giwa School

"I Hope You Will Write Down This Story for Him"

This may sound odd, but each time I read Baba's life, I feel sad. It is not that people die and cultures change; I can accept that. But I think about how much richness and potential the world has lost because of systems of slavery and colonialism.

The Nigeria that Baba experienced no longer exists. Hausa peoples are part of the postcolonial nations and history of Africa. Their contemporary story contains civil wars, droughts, and economic, political, and social changes unimaginable in 1950.

The book was written for anthropologists, and it retains some limited value for specialists. Ironically, however, the meaning or relevance of this and similarly obscure works may belong to Baba's descendants. Recently I met a number of Africans at a conference. These days anthropologists have many reasons to be defensive about our connections to colonialism. We have much to account for. However, these colleagues laughed at my false sense of responsibility. They told me they found obscure monographs about death customs or dull articles with lists of titles or places in one tribe or another very useful. They want to write personal and national narratives on their own terms and in their own ways. So they are searching libraries and archives for accounts like Baba's. Somewhere her grandchildren and their families live on. In the larger context, the customs alive today are descended from those of the past, just as people are.

They asked me, "Wouldn't you like to know something about the lives of your great grandmothers or great, great grandmothers? Would you be glad someone wrote their story down so you could read it?" You bet I would!

As Told To: The Value of Autobiography

There is a long and honorable tradition of anthropologists' wives writing great ethnographies and collecting astonishing autobiographies. Some women have achieved anthropological immortality just by helping out a husband or keeping busy while he did fieldwork. The most obvious and perennially popular example is Marjorie Shostak's famous autobiography of an African Bush woman: *Nisa — The Life and Words of a !Kung Woman* (New York: Random House, 1981). Not only is the book emotional, earthy, and vivid, but we are treated to the collaborative energies of two extraordinary women. Naturally, the account of !Kung life is also a major contribution to anthropology.

The most riveting "as told to" book to come along for some time is by a Somali woman named Aman. She was born in the bush as her mother was taking the herds to water. At nine she underwent a ritual clitoridectomy (genital surgery). She was given away in marriage; she ran away. She became a street person and braved the dangers of Mogadishu. She had many adventures and escaped from the national upheavals of Somalia. It's a long story, but anthropologist Virginia Lee Barnes found Aman, listened, recorded, and encouraged. When Lee died too young, the story found its way to anthropologist Janice Boddy who finished it and arranged its publication. It is called *Aman: The Story of a Somali Girl,* as told to Virginia Lee Barnes and Janice Boddy (New York: Vintage, 1995).

Mary Prince was the first black woman to escape from slavery and publish a record of her experiences. Her book came out first in 1831. The horrors of slavery, through the eyes of a woman, never looked more awful; her book helped bring that system to an end. Professor Moira Ferguson edited this recent edition, *The History of Mary Prince: A West Indian Slave, Related by Herself* (Ann Arbor: University of Michigan Press, 1993).

Unfortunately, in this chapter we did not have the opportunity to explore the elaborate systems of women's healing, magic, and divination or female-centered groups devoted to spirit-possession and the worship of spirits. These appear central to Baba's religious or emotional life in ways that Islam, the official and formal religion, was not. The closest and best book I can find is by William L. Andrews. He edited *Sisters of Spirit: Three Black Women's Autobiographies of the 19th Century* (Bloomington: Indiana University Press, 1986). These autobiographies are significant literary and historical documents and invaluable portraits of three women centered in the black feminist and black spiritualist traditions in America.

Some Questions to Ask an Anthropologist:

1. How could Baba marry her cousin? The answer you will receive will sound something like this: because cousin-marriage is very common in the world, because it is a useful practice, and because couples are probably not marrying all that close biologically. Cousins are often what we call "classificatory kinfolks."

2. These women seem to have very close friendships. Were they ever what we call lesbians? Well, some probably had sex with each other, made love on occasion, took care of each other's kids, or loved each other in many ways. That doesn't seem to be what we call lesbianism. How did Baba and her co-wives act with each other and define their relationship? What seemed to be the advantages, the disadvantages? That's what matters.

3. What about anthropologists who don't have such dutiful wives? What about the reverse — female anthropologists with husbands? What happens in their fieldwork? These questions are very open, even painful, issues in the field of anthropology. There are no set answers, or perhaps there are as many answers as couples who go "into the field" together.

4. So how many husbands did Baba have? And why did she need those husbands? Baba had four husbands. She needed them for the same reasons most women in all human cultures have husbands.

Endnote to Chapter 4

1. From Mary F. Smith, *Baba of Karo: A Woman of the Muslim Hausa,* with introduction and notes by M. G. Smith (London: Faber and Faber, 1954), 7.

Everyone's life in Havana, Cuba changed after the revolution.

Photo courtesy of A. Ramey, Stock-Boston.

Inocencia

"Expecting Something Good to Happen"

Inocencia participated in a successful revolution. She is, therefore, a "liberated woman." That we happen to have her autobiography is, in itself, another singular story.

Americans know little about the island-nation of Cuba, only forty-eight miles from Key West, Florida, or about the socialist revolution now in its fifth decade there. We have even fewer personal accounts of women who have lived in such dramatic times or places.

Before reading about Inocencia, you need to know that between 1924 and 1959 assorted dictatorships ruled Cuba. Then in 1959 the socialist revolution of Fidel Castro overthrew the last dictator, Fulgencio Batista. The Communist Party of Cuba took control at that time. But even communists must adjust to the harsh demands of the island's dominant industry — sugar. Raising sugarcane means hard, seasonal labor for low pay. Crops fail; the prices for sugar rise and fall randomly on the international market. So sugarcane, hard work, poverty, Communism, and revolutionary politics color all of Inocencia's autobiography.

The word *liberation* in Cuba, as in China and Russia, meant being free from bourgeois, middle to upper class, or capitalist domination. In these socialist countries, being liberated had a very different meaning from the Western liberal or feminist ones. First, there was no self-realization or individuality except through service to one's state and society. Cuban women were freed from traditional gender roles to serve their nation better. They were expected to participate in mass organizations and in the labor force. Second, in Cuba as in other socialist countries, the energy behind movements for women's equality came from the government itself. So the Federation of Cuban Women, the principal women's association, was a branch of the central government. In fact, a handful of men in one of the political bureaus wrote the objectives and decided on the agendas liberated women followed.

At the same time, the women's movement had full legitimacy. Women had more access to such venues as mass media and school curricula than women in North America have experienced.

> It may help to keep in mind that the Cuban women's movement is not primarily a feminist movement but a movement for equal rights, and it is much easier for a man to comprehend equal rights for women than it is for him to develop a feminist consciousness.[1]

In effect, women became "free" to commit themselves wholly to the socialist economy and society, and "free" to engage in socially productive labor.

Liberation meant many things to many people. To women who grew up in the lower-class slums of Cuba, being liberated meant freedom from working outside their homes. It meant having homes, and taking care of them instead of working in someone else's house. It meant "staying at home" and having the resources to take care of their own children. Such women didn't want a job, child care facilities, or independence from husbands and children.

Revolution meant joining study groups or "circles." Once again, we see the difference between the United States and Cuba: these were not consciousness-raising groups at all. Women did not seek these out and find other women to share their common problems. Instead the central government set the topics for discussion. They did not use personal perspectives or individual psychology to discuss their lives or their problems. Instead they asked how the ideologies of the socialist movement applied to their collective lives and how they could work together better.

Ironically, women in revolutionary Cuba did not flock into the labor force. Most husbands were suspicious when their wives were out of sight, forming friendships with men or other women, or earning money for themselves. Many women resisted the revolution; they had grown up with traditional expectations. More to the point, the revolution made housekeeping and family maintenance much more difficult than it had been. Food and other necessities were rationed. Women had to stand in slow lines to buy basics. At the same time, growing national groups such as the Federation for Cuban Women or the Committees for Defense of the Revolution demanded time for meetings. Moreover, in the new socialist regime, one could not hire a servant or a helper, and child care facilities were generally inadequate. So the revolutionary government had quite a struggle to incorporate women into the labor force.

We see these new imperatives acted out in Inocencia's life. For example, the young socialist government of Cuba tried to abolish the practice of hiring private servants; only capitalists did such a bad thing, they believed. Families were forbidden to hire or retain servants. The government retrained prostitutes and domestic servants — women who were among the most exploited under the former capitalist regime. The women were given jobs in hotels, schools, hospitals, or in homes for state-approved foreigners. This was a major advance in salary and status for them. So Inocencia was sent to work as a "maid of the state." You will note the singular conclusions she draws from her experiences of working for both capitalism and communism.

Why Do We Have Her Story?

An anthropologist-sociologist named Oscar Lewis wrote a number of best-selling and highly readable books about poor people in Latin American countries. He used autobiographical methods in unusual and challenging ways and developed theories about poverty.

Lewis was a *wunderkind* — he finished his Ph.D. at twenty-five and began to publish books and articles rapidly. He collected prestigious grants and achieved professional eminence. He spoke of a new purpose in anthropology: to serve as students of and reporters on behalf of the great mass of peasants and poor urban dwellers who make up 80 percent of the world's population.

The notion of "the culture of poverty" was his idea. As he saw it, poverty was somehow a natural and integral part of life. Every country has such a culture, passed down in families from generation to generation. These cultures are typically marked by unemployment, underemployment, low wages, unskilled occupations, child labor, alcohol, violence, informal marital arrangements, money lenders, mother-centered families, authoritarianism, resignation, fatalism, male superiority complexes, female martyrdom, and innumerable psychopathologies. In short, too little money and too many problems. This sounded good at the time.

Many scholars saw his work as a new literature of social or ethnographic realism. He wove the lives of down-and-outers into deep and beautiful stories. The interview methods he used called out their energy, cunning, cynicism, loneliness, self-pity, selflessness, and the craving for meaning in their lives. *The Children of Sanchez: Autobiography of a Mexican Family* (New York: Random House, 1963) was a blockbuster. Another book followed up on the fortunes of this family with *A Death in the Sanchez Family* in 1969 (Random House). His book, *La Vida: A Puerto Rican Family in the Culture of Poverty* (Random House, 1966), earned Lewis a National Book Award for nonfiction in 1967.

Other scholars believed Lewis was doing less social science research than literature, perhaps even creative writing. Critics in anthropology and other social sciences often attacked him. They found many contradictions and called him out on them. An exasperated Lewis proclaimed that poverty produced pathologies and the pathologies produced poverty. "You're blaming the victims, you're saying they have only themselves to blame," proclaimed the critics. Most important, they said that his stories failed to prove his theories. In fact, many observed that the autobiographies had acquired a life of their own apart from him.

Oscar Lewis was fascinated with the revolution in Cuba and longed to do research there on how ordinary people's lives had changed. He conceived an ambitious project he called "an oral history of contemporary Cuba." He wanted to use his standard intensive interviewing methods that focused on individuals — asking specific questions and using free association in multiple interviews. When these interviews are collated for each individual, an elaborate form of autobiographical analysis emerged. Lewis did not set out to study women anymore than he usually did or to highlight women in a separate volume. In 1969 and 1970, when this research was done, the women's movement in places like Cuba and North America was still a distant drumbeat.

In February of 1968, Lewis arranged a meeting with Fidel Castro. The revolutionary leader had read his other books; he wanted Lewis to do for Cuba what he had done for Mexico and Puerto Rico. In February of 1969, Lewis received a major Ford Foundation grant for his dream research. He returned to Cuba with his wife and non-Cuban staff. They were treated like royal capitalists — a lovely house, telephones, privileges, bus, car, gasoline, and servants, chauffeurs, typists, and interviewers.

The Cuban Revolution was only a decade old. And 1970 was their worst year yet — a time of economic and social crisis, particularly in sugarcane production. For Oscar Lewis, the problems in his research project also multiplied. The man who was his link to Castro died. Lewis apparently was not careful or discreet about some people he interviewed. Surprisingly, Lewis grew bored with all the success stories he heard about the Cuban Revolution. His health was getting worse. Even his loyal wife commented that Oscar was difficult and demanding.

Government officials supervised the tiniest details of their lives. Some Cubans suspected him of spying for the American CIA; others apparently used these suspicions against him. Then agents of the State Security visited the Lewises and removed many sets of papers and interviews.

In midsummer of 1970, the Lewises left Cuba. The project was unfinished; they had not even started the rural portion. They never recovered some 20,000 pages of data confiscated by the government. Moreover, Oscar Lewis had not found a clear framework in which to explain the people and processes of the revolution.

By Christmas of that year Lewis was dead of a heart attack; he was not quite fifty-six. It seemed the project he imagined would never come to life. So his wife, Ruth Lewis, who had worked at his side for thirty years, stepped in to organize and save what she could. She gathered colleagues and assistants to help. She followed the editorial methods he made so successful. She wove the interviews into "autobiographies" that preserve the integrity and individuality of those interviewed.

Three books came out of this collaboration: *Four Men, Four Women,* and *Friends,* each subtitled *Living the Revolution: An Oral History of Contemporary Cuba;* all were published by the University of Illinois Press.[2] Susan Rigdon, a political scientist, assisted in the lengthy analysis of the data and wrote helpful introductions for the books. Inocencia's story comes from the second volume about four selected women.

Ruth Lewis did a heroic job of saving the project. In fact, one suspects that much of the humanism and humanity that ordinary readers appreciated so much in Lewis's books may somehow have come from his wife. In fact, she is the one who interviewed Inocencia and translated her delightful Spanish into colloquial English. Inocencia was her favorite; Mrs. Lewis wanted to make this particular woman's life come alive for people who would never meet her.

In Ruth Lewis's hands the stories that make up *Four Men* and *Four Women* become "salvation narratives," or dramatic personal tales of suffering, sin, and redemption. In her construction of their stories, these women and men are not just struggling to survive, not just getting by or coping. They have joined a revolution to save their souls, to live as responsible citizens and as comrades with each other. They have found an unexpected liberation.

No person in these three books is average, typical, representative, or was located through any sampling methods. Moreover, their lives tell us very little about the Cuban Revolution itself. So much happened so fast and so unpredictably, that any book about these events would be out of date faster than it could be printed.

Moreover, Oscar Lewis's theories had never looked sadder. He seems to have missed the central themes revealed in his own research: that work for a purpose has power and that validation for that work empowers entire social groups. For all the elaborate research, the most enduring or endearing parts are the individual stories such as Inocencia's. Ruth Lewis managed to salvage only fifteen long life stories and thirteen partial ones. The only element these Cubans have in common is managing to live through a revolution. In fact, taken together, they seem to have lived through at least eight different revolutions! Inocencia's responses are radically hers — no one else seems to have shared these events or had these interpretations.

Inocencia was the ninth of twelve children. She was fifty-four years old when the Lewises met her. Cuban-born of Spanish parentage, her beloved father fought in the War of Independence from Spain; later he became a small sugarcane farmer. She remembers her childhood with great fondness; she idealized her father and felt her best years ended with his death.

Yet another sugarcane crisis in Cuba and the death of her father when she was eight changed everything. Inocencia was sent to live with relatives. In the homes of her aunt and married sisters, she lived as a servant. At twenty-one she was working as a maid in Havana. Of course, she dreamed of greater independence and freedom. She felt frustrated and humbled by years of domestic service.

It is no wonder she thought marriage would allow escape, freedom, and self-realization. It is no wonder she loved being a saleswoman, a successful capitalist in the midst of a socialist revolution. It is, however, a wonder that she finds an unpredicted and unpromised liberation through the Cuban Revolution.

Inocencia frames her response to liberation and revolution in terms of love and work — arguably the two most important aspects of being human on the planet. Many of the values she learned as a child — work, service, and sacrifice — were easily translated into and validated by the revolution. She talks of helping others, and she expects others to have similar standards of morality, hard work, dependability, and frugality. Whether these kind impulses come from religion or revolution, from God or from Castro, is immaterial to her.

I like Inocencia so much; she sounds like I feel sometimes, like friends or relatives I have known. She talks a mile a minute and tends to repeat herself. She stops to analyze and then contradicts what she just said. She manipulates the philosophical conflicts between Catholicism and Communism with a funky brand of common sense. Her discussion (or dissection) of her husband is one of the funniest and frankest moments we are likely to see in an autobiography. Thank you, Oscar and Ruth Lewis. You may have lost the project but you saved the stories.

Paradise

Before the Revolution, a servant was like a dog — at the bottom. That's what I was, a servant, and even my family looked down upon me. At our reunions I always felt inferior. Their clothes were good, mine were not, and I could never afford to go to beaches or on outings as they did. But what else could I work at? I wasn't trained for anything. Out in the country we couldn't go to school because it was a long ride on horseback. Later, when we lived in a town, I got through only the first few grades. I loved to study but it wasn't until after the Revolution that I went to high school.

I'm a servant again, but working for the revolutionary government is a different matter. I'm no poorer than anyone else and I'm not treated like an inferior. I feel the same as if I were a clerk in a store.

Before the Revolution women didn't have the opportunities we have today. No matter how intelligent a woman was, if she weren't pretty or well connected, she couldn't get along on her ability alone. Nowadays you work at what you're fitted for, and above all, at what's in keeping with your dignity. I would not have suffered so much in the past if there hadn't been such prejudice. I'd have had a different kind of job, and a pension. I might even have remarried and had children instead of having to put up with a husband who didn't give me a single pleasant memory in twenty-three years. That's why I'm interested in women's liberation. I was reading a book — I can't remember the name of it — a lovely book that tells when Lenin first began to see that women didn't need to go on being merely dishwashers.

When I became engaged to Reinaldo Serrano, I was very hopeful. I, who'd been a slave all my life, thought that at last I'd be able to say and do what I wanted. But Reinaldo killed all my dreams; the only difference marriage made was to give me an even tougher boss. His nature was very different from mine. I tried to fight it, but it was like banging my head against the wall.

Reinaldo thought of no one but himself. I, on the other hand, was brought up to feel I had to sacrifice myself for others. I've made it my aim in life never to ask anything of anybody; helping others makes me happy. And I've never consciously done anything bad.

Even though I'm for the Revolution, I believe in God. Fidel never said that if you believe in one you can't believe in the other. He doesn't interfere in religion. But I don't go to church anymore because I'm not sure how the Revolution would look at it. It seems to me that the principles of the Revolution are the same as those of religion: to share all one's possessions, to love one another as brothers, to become as one. That way there's solidarity, unity, like in a family. It would be a fine thing if everybody assimilated these principles, yet one doesn't necessarily have to be a revolutionary to be good. I don't judge people by their political position but by their feelings.

If you really feel the Revolution inside as I do, you make the necessary sacrifices and stay with it. I know we Cubans are going to be all right, because when I'm with a group of revolutionaries I can feel something that joins us to each other. It used to be faith in God and in the organized Church that kept us united; now it's a political policy. The Revolution is like that religious faith.

My earliest memories are marvelous. As long as I had my father, I was happy. Of all that has happened to me since, the misery and misfortune and the good things too, I only remember what was good about those first eight years with my father. My life consists of the present moment and of my memories of those early days. It's like reading a fine book that you never forget no matter how many others you've read and forgotten afterward. Someday I'd like to ask a psychiatrist why this is.

Painful Memories

The year 1936 was very hard for me. My brothers went off to Camaguey, and Mama, Honoria, and I moved to my sister Felicia's house in Colon. Felicia and her husband, Emigdio, were lower middle class and Emigdio earned quite a lot of money as a produce wholesaler. Later, business in Cuba started going downhill and only people in politics prospered. When his business failed, Emigdio went to Havana and ran a flower stand that did quite well.

I hadn't really known my sister Felicia until she was a grown woman, but I think she was always the same selfish person she is now, the kind who looks out for her own. For instance, my sister Alicia was raised at Felicia's house because Felicia claims she was sick. She's a sharp one, Felicia. Sick indeed! Well true, she'd sometimes get paralytic attacks and become unconscious — that's why Mama sent Alicia there — but with that excuse Felicia used her to take care of the children until Alicia was married.

Felicia didn't treat us well, because we were in need. I was a big eater, and though I worked hard in her house and was always ordered about, she served me very small portions and gave large portions to her own children. I didn't complain — to whom could I complain? — but at night I cried. Honoria wasn't used to being scolded, and she and I wanted Mama to let us get a house of our own and work for wealthy families in town, although Honoria wasn't allowed to wet her hands or work hard. But Felicia wouldn't hear of it. It was to her advantage to have us there working for her, so she said, "What would people say if you became servants!" and "How could you go off and live by yourselves with me having such a big house?" She was very domineering, and Mama didn't contradict her.

There seemed to be no possibility of our getting out of Felicia's house, and that's why Honoria killed herself. I'd gone to the post office to pick up some letters, and by the time I returned Honoria had taken poison, something called *Rompe Roca,* that Emigdio kept for spraying the cattle against ticks. When Honoria saw me, she started to cry and said, "Cencia, I'm sorry on account of you and

Mama," and she squeezed my hand and asked me for water. Then she died. By the time the doctor got there it was too late. I was carried away by grief.

Mama took it badly. My brothers didn't say anything, but everyone knew it was Felicia's fault. Yet she wasn't affected in the slightest. She went to town to see the judge about getting the autopsy waived — an autopsy was such a botched-up business at that time — and she succeeded on the grounds that the doctor had already reported the cause of death.

Had my little sister died in an accident I might have accepted it better, but this way was so senseless. Honoria had no reason to take her life. Everybody has troubles, but one should struggle and overcome them. I felt God could have prevented it, and at that moment I almost lost my faith. I had serious doubts, but even in my desperation I didn't curse or blaspheme. I cried out, "My God, why have You done this senseless thing?" It filled me with despair to think that it could have been avoided if only Mama had agreed to leave Felicia's house. Then the priest told me that true Christians were formed through such tests. "It's a harsh trial," he said, "but those who overcome such trials are the true believers." His words comforted me.

When Honoria died, I sent my sweetheart, Ramon, a telegram asking him to come to me. But to achieve his ambition to become a soldier he'd vowed to hold a vigil before the Virgin the day he returned to Cuba, so instead of coming immediately when I needed him, he and his friends arranged to hold the vigil that night at his mother's house. It's true he had an obligation to the Virgin, and there was nothing he could have done for me, but still he should have postponed the vigil. It didn't have to be that very day. Anyway, he didn't answer the telegram but appeared two days later with my wedding gown, shoes, purse, and everything. I was burning up, not so much with anger as with disgust, and I wouldn't accept any apology. I thought he didn't sympathize with me and I didn't want him back. Well, he returned to the Isle of Pines and kept writing me from there but I never answered him. When he came back I gave him all the wedding presents — the initialed sheets, the tablecloths, and everything else I'd worked on — and called off the marriage.

Later I regretted my action. I would have been happy with Ramon and would have had a lot of children because he was just like me. He was the kind of man I dreamed about. But he'd hurt me so much, my pain at the time of my sister's suicide was so deep, I couldn't forgive him.

I'd known Reinaldo Serrano Balseiro since 1939, the last year I worked for Señora Merida. We met when he came to take the girl next door to a fiesta. He soon dropped her and began to send me postcards and call on me. That's how our courtship began. Reinaldo was a handsome boy with regular features; he was white with medium-brown hair and brown eyes like me, and a straight nose. Before we married he looked quite thin but afterward he filled out.

As for me, I'd always been considered *hermosa* but not *bonita*. *Hermosa* means you aren't thin or sickly; *bonita* means having a pretty face. But by the time I met Reinaldo, I think I was pretty. Everybody complimented me on my good skin and beautiful hands, and on my figure, too. I never worried about my looks, though, because I've always had such determination and ambition that I never thought about how tall or short I was or whether I was beautiful. I've seen very pretty women who were useless. At least I've been of service to everybody and have always felt satisfied with what I've done with my life, and I never had complexes about anything.

Reinaldo and I kept company for four years, and all that time he was very attentive, and a bit jealous, but he waited patiently for us to be married. He was rather severe in temperament and critical of everything — how I looked, the fit of my dress, or if my collar or my kerchief were right. We were really very different from one another.

Nor were Reinaldo's sentiments toward me all I would have liked. It's true that he always seemed to be in love with me, but he wasn't loving. Before we were married, I let him know all the defects I found in him and said, "I don't think we're going to be happy on account of this." I faced him with it but he kept saying that when we were married he'd change.

Reinaldo worked as a dispatcher for a taxi company, and during our four years of courtship he earned a little over one peso a day. Out of this he had to give his mother money for his food — his family was worse off than mine — but with my earnings and what remained of his, we began to buy things for our future home. As soon as we'd accumulated twenty pesos we'd go off to the store to buy dishes, pots, sheets, blankets, and clothing. We kept the things at his mother's house in Santa Isabel.

About two months before we were married, an apartment in a little wooden house in a *solar* (sunny yard) across the street from his parents became available. The old couple who owned it lived next door and were close friends of Reinaldo's parents. They needed the money and had to rent the apartment immediately. It had one room and a tiny kitchen. In back of the solar there was one toilet, without water, for all three tenants, and they had to bathe in the tiny kitchen, pouring water over themselves. Later a toilet and shower were added to each apartment.

Well, we rented the apartment for five pesos a month and decided to paint it and fit it up before getting married. Little by little we furnished it with a few pieces: a bed, two little tables, a chair, a china closet, and a used wardrobe in very bad condition. Later on we got a new bedroom set, hung curtains, and furnished it completely. We had everything, down to shoe cloths on which I'd embroidered Reinaldo's initials. A week before the wedding I stopped working so I could finish my trousseau and a few things for the house.

We were married late in 1943, when I was twenty-seven and Reinaldo twenty-nine. At 6:00 A.M. on my wedding day I washed my hair, got everything together, and started off with my nephew, who was to act as witness and as best man. We were married in the Toyo courthouse at 7:30 in the morning, and again in the church in the afternoon, because during the war, weddings had to be held in the daytime to save electricity.

After the wedding we went back to Felicia's house for dinner. Later, friends and neighbors came over and had cake and refreshments and danced until 10:00 o'clock. Naturally I felt happy that day, with the radio on and everyone dancing. The guests stayed at the fiesta but Reinaldo and I left. One of his cousins drove us to our own home because we had no money to go to a hotel. Reinaldo didn't carry me across the threshold or any of that. He wasn't very romantic.

I was a virgin when I married, completely without experience. I knew only what my girlfriends had told me. Reinaldo enjoyed it — he adored me — and treated me well that night, but he didn't make love tenderly. He wasn't really affectionate; he was hard and abrupt. That's the way he was and he never changed. He felt passion for me and still does, but I never did, nor did I ever feel much pleasure. Maybe that's why sex didn't mean much to me.

I'm not altogether sure I loved Reinaldo because I found it very difficult to adapt to his ways, though I was a good wife in every sense of the word. I'm sure that he was more in love with me than I with him. He wasn't a skirt-chaser; I've never known him to go with another woman. The main problem, I guess, was his character — our temperaments were very different. In my family we were affectionate, especially when we haven't seen each other for a while. But Reinaldo and his family are very cold and unexpressive; they love, but in their own strange way. They're very withdrawn and the brothers and sisters never kiss each other, not even their mother.

So I was very affectionate and Reinaldo wasn't. I looked after him and his things, I waited anxiously for his return, I called him pet names, like "Little Fatty" when he began to put on weight, but he had no such way of showing his love for me. And the times when I felt romantic and hopeful and most wanted him, he'd excuse himself by saying he had a headache or was ill, or he'd come home in a bad mood and begin to quarrel over the least little thing. But the day *he* wanted *me,* I had to give in no matter how I felt.

From the outset sex was when he wanted it, about once a week. I didn't want children by him so I used *Corome,* a Swiss contraceptive. He agreed to this because he's so self-centered he didn't like children. I had no guilt feelings about it, because I thought that it wasn't worth having a child who might grow up bitter and unsociable like his father. And feeling as I did, that someday I would leave Reinaldo, it would have been foolish.

All through the courtship I knew we just didn't belong together, but I believed with God's help I could change him. It was my error, my weakness, not God's. I knew I should have married an atheist. It's unpleasant for me to admit these things, but I suffered so much with that man all my life. I don't know how I bore it.

Reinaldo is the kind of person you have to say yes to in everything. "Do this, do that!" I'd always had somebody giving me orders and had never been free to say or do what I wanted. It turned out that after I married and had my own home I was more a prisoner than ever. I couldn't even hang a picture where I wanted. It had to go where Reinaldo said. I had everything in the house so pretty, but it all annoyed him, even the china closet where I kept the glass wedding gifts. It bothered him so much we sold it. The curtains annoyed him, the flowers annoyed him, and little by little everything was replaced by what *he* liked. It was humiliating to have to always bend to his will.

As a child Reinaldo had been very ill with asthma and parasites and lots of colds. He spent much of his time sick in bed, but he was simply coddling himself, complaining and saying this or that hurt. Tending sick people isn't something I enjoy — that's why I never wanted to work in a hospital. It disgusts me to see someone vomiting and I hate the smell of sickness and of medicines, though when Papa was sick I felt differently about it. I wanted to be near him all the time.

Of course if there were no one else to do it, I'd take care of a sick person, as long as he didn't have tumors or other disgusting symptoms. I can't bear skin diseases. Reinaldo was always getting horrible rashes all over his body, and little by little that made him repulsive to me. The doctors said the rashes came from an allergy, but they never found out what caused it. All I know is that Reinaldo's feet were always rotten with fungus infections and he had some sort of rash in the groin. Or his eyes would get red and sore, or his lips cracked and peeling. He always had something disgusting the matter with him, but the doctors never really found anything wrong. He bought all kinds of medicines — that's his hobby — and if he read about a disease in a book, then he had it.

I believe men are superior to women — that is, they're more intelligent and stronger — but that doesn't give them the right to do what they do. It's not that a woman is inferior, but she's weaker and easier to impress; there are times when she simply has to depend on a man. Women fall in love, have children, and have twenty difficulties men don't have, and no matter how intelligent a woman is, she feels more protected if she has a man. And yet, no matter how much I needed my husband and how hard I tried to please him, there's no moment I can think of and say, "Yes, he made me happy then."

At first I handed over my pay to my husband because we had to pool both our wages to meet expenses. But he came to look upon taking my money as his right even when it was no longer necessary. I let him do it to avoid trouble. He'd even keep track of how much sewing I'd done. Later, when I was a saleslady, he also wrote down how much commission I received. On payday he was the one who got my money and decided what to do with it. Even the bank account was in his name, but those were *my* savings he took over because, actually, I was the only one who saved.

Reinaldo was always supervising me, asking how much I was going to spend and why. If I bought a birthday gift for someone, or wanted to take a child to an amusement park and spend ten pesos or so, Reinaldo just couldn't see that. When I picked up some little things in the dime store, he'd tell me I was spending money on crap. One day I bought some flowers to put on the television set and he said, "How much money do you want to throw down the drain?" But if *he* was interested in any antenna or a camera, he'd go and buy it for himself. He was piggish that way; any money he spent was fine, but I was always wasting money.

I quit sewing at El Encanto in 1949 because I was still only a temporary worker, without the right to retire on a pension. I found a job with the Phillips Company selling electrical appliances — refrigerators, television sets, radios, and sewing machines — on a commission basis. I got 20 percent on every sewing machine and 28 percent on the refrigerators. Selling was my passion — I'd sell anything, even if it were only a single sweet potato. It never embarrassed me to go to someone's house to sell something. When Papa was a peddler he felt defeated and humiliated, but I was very proud of my work. I loved to win clients, overcome their resistance, and make a sale. Never before or after have I worked so hard or enjoyed it so much.

Selling was not only my work, it was my social life too. I knew every street and alley in the barrio and everyone who lived there. All the neighbors were fond of me, and anybody I talked to was apt to become my client sooner or later. The housewives were friendly when I called on them because I never deceived them or took their money without delivering the goods, and I helped them as much as I could when they were in difficulties. Many of them were afraid to get in debt but I convinced them, not so much to earn a commission, but because I knew what I sold was quality equipment and would be useful to them. Many have me to thank that they learned to sew or that they have a frigidaire or some other piece of scarce equipment today. They're grateful to me now; the others regret that they didn't let me talk them into buying while the getting was good.

Getting Involved

I didn't bother with politics when I was young, but my awareness of the tragedies of others, especially those caused by economic misfortunes, caused me a great deal of suffering. I had a vision of a Cuban government led one day by a man who would do something more than play the usual corrupt politics, who had no personal interests or prejudices, and who would accomplish something for the people. It was like waiting for your dream prince — your lover — to come, like being in an ecstasy, expecting something good to happen.

That's how I got to know Mario Ramon. He was one of the chief people in Pereira's office — he kept the books, the records of sales, the checks, and all that. I'd been selling refrigerators for almost a year and was getting a lot of commissions when Mario began to take me into his confidence. He told me Pereira was secretly involved with the *Ortodoxos,* Chibas's party, and was giving them money.

Then he told me what they were going to do in Santiago. Imagine how I felt! I didn't think he had a chance. It seemed like a crazy dream that could never be realized. How could a small movement to overthrow the government begin by attacking a military garrison like the Moncada? It seemed impossible, a useless action. But I was mistaken. Though it failed and he and many others lost their lives, the spark was struck. Their attempt to improve the situation in Cuba remained a strong inspiration to our people.

It was a terrible blow for me that Sunday in 1953 when I read they'd been killed. My close friend Mario Ramon had become a martyr of the Revolution! That's when I really became a sympathizer of the Twenty-sixth of July Movement, a *patria o muerte* [freedom or death] revolutionary. My being a member of the poor working class had nothing to do with it. I'd have made the same decision had I been rich, if I had known Mario. That was crucial. Although I expected someone to turn up who could improve our lives, I never dreamed it would be Fidel. Mario's death woke me up. I said to myself, "If he died for this cause it must be something very good, therefore I too am willing to die for it."

With the storming of the Moncada the real struggle began. I was part of it because after Mario's death I pledged to do everything I could. Furthermore, I'd come to believe in the principles of the Revolution and I had faith that they'd win. From then on I cooperated with the Movement. The events of the Revolution itself convinced me even more, for if they hadn't been honest and good I would have had to break away.

During the struggle my husband was afraid to attend meetings, although he was a sympathizer and a lifelong communist. He'd been a member of the Communist Party since 1937 or 1938, before I met him. He had his membership card and he'd attended meetings before the Batista presidency. He got out because he couldn't meet all their demands and at the same time support his family. He was still with the communists in his ideas, but as time went by he grew further and further away from them. Perhaps that's why he did nothing for the Twenty-sixth of July Movement. Or maybe he didn't think it was going to lead to communism. Anyway, he was a very cowardly man of no conviction, and he was afraid of Batista's persecution. I myself was not able to do much for the Movement because I lived under my husband's thumb. Had I not been married, I would have followed my heart and gone into the mountains.

When victory came, we hung out Twenty-sixth of July flags, scaring and surprising a lot of people. When they saw my flag they said, "How do you like that! Inocencia belongs to the Twenty-sixth." A group of us women began holding meetings at each other's houses, and when an order came to close all stores to prevent looting, our entire group went through the streets with flags, closing up the shops. The next step was to take over the police stations, so our group occupied the neighborhood station and stayed there every night until things returned to normal.

I was at home on January 8, 1959, when Fidel rode into the city. I had to see the whole thing on television because my husband wouldn't let me go out. I never went to any mass meetings or anything. Nor could I join the women's militia at that time because he didn't want me to stand guard. But I *was* a member of the Twenty-sixth of July from 1959 through 1961, and I *did* support the Revolution.

The first big CDR [Committee for Defense of the Revolution] activity was the lard census, which was the first food census in Havana. Lard [pig fat used in cooking] was rationed and the census had to be done to find out how much of it would be needed. There was a shortage because we never had a hog-raising industry in Cuba; it was cheaper to import lard from the United States. So hog-raising had to be introduced and it wasn't easy. It took proper planning.

The census was quite complicated. It worked like this. After we set up a CDR, we'd tell the members, "Look, make a list of all the families living in each building on the block to show how many adults and children are there." All the available CDR members were sent from house to house to collect the information, and they'd turn in their lists at the neighborhood social center where the group heads met. If there was no CDR on a certain street and no possibility of setting one up, those of us in charge would have to go there ourselves and register each family.

The lists were then handed over to the local grocery stores to which the families were assigned. Each individual was allowed 1 pound of lard per month, and with this list the warehouses knew that in one store they needed 300 pounds, in another 200 pounds, and so on. Sometimes there'd be a surplus in one store and a shortage in another, and we'd have to juggle the lard to distribute the ration properly.

The Revolution began new fronts or campaigns as it required them. After the lard census we were busy with the vaccination drive. Later the Public Health Front organized. It had both a cleanup and educational function. Then an education campaign was set up to deal with children who were absent from school, and I participated in that too. We visited parents to discuss the reasons for the absence.

When I first tried to join the Federation of Cuban Women in 1963, I had trouble being accepted. I was told by a *companera* that to be a member in good standing I had to take a turn at guard duty. So I said, "Suppose my husband doesn't let me?" The *companera* replied, "Well, then you can't join." She allowed me to contribute one peso a month as a voluntary donation, but wouldn't grant me membership. The fact is, this comrade was politically uneducated and deficient in understanding other people's problems. Furthermore, as I learned from a schoolteacher member of the Federation, she was mistaken in denying me membership, because only those who can freely stand guard are required to do it. The schoolteacher then made me a member of the Federation.

As a volunteer for both the Federation and the CDR, I've always gone to the Sunday activities of both groups — the CDR in the morning and the Federation in the afternoon or at night. But all along I've been more devoted to the CDR, which is highly political. Just the same, I'm the secretary-general of my delegation in the Federation and of the whole bloc too. I like it because it had an Education Front. Finances and education are activities I'm always involved in. In fact, when I went back to school, I was the president of the school board and was in charge of raising all the money and getting the school supplies.

My personal affinities aside, I must admit that though some of the CDR and Federation fronts are the same, the Federation's is more effective because it always has some specific, practical purpose in mind, like helping a comrade, or sewing kitchen cloths and aprons for the nursery school. Maybe because it's composed entirely of women, the Federation has greater unity than the CDR.

Just now I'm president of my CDR. There are twenty-seven members; only eight people on the block don't belong. The many contacts I'd made while selling appliances turned out to be very useful. Everybody in the barrio knows me. When the judges for the People's Courts were elected, I was number one, the very first in my barrio to be chosen. I couldn't accept, though, because being a judge involved a lot of duties which Reinaldo wouldn't allow me to undertake. Those People's judges sometimes have to preside over a trial until the small hours of the morning. But oh, how I'd have loved to accept! It's too late now, that stage is past. They've already given the course of instruction and graduated a batch of judges, so if I wanted to become a judge I'd have to wait for the next stage.

Family Matters

The crisis between Reinaldo and me took place in 1966. I guess it was my being away from home so much that finished us off. I wanted a divorce but Reinaldo didn't because he would have had to contribute to my support. I would have divorced him anyway had it not been for my family; they said it was foolishness at our age, after having been together for so many years. But it was a big mistake on my part to have let them influence me.

I should never have put up with my marriage all those years. My life with him was impossible — like a nightmare — and every time I tried to change to suit him, it was worse. The woman who struggles to free herself and succeeds is more to be admired. Had I divorced my husband twenty years ago I would not have been tied to a lie, to something I didn't feel and didn't want. Instead I waited for him to change, and of course, he didn't. Such men don't change.

One of the reasons I didn't get a divorce before the Revolution was that I was afraid of some dirty work, such as someone making an accusation against me. He could have gotten a politician to do it for him. So I was very scared. But since the Revolution they play very clean here. If you're straight, nobody bothers you. Only wrongdoers are punished.

Instead of going my own way, I went on living in the same house with Reinaldo for three and a half more years, keeping up appearances, although our obligation to each other no longer existed. Only the members of the family knew of the separation; everyone else believed we were still married. During all that time I was very miserable, with nobody to confide in, no place to go, and nothing to do. Reinaldo didn't give me any money and he made life unbearable. He'd litter up the house, throw things on the floor, turn the place upside down. He kept it filthy. He tried to make life impossible so I'd be the one to leave and he wouldn't have to pay me alimony. If he'd been the man he ought to have been, he'd have gone to live in his aunt's or mother's house and I wouldn't have had to go through all that.

One day I did something the Revolution doesn't like. For the first time since I married, I went to church and confessed to the priest all that had happened to me. As the saying goes, "People remember God when it thunders." I was in such a state I muddled my confession, so I went back to confess again. The priest said it was more dishonest to go on living under the same roof with a man I didn't love or even like than to get a divorce. They almost never advise divorce. But to me the priest's words came as a great truth and made me wish I'd gone to him twenty years earlier, though whether or not he'd have talked that way before the Revolution, I don't know.

So I went home and said to Reinaldo, "I'm going to sue for a divorce." At first he didn't agree. Then, when everything looked blackest and he was treating me worse and worse and making the house a hell, I prayed to God. I was very confident that He would help me as He always has. I said, "God, You know I believe in You and Reinaldo doesn't. If You think I'm the one who should keep the house, then do Your will. It may be nothing but a box but it's all I have." That's how I left it. Then one day out of a clear blue sky, Reinaldo told a friend that if I waived alimony he'd leave me the house. What did I need alimony for when I'd lived on practically nothing all my life? A few days later Reinaldo told me he was moving to his aunt's house.

I got together with my family and told them I was suing for divorce without alimony. I was capable of working, had worked all my life, and would continue doing so. Then, with the help of a lawyer, who charged me forty pesos, I went to court and within sixteen days was divorced.

When Reinaldo left, he took everything he said was "worth his while," including the refrigerator that cost me 570 pesos, paid off in eight months from my commissions. He also took the mahogany wardrobe that cost 195 pesos, the radio, the record player, the television set, and even the books. The only things he left were some furniture, the electric iron, the sewing machine with its new motor that cost me 120 pesos, and the house itself.

Reinaldo didn't claim the house because he knew the agony it had cost me to live with relatives. The title was transferred to my name, and even though it's just a tiny room, at least it's my own. And as far as the divorce is concerned, I don't feel any guilt. It was like getting rid of a cancer that was destroying me. I'm very satisfied with what I did. After all, I fought to save our marriage and nothing happened that was my fault. In spite of everything, I was good to Reinaldo and affectionate, taking care of him up to the end in a way he never deserved and as nobody else had ever done. But his conscience will kill him, of that I'm sure.

It's been almost six months now since I've been living alone and I feel very relaxed. At least I'm the mistress of my own home. When I was younger I never had a chance to spread my wings. I was always under someone's thumb. But now I have nobody to order me around, to tell me not to go out, to go to bed, or if it's raining, not to get wet. If I want to go to the movies, I go to the movies; if I want to cook, I cook; if I'm not hungry, I don't eat. I have something I've never had before, peace and freedom, and in that sense I'm very happy.

My greatest concern after the divorce was supporting myself. At first I did it by sewing at home. I received no cloth ration as I had no shop, so I could do only alterations. Otherwise I'd have had to pay the government a percentage of whatever I earned. Doing alterations, I sometimes earned as much as thirty or forty pesos a week. It wasn't enough but I managed quite well.

To get a job, I had to go the Women's Federation, where I was classified as unemployed. I put down that I'd worked as a domestic, and they said there were openings in the government protocol houses. As guests of Fidel, naturally not just anybody could be assigned to them. Honest, reliable people, good revolutionaries, were needed, so I agreed to take a job.

Today in Cuba it's no shame to be a servant, but nobody else I know who'd been one before the Revolution will do that kind of work anymore. The fact is, I enjoy doing housework. I pretend I'm in my own home doing the work for myself. I earn eighty-five pesos a month, the minimum wage, and I get a good lunch and dinner, which is a savings for me. In the past I had no security at all as a maid, but now, the day I stop work in one place I'm sent elsewhere, so I'm never without a job. Soon, I'll be getting a pension. I have to work until age sixty to qualify for retirement at my full salary. Of course if I were very old, the government would pension me off right away, but I'm happy to work as long as I have the health and stamina.

Nothing about the shortages today really bothers me. I guess I'm not very demanding, though I do wish there were a larger supply of goods so everybody could have what he needs. But before the Revolution, when there were a lot more things in shops, most of us couldn't afford to buy them. Now sometimes there's a line for food, but at least you know there's enough for everyone.

I no longer worry about the future and have no intention of marrying again. I've gone through too much, I'm old, and besides I don't need a man. Yet my first Christmas alone after the divorce was very sad. I was invited to many homes but I refused them all and went to bed. Reinaldo and I had always gone together and I was embarrassed to show up alone. Furthermore, I couldn't contribute any food because on my single ration book I get so little. And Christmas is a bad day for going out anyway.

The one thing I really regret about the past is not having had children. I couldn't adopt any because I was never in a position to. Still, I have lots of godchildren — practically all my nephews and nieces and many of the neighbor's children. I'm the godmother of Leida's son Pancho, though he hasn't been baptized. His father is a revolutionary and doesn't approve of it. For me, though, and for Leida, ceremony or no ceremony, I'm the child's godmother.

In spite of the fact that I live alone, I get along. For example, I find it perfectly easy to get things fixed. Once I needed some boards to replace some rotten ones on the porch wall. The house was falling apart and Reinaldo wouldn't fix anything after we decided to separate. On the contrary, if something fell down, he'd smash it so I couldn't get it fixed. Well, after the divorce I decided to repair the wall myself, and I asked a boy I knew in *Poder Local* [community agency] for boards four meters long. He got me six boards from a house that had been torn down, and he also got me some pink paint. I didn't even have to pay for the boards, because when a house is condemned, the materials from it are distributed where they're most needed. A friend of mine, the driver of an ice-cream truck, picked up the boards for me. Everybody is so helpful here.

Reinaldo had taken most of the nails, but before he left I filled a jar with some of every kind, so I was able to do the job properly. I don't know if it was good luck or my self-confidence, but those four-meter planks fit that wall as though they were especially cut for it.

I've done a lot of household repairs myself. If the sewing machine is dirty or needs oiling I can take it apart and assemble it again. But if a part is broken I have to call the central repair service to replace it. The repair *consolidado* is very efficient. They usually come right away.

The one thing I don't repair myself is the electric wiring, because I'm terribly afraid of getting a shock. There's a man in the neighborhood who can't work because his nerves are a bit shaky; he's very useful to all us neighbors because anytime we need a socket or a cable installed or something like that, he comes right over and does it. Of course it's against the law to work privately and we know he won't charge us, so we figure out how much the job is worth and say to him, "Here, take three pesos to buy yourself some medicine." We never let on that we're paying for the job, but pass it off as a courtesy gift.

There are no private plumbers either, so for plumbing repairs I have to call Poder Local, or a neighbor who knows about such things. There aren't many good plumbers but we manage one way or another. Everybody knows a little of everything and neighbors help each other without thinking of money. In these times Cubans are plumbers one day, masons or electricians the next.

Other than plumbing, Poder Local hasn't made any repairs in my home. The house gets soaked every time it rains, but whenever I go to Poder Local to ask for roofing paper they tell me it isn't my zone's turn for it. I don't have time to hang around all morning so I haven't been able to get them to do anything so far.

One Foot in the Past

I've always been religious although I've never been much of a churchgoer. Nor did I have faith in the saints, or visit shrines, or join any Catholic organization. All I did for the Church was sometimes make an altar cloth or bring a vase of flowers for the altar. I went to Mass once in a while to please my employer, Señora Zaldivar. I went to Communion only about once a year during Holy Week or sometimes at a Sunday mass, and I went to confession only when I had some problems, for consolation.

You see, my husband didn't believe in anything and constantly ridiculed me about God and religion, and that discouraged me. But when I finally stopped going to church, it was because most people had stopped. I thought, "Why should I go if it offends the Revolution?" It's not that I'm afraid to take part in religious ceremonies for fear of being seen by some revolutionary. When I'm asked to be a child's godmother, I still accept. If I'm invited to a church wedding, I go. I no longer pray the rosary or even own one, but that's merely a change in customs, not in principles. I still say grace before meals and pray before going to bed, and every time I begin a new task, whether for the Revolution or for myself, I place it in God's hands.

I have no clear idea of what the soul is — I believe there is nothing after death. We pay here on earth for everything; that's what kills people, what makes them suffer and frightens them. A person's behavior decides his destiny. If he's bad and plants bombs and is against the Revolution, he must be punished.

I must admit that there are many confusing contradictions between religious faith and the Revolution. Sometimes I wonder if there isn't a conflict between those two allegiances. But I can believe in both at the same time because what is now called communism I've always practiced and learned as the principles of the Church. The difference is that now these principles and practices are general, whereas before, not many followed them. At the same time, many people make the mistake of believing that to be in favor of the Revolution is to be against God.

When I joined the Women's Federation nobody asked whether I believed in God and there was no conflict. The first thing I did as a member of the Federation was to cooperate in making layettes for Mother's Day. That was nothing new to me. All my life I'd been taught by the Church to give clothes to those in need. When we heard that a poor woman was expecting a baby, we sewed shirts and baby blankets for it. To this day, half the things I sew for people I do for free.

After all, it was God who said you shouldn't wish on your neighbor what you don't want for yourself. And He always spoke of doing good to others and sharing what you have. What is that if not true communism? Doesn't the Revolution require you to sacrifice yourself for others? And isn't that what religion is all about — kindness? So where's the conflict? I can't see how anybody can be required to renounce God in order to follow God's doctrine.

When women's liberation was the topic in our study circle, it stirred up so much controversy we had to continue the discussion in another session. Some husbands thought one thing, others another, and the women were also divided. Some of the women equated the function of a housewife with that of a servant. They believe that men should help with the dishes, housekeeping, and so on. And some of the men said they usually help their wives with general housecleaning, that they often wash dishes and sweep floors. But I don't like to see a man doing that kind of work, unless a woman is ill. Otherwise, I think it's a woman's duty to organize her housework so she'll have time to engage in revolutionary tasks. The trouble is that many women start gossiping with neighbors and it gets to be 10:00 in the morning and they haven't made the beds. By noon they're rushing around like mad. Naturally!

Personally, I would never renounce woman's work though I wholeheartedly approve of women's liberation. I do any work I can for the Revolution, cutting cane or whatever, but I enjoy housework so much I don't want to be freed from it. I suppose I differ from most women in that respect. Of course I like to go to movies, to a party now and then, but I also like to have my clothes nicely ironed and I prefer to do the work myself. When a housewife says she's no better than a servant in her own home, it seems to me she doesn't love her husband or her children or her home. In fact, I think she's disappointed in being a woman.

To me, women's liberation means that a woman shouldn't have to submit to a man while he runs around doing whatever he pleases. Also, that women have the right to participate actively in the Revolution and to work outside the home, though I don't believe that the mother of young children should go off and work on a farm. But the Revolution would never ask that of her.

The truth is, women in Cuba are rarely integrated into the Revolution and most of them don't have jobs. Aside from male prejudices, conditions here make it difficult for them to work. Women run into an infinite number of problems if they want their children to be fed in school or in public dining rooms, or to attend nursery schools or kindergarten, or to have laundry done outside the home. Such facilities are readily available only in cases of urgent need, like when a woman must work to support three or four children. Still, I believe that every married woman should have as many children as her health and circumstances permit.

As old-fashioned as it may seem, I also believe that a woman should obey her husband, within reasonable limits. Every woman with a home and family is aware of her duties and responsibilities and need not be dictated to, as I was. It's not necessary to tell her, "Do this, do that." That's a kind of slavery. Instead, mutual understanding and agreement ought to be involved in everything a couple does.

A woman has the right to demand faithfulness of her husband. No woman can accept her husband having an affair with someone else. However, I don't go along with those who see women's liberation as equality with men. A woman should be free to form her own opinions and make her own decisions, but that doesn't mean she has to act like a man and have one lover today and another tomorrow. She should never under any circumstances have two men at the same time. Some women claim they stay with their husbands for the sake of the children, and then secretly carry on with other men. I think that's wrong. When a woman stops loving a man she should give him up. So when I speak of women's liberation I don't mean sexual freedom or freedom derived from use of the pill or the ring. I don't think they've had much of an impact here. We've been brought up to believe that a man loses nothing by being promiscuous but a woman loses everything.

Before the Revolution I didn't feel any great love for my country. Of course I felt a kind of love for my province, Matanzas, the love anyone feels for home. No matter where I might be, I'd feel that. But since the Revolution, I've changed completely toward the country. Now I feel for all of Cuba because I know the country is everybody's equally, and not in the hands of a monopoly or of someone who just wants to get rich or ride roughshod over the rest of us.

We Cubans will solve our difficulties little by little. Despite the problems, I have no fears for our future. On the contrary, I'm enthusiastic about the way things have progressed since the government took steps to increase agricultural production. There was a great deal of turmoil at the beginning, but the government has become more mindful of conditions in the countryside and the economy has improved. Our land is very productive, and if we work hard enough we can produce practically every agricultural product. Soon we won't have to depend on imported foodstuffs. After the 1970 sugar harvest, I expect the food situation to be much better here. The housing situation will also improve, but our energies should be directed to the production of cement and other building materials.

If we weren't blockaded, our development would be more rapid and efficient. But in spite of obstacles, I believe that Cuba's future will be prosperous and happy, with all Cubans cooperating with each other and sharing everything. I also have confidence in the Communist Party now that it's putting Fidel's ideas into practice. I know that he needs a lot of good people on his side. Perhaps now that the stage of persuasion is completed, we the people, along with the Central Committee, will be able to help Fidel achieve everything he wants.

The Aftermath

Inocencia's story seems innocent enough. But Ruth Lewis, who compiled and edited it, attributes a stronger, stranger kind of power to autobiographies of this kind. She suggests that the simple life histories of seemingly ordinary people may have the power to frighten authoritarian governments and threaten revolutionary gains.

> Why was the project ended in this manner when it would only have been necessary to ask us to leave? The immediate, obvious motive was to prevent publication of the data . . . In previous research, we had found that family studies and life stories told by even the humblest, least powerful people were often seen as very threatening by those above them. This was true in Mexico, Puerto Rico, in our own country, and now again in Cuba. The range and depth of topics touched upon in the autobiographies, the direct and indirect expression of opinions and attitudes on controversial matters, the reference to public figures and private matters, the involuntary involvement of relatives, friends, neighbors, and other persons whom the informant wishes to talk about, and the simple personal account of daily life with its frustrations, anxieties, and social injustices — all these make the data unpredictable and hazardous, sometimes explosive in effect, with far-reaching repercussions.[3]

Fascinating. One wonders how the lives of four men and four women, including Inocencia, could possibly frighten the powers-that-be. But Mrs. Lewis quotes from a 1972 speech of Raúl Castro, younger brother of Fidel and then Minister of the Revolutionary Army. He speaks of

> dangerous foreigners connected to the Ford Foundation . . . who established ties with counterrevolutionary elements . . . and members of mass organizations who unconsciously volunteered interesting data . . . intellectuals who have conducted political, economic, social, cultural, and military espionage, making use of their progressivist facade. . . . This has been possible, of course, because they have approached comrades incapable of seeing beyond the outward appearances.[4]

This brings up other questions. Did the Lewises put their confidants in danger? Was giving an interview a counterrevolutionary act for these Cubans? What should anthropologists do in difficult, morally ambiguous, or outright dangerous situations? As Ruth Lewis observes, she and her husband felt that they could do more good with their research and publications than they did harm.

> Oscar had nowhere in print raised the ethical questions posed by doing family studies and tape-recording life stories. However, because of our continued interest and involvement in them it is fair to say that we had committed ourselves, at least implicitly, to the position that the knowledge and insights gained from this kind of research outweighed the consequent invasion of pri-

vacy and the risk to the informants and to ourselves. Even though we believed greater risks existed in Cuba, we did not change our attitude.[5]

Many anthropologists of that time and worldview agreed with the Lewises. They resolved these questions in favor of doing the research — regardless of known or unknown consequences. They decided that the goals were justified. Of course, Ruth Lewis changed names and other identifying characteristics for publication and made other safeguards.

This was no casual project; enormous amounts of money and effort were spent to collect these autobiographies. Lives changed. It was to be the capstone of Lewis's career. Yet the three books are now out of print and far too long to digest and absorb easily.

Reviewers and critics did not respond favorably to any of the three volumes. They lamented an extraordinary career cut short, but noted that the three volumes provided no new insights on the revolution, on work, or on poverty and class structure. They did not seem to think that the autobiographies alone justified the project.

However, when contemporary readers go searching for women's lives, even in unexpected places, we are delighted to find Inocencia and her friends. We can hear her story and see a revolution at work in ways Oscar Lewis never anticipated. Once again we can wonder about the extraordinary act of offering one's life for strangers to ponder.

Women, Revolutions, and Some Good Books to Read

A number of compelling autobiographies are available to us about women and the appalling social conditions that seem to produce revolutions — especially in Latin America. In listening to these women, we may be learning more about their countries than a dozen social science books could teach us.

It is easier to find good material on women in Brazil, Central America, or the rest of the Caribbean than on Cuba. Daphne Patai has organized an enormously appealing collection of life stories, *Brazilian Women Speak: Contemporary Life Stories* (New Brunswick, NJ: Rutgers, 1993). The women come from different political and social backgrounds; each of twenty women speaks in such a direct and authoritative way that we are provoked beyond any easy assumptions.

A woman living in the slums of Sao Paulo, Brazil, kept a raw, primitive journal on scraps of paper picked from gutters. The main characters are herself, her three illegitimate children, Hunger, Scavenging, and the Slum they live in. David St. Clair recognized how compelling her story is and translated it from Portuguese. It is called *Child of the Dark: The Diary of Carolina Maria de Jesus* (New York: Dutton, 1962). Her terrifying outcry from the barrios of Brazil moved countless readers; the sequel or end of her story comes in *The Life and Death of Carolina Maria de Jesus,* edited by Robert Levine and José Meihy (Albuquerque: University of New Mexico Press, 1995).

Domitilia Barrios de Chungara told her story to Moema Viesser who edited it and arranged publication. It's called *Let Me Speak: Testimony of Domitilia, A Woman of the Brazilian Mines* (New York: Monthly Review Press, 1979). Mines and the conditions of mine workers' lives are another of those capitalist, colonial systems of exploitation that produce radical, revolutionary responses in men and women. Social conditions that affect men in such situations seem to fall even harder on women.

A classic autobiography of a woman turned revolutionary is *I, Rigoberta Menchú: An Indian Woman in Guatemala* (Monthly Review Press, 1984). Anthropologist Elisabeth Burgos-Debray, herself a Latin American woman, arranged a series of interviews with Rigoberta. She is a young peasant woman, an Indian who learned Spanish so she could join the revolution after the army killed her brother, father, and mother. Rigoberta Menchú won a Nobel Peace Prize for her leadership.

The socialist revolution in Cuban tried to solve "the woman question" and offer equality between genders. Did their revolutionary strategies work? Here is a beautifully reasoned and researched answer by Lois M. Smith and Alfred Padula: *Sex and Revolution: Women in Socialist Cuba* (New York: Oxford University Press, 1996).

Other Points to Ponder

1. Sociologists, anthropologists, and psychologists (among others) often speak of "maternal thinking." They mean that many women act like mothers even when they have no biological children. Being foster parents or godparents are good examples. In what other places does Inocencia apparently act or think maternally? How does it give meaning to her life?

2. Sometimes, it would seem, the government (or the church) can act like a husband or a boss. Inocencia's story illustrates this at a number of levels. How does such a notion explain her relationship to the revolution?

3. In analyzing life stories, we often see a turning point or key event that shapes the storyteller's life ever after and even colors what went before.

Divorce seems to fit this description in Inocencia's life. Why is divorce such a unique moment in many women's lives?

4. Today, researchers would probably not be able to "collect" autobiographies the way Oscar Lewis did. What has changed and why in the way someone hears, understands, or publishes another person's life story?

Endnotes to Chapter 5

1. This quote is from the introduction to Oscar Lewis, Ruth Lewis, and Susan Rigdow, *Four Men: Living the Revolution, An Oral History of Contemporary Cuba* (Urbana: University of Illinois Press, 1977), xi.

2. *Four Women* was published in 1977; *Friends* in 1978.

3. Introduction to *Four Men,* xxiii.

4. Ibid., xxiv.

5. Ibid., x.

Amiria with pigeon.

From *Amiria Manutahi Stirling,* Amiria: The Life Story of a Maori Woman, *p. 142.*

Amiria

"The Place Where You Fed at Your Mother's Breast"

The setting is New Zealand. A woman descended from the Maoris, the original Polynesian inhabitants of that island chain, befriends a young *pakeha* woman who traces her descent to European settlers who came later. They travel the splendid countryside together, the older woman teaching the younger one about Maori traditions. Then one day the old lady turns to her young friend and says, "Hey, Ani — what do you think of a book about my life?"

Who could resist! Anthropologist Anne Salmond had met Amiria Stirling at a party the first year she taught at the University of Auckland.

> Usually the anthropologist goes into the "field" with a project in mind, recruits his informants and then if he's lucky, makes friends with them, but in this case the Stirlings and I had already moved to a sort of "grandparent-grandchild" closeness before we ever did fieldwork together. When I came back to New Zealand in 1970 after finishing my doctoral papers in anthropology at the University of Pennsylvania, Eruera and Amiria took me to visit *marae* [ceremonial centers] throughout the country so that I could study Maori gatherings or "hui". For two years we traveled together, and it was towards the end of this research that the idea of this book emerged.[1]

When Amiria Stirling suggested the idea of recording the stories she had told on so many occasions, Anne Salmond agreed. So in 1973 Amiria and Anne as friends set to work. Mostly they taped in English. But when Amiria spoke of matters at the core of Maori life, she used that language and Anne Salmond later translated.

Amiria's life story as it emerges reveals the deep and inseparable connections between two cultures on this magnificent sweep of islands. First came the Maori ancestors, Polynesians who sailed across the Pacific Ocean in immense canoes and built a vivid culture. Then came the Europeans. A Dutch sailor named Abel Tasman sighted this land in 1642 and wrote the name New Zealand on his charts to honor the lowlands of the Netherlands from which he came. Captain James Cook visited the area in the 1770s and claimed the lands for England. Missionaries came in the early nineteenth century, and systematic settlement and colonization followed.

In 1840 Maori chiefs acknowledged British sovereignty in exchange for recognition of their tribal rights. However, the European settlers did not keep the promises of the treaty; so for the thirty years that followed, the first inhabitants and the new settlers fought fiercely. Two new histories were forged in those unstable times. Maoris became an impoverished minority in their native land. At the same time, many Europeans and Maoris married each other and raised children within their shared cultures.

European-descended New Zealanders — *pakeha* — are proud of their innovative social policies; in 1893 they were the first country to give women the chance to vote. But they also brought with them the patterns of prejudice and oppression that European settlers in North America practiced against the Native Americans of this continent. Maoris had to adjust with their very lives to a colonial situation they had never chosen and in which entire arenas of an ancient and integrated culture were destroyed. It is at this historic point that Amiria's own life begins.

Place and People

Amiria grew to adulthood on the East Coast, a formidable, mountainous area that faces the Pacific sunrise. At the time Amiria's story begins, most of the people in the region were Maori.

New Zealand is exceptionally beautiful. This may be one of the reasons that places and place names loom so large in Amiria's account. You will notice her strong sense of geography. In addition, the Maori language specifies locations, directions, positions, and the qualities of places more than does the English language. So she talks spontaneously about going to this place, coming back from another place, or living in specific places. Her entire narrative is grounded in places.

Genealogy, as well as geography, is embedded in Amiria's sense of herself. Maoris can recite long lists of their ancestors, names, deeds, and places where they lived, died, and were buried. Pedigrees and family trees are who they are.

Amiria's marriage, for example, was a way of affirming these traditional and very complex genealogical ties — both for herself and others. She includes elaborate genealogies with the book and she mentions these connections frequently.

Like the other women in this book, Amiria grounds herself in relation to other people — but she does it with a distinctive Maori touch. She also invokes or calls out the profound themes of Maori culture: "the sacred" or *tapu;* "value, prestige" or *mana;* honoring the traditions or *maoritanga,* as well as the universal experiences of marriage, raising children, death, earning a living, and putting meaning in our lives.

Amiria sprinkles Maori words throughout her narrative. She has clearly been trained in and loves the Maori way of talking, speaking, listening, reciting, and remembering. Look at the extraordinary conversations that mark her entire account. Some of the best conversations she recounts she didn't even hear. Others are amazingly detailed and still hold the flavor and feeling of the events decades later.

We must not underestimate the impact of oral tradition. Amiria came from a culture where people knew how to tell tales, recite genealogies, and sing songs they composed in their heads. In these cultures, older women always have the best proverb to sum up a problem. In moving from the spoken to the written accounts, Anne Salmond retained idioms and turns of phrases that mark New Zealand English as Maoris use it. She left in the exclamations, the idiosyncratic grammar and phrases. It is possible to fall into the rhythm of Amiria's tales and allow the rhythm to carry us.

Anne as anthropologist resisted the temptations to fiddle with the text. She translated some of it, arranged sections in chronological order, and added explanatory footnotes. As do many anthropologists, she believes that human lives, like human societies, contain the seeds of their own interpretation. Moreover, interpretations can and will change. New readers will find new ideas.

Anne and Amiria made no effort to fill in obvious gaps in the story, nor to dive deeper for the kind of analysis Westerners often think is needed. Therefore the short selections included here have the same texture as the entire book has.

In common with many autobiographies, Amiria's is packed with details. At the same time, many pieces — even things obviously at the core of her life — are simply left out. In fact, I have the feeling there is another kind of autobiography just below the surface of this one. For example, Amiria recounts very few conversations with her husband, Eruera, particularly ones that might allow the reader to intuit what their unusual marriage was like. George is the only one of Amiria's children whom she talks about in detail — the only one whose life comes through to us; yet mothers like Amiria could talk for days, probably months, about each of her children, their special personalities, her memories of them. But who would listen? Would that still be autobiography?

On another level, this is a specialized history of the enterprise and vigor of the East Coast Maori tribes and the story of how they gradually moved into urban areas, leaving their *maraes* (ceremonial centers) to grow cold. On the level of autobiography, however, it is a woman's story — births and deaths, seasons and gatherings, love and work. Her dying father exacts a promise from her mother. Relatives who feel Amiria is their investment in the Maori future start to plot on her behalf. Then, in a most dramatic scene, she meets her future husband. The events of her life seem to be framed in the pervasive and permanent linkages between Maori and European.

For purposes of this chapter, Amiria's story starts off with her marriage, negotiation for which was begun in her infancy. The middle section concerns her first son, George — for reasons that will become obvious. The selections are topped off by her stories of old age. I have added short bridges that connect the long pieces of her life. If this book were literature or a movie, we would probably call it magical realism. I cherish the undercurrents — the feeling that things are more than they seem, that perhaps spirits lurk just out of sight, or that life is in its odd details. Prepare to be surprised about the style of the narrative.

My Young Life as a Child

In those days, Tuparoa was the township, Ruatoria wasn't even started. It was a *beautiful* town too. There was a big hotel and the Farmer's and the big Williams' shop which was run by the Lubrooks, and the blacksmith's. Then of course, there was my father's business — he was the only tailor there, and when he died there was no more. He did these divided skirts and riding breeches, and my mother used to go there house-keeping and that's how he fancied her. Harry thought, well, he'll come to Auckland and ask his parents about his marriage to this Maori girl. He came to Auckland and told his mother that he was going to get married, and his mother said,

"Oh yes Harry, what is it? The *pakeha* [European] girl?"

"No, it's a Maori."

When he said it was a Maori, oh . . . she shot up, she didn't like it.

"No," she said, "No!"

They wouldn't have a Maori, not a Maori.

"You'll have to marry your own people."

And Harry said, "Well, I can't help it. I *am* going to marry this woman! You don't know the Maori people; you've got to live with the Maori people, Mum, to understand them. They're lovely people if you know them, and I know them because I live there amongst them, and they're the people that got me on my feet. I'm the only tailor in the district and most of my customers are Maoris, so I'm all right. But I just want you to say 'yes' about this."

"No!"

"All right, well you go your way, I'll go my way. I can't help it, I am going to marry that woman."

"If you do, we won't have you, we're finished with you. We don't want to have any more to do with you!"

He walked out, then he thought, so he went back again.

"Mum, what about my family? If I have children would you accept them? I have made the mistake, but what about my family?"

"No." She would not have anything to do with a Maori family. Then Harry thought — his is the end, so he left and came back to Tuparoa.

He took sick a few years afterwards, not long after I was born. He asked my mother to get a doctor, and she went and got a *tohunga* [a priestly expert]. The tohunga came and started to do water and all this sort, and Dad got wild, because he said he wanted a doctor. But you couldn't get a doctor in the country in those days and that's how he lost his life.

Before he died, he asked Mum to come over to the bedside. He wanted a quiet talk with her, because he didn't want the tohunga and all the other Maoris sitting around to hear what he was saying. He was talking to her quietly about me, about the baby, to make sure I marry back, marry a pakeha.

"When she's old enough to get married, Ani, promise me that you will see that she marries a pakeha — I was the one that made the breakage with my family, but perhaps my daughter will mend that break. If she marries back, then maybe my family will accept my daughter."

My mother said, "I will Harry. I'll do that for you. I'll see that your daughter will marry back. I was the cause of the trouble, so you leave that to me."

They hugged one another, and shook hands on it. He was happy before he died. And he left all the money from his business to see that I get the best of education at a good school, not just the Maori school.

After he died Mum couldn't keep up the business, she didn't know how to do tailor's work. She cleared up the shop and sold everything, then she travelled around and stayed with relations for a while. Her elder sister Hera Kaiwahie came and took me to Waipiro Bay.

[Amiria was sent to live with her grandmother and the rest of her mother's relatives, as immersed in Maori life as was probably possible in New Zealand in this century. Then she went away to pakeha school when she was eighteen. But she left and returned to the east coast just as a typhoid epidemic was starting. A good friend, Kareti, told her that the relatives were keen on arranging a good Maori marriage for her. Amiria's mother apparently hoped to forestall these plans, so she assisted Amiria to enter nursing training. As the epidemic waned, Amiria left nursing to be a housewoman (maid) on a pakeha estate. She liked the job very much. By this time she is in her early twenties. Then she caught typhoid fever.]

My *Taumau* Marriage

Even while I had typhoid, the old people didn't give in; they were still working on my *taumau* [arranged] marriage. Kareti was the one who told me about it. One time we went to a dance at Hiruharama and she said, "Amy, remember that taumau marriage I told you about? They're still planning it, you know."

"Kareti, I'm sick of that! What are you trying to do?"

"It's not *me,* Amy, it's the old people."

"Oh, what do they want now?"

"They've got a man for you; Eruera Kawhia."

"Don't be silly, that fulla is an old man!"

Eruera Kawhia was an old man in Ruatoria, and I thought Kareti was joking me for all my floating around. I didn't realize that the chap they wanted me to marry was named after that old man.

"It's not this old man in Ruatoria, Amy — it's Eruera Kawhai Whakatane *Stirling.* Remember . . . he came here one time, and called in to Taumata-o-mihi." I did remember that one time when I was at the Williams, I went back home and there was a young boy running around on the marae. Aerta told me then that he was their cousin, he was going to Te Aute and his name was Dick.

"That can't be the same fulla. That's Dick . . . "

"It is the same man. Eruera Kawhia — Dick Stirling!"

"Oh well, forget about it!" I said. "I don't want you to talk to me about it . . . he's still at school!"

They kept on planning this though, and all the time my mother was fighting with them. She told Hakopa Haerewa and them to stop it and they told her off. They said it was none of her business.

"You didn't look after this child — we did!"

Then another would say, "Ae. When her grandmother went to work, Tapita and I kept her. She's *our mokopuna* [grandchild] — you left her behind. So don't talk to us, we have the right!"

There she was, with everyone hoeing into her. She started to think up something to get me right away from this; she thought to herself, the best thing would be to get me to come to Auckland and stay in Auckland — maybe then I'll meet a pakeha, or I might meet some of my father's relations, and they would keep me away from this Maori stuff. Anyway, she planned to take me to the Exhibition in Auckland. She knew that I generally had Wednesday afternoons off from the Williams, and one Wednesday she came up from Tupaora on horseback. She rang Mrs. Williams to ask what time I'd be leaving.

"She generally goes off at three o'clock," Mrs. Williams said. "She'll be leaving here soon."

So Mum came up to the Williams place. We didn't go, we sat out on a bank near Taumata-o-mihi because she wanted to have a quiet talk with me, she didn't want anyone to know. When we sat down on the bank she said, "Taku korero ki a koe, Amiria . . . do you know your elders want you to have a taumau marriage?"

"What's that, Mum?"

"Well you see, it's not for you to pick the man, it's for them, they pick the man for you. All you have to say is 'Yes,' and they'll do everything. It's not your marriage, it's the people's."

"But this Dick Stirling they want, he's only a boy, he's still at Te Aute!"

"That's it. They don't care about anything."

"Oh no, I don't want it, no!" I said, "I don't want it, I want to get away. . . . I want to find my own man, I can find a man myself. I got a lot of boyfriends, pakeha friends and all that. If I want to get married, well, I can choose which one . . . " I was getting all upset.

"Well, this is what I've done for you — I've got your ticket, and we're going on the boat. I'll pay the taxi here from Ruatoria, and we'll go to Tokomaru and get on the *Arahura* and go to Auckland. You pack all your things and everything, and we'll go. I'll stay with you in Auckland until you're really settled down, and then I'll come back."

Poor Mum. She said to me, "You've got to get away from here. *Never* let those people have what they want!"

Then she told me about her promise to my father on his deathbed, how they shook hands on it, and she promised him that I will marry a pakeha not a Maori.

"So, Amiria, you have to help me keep my promise to your father. If you agree, I want you to shake hands with me too. Will you promise to marry a pakeha?"

"Yes," and we took hold of each other's hands, and she put her nose to my hand, like that.

"Well, kai kaha! You be strong. Your elder sisters have all married Maoris, but you must return to your pakeha side, your father's people."

Then she asked me to meet her in Ruatoria the day after next.

"Get all your things, but don't tell your grandma where you're going . . . If you do, they might know that you're leaving. Might be better if you tell her that you're coming to Tuparoa."

"All right, Mum."

She went back to Tuparoa. I went home and started sewing, I wanted to make a nice dress for myself and that, so I started sewing, ironing, and packing up my suitcase.

Old Hakopa had seen her though, and he thought, I'll bet Ani has been here to talk to Amiria about our plans.

He talked to my uncle Tamati, and Tamati said, "If I see her doing that . . . *nati au te kaki,* I'll squeeze her neck!"

The next day old Hakopa marched into the house, and there I was, sewing and ironing.

"Oh. Hello mokopuna," he said. "How are you?"

"I'm all right."

"It looks as if you're packing — where are you going?"

"I'm going to Tuparoa," I said.

"What's the use of *that*? What do you want to go to Tuparoa for? There's nothing to do there except to look after all your mother's kids! You needn't slave for her . . . She got married, and brought all that family to the world, let her look after it! Stay here with your *tipunas* [grandparents, ancestors] — you belong to us, not her."

"Listen, Amiria Manutahi . . . it wasn't your mother who brought you up, it was us, your tipunas. We were the ones who loved and cared for you. As for your mother, what's the use of that woman! She married another man, had another family — and then she has the cheek to come and lecture us about you. Today, we love you as we always have. We don't want you to be like your mother, one husband dies so she marries another, then he dies and she marries someone else . . . "

Which was right. Wirihana Tatai was her fourth husband, and they didn't like that. They only wanted me, and that was all — she could go her own way. Then they told me why they were so keen on this match, and they explained all about Eruera Kawhia and how his namesake must marry a Ruatoria woman.

"We want you to marry Eruera Kawhia Whakatane, your cousin. He's from here, just like you. On one side he's Te Whanau-a-Apanui, and on his mother's side he's from here. So that is our wish. We only want you to say 'Yes.'"

Hika ma! I didn't know what to say.

"I don't know this man! It might be all right if I did — if a woman sees her man, that's better. You're the ones that know him, not me."

"Never mind that! All we want is for you to agree . . . As long as you say 'Yes,' that's it. We'll be happy then."

"But if I say yes now, I don't want to get married straight away . . . let us be engaged for two years, so we can get to know one another and that."

"Well, all right."

I thought, that fixes that. As soon as I get my bag, I'm off, I'll never come back.

"All right," I said to them. "Now I'm going to the Exhibition in Auckland with my mother. I will remember about this two years — that's quite a time from now."

"No," said Hakopa. "We don't want you to go. We want you to meet this man now — he's in the Bay of Plenty."

"Why? We've got all this time — two years — to meet him. When I come back from Auckland!"

I knew they'd keep nagging at me, so I came away and went to bed. Next morning I got ready, and I called out to Kareti to tell the old man that I wanted my bag. He came walking over to our place.

"Now, I want to talk to you, Amiria . . . You say you're going to the Exhibition in Auckland? Well, Kareti, Areta, and I are going there too. We're not going on the launch though, we're going on horseback. Why don't you come with us? I know you haven't got a horse, so I've bought one for you."

I looked at him. "You've bought me a horse?"

"Yes — new saddle, bridle, everything. You're a *rangatira* woman [chief] now, Amiria Manutahi."

"Oh!" said Kareti. "Fancy that. She's got a horse and I haven't even got one . . . You blooming lucky beggar! He's never bought me a horse."

Then I got excited. In those days I suppose, getting a horse was like getting a motor car. I thought, gee, I never owned a horse, and now I will have a horse, and a saddle and everything.

"You don't have to pay any money out either," Hakopa said. "No fares — and when you come back you've still got your horse. You're a lucky girl."

Then Kareti went and brought the horse. And when I saw this horse . . . gee whiz! *Ka rawe* — beautiful! It was a racehorse, too. He told me he bought it from K. S. Williams; but I think Mr. Williams only lent it. Kareti saddled it up.

"Come on then! Get on the horse. We're going to Ruatoria." Both of us got on the horse, she came on the back and we went cantering down to Ruatoria — whee! We forgot everything . . . we went right to Mangahanea, came back on the horse whistling and singing all the way home. When we got home and let the horse go out in the paddock, she said, "Gee you're lucky. You're coming with us?"

And I said "Yeah!"

That was it. That afternoon Hakopa asked me if I was coming with them on horseback. I said I was, and he packed everything for me. That was how we came to Raukokore.

When we got there they made a big fuss of us, and it's nice to be fussed over instead of having all those fights, so I felt happy.

But when Kareti and I went to our bedroom, I noticed everything was different in this room. There were two single beds for us girls before, but now there was only one big bed in it. I thought, oh well, they might be putting us all in one bed, and that's less trouble for the old lady . . .

That afternoon there was a service. The old man Duncan Stirling always held his service, whether there was anybody around or not. I give the old man credit for that, even if the family didn't want his service, and they all ran away to a dance or something as soon as they heard the old man bang! bang! on the wall, well, he'd stand in the sitting-room all by himself and hold his service. I used to like it though, because I was brought up that way when I lived with the Williams, there was always a service in that house . . . And I still respect service before everything.

After service, the old man Hakopa stood up and started talking to me.

"Amiria, Mihi Kotukutuku is a chieftainess here. And remember the taumau you agreed to in Ruatoria? Well, Eruera Kawhia is her son. Mihi doesn't agree with the pakeha way, the engagement. What we want is for you to sleep with your cousin tonight."

That shocked me, of course. I thought, now what's this!

"No!" I said. I couldn't make it out — I thought he was still at Te Aute. I was getting very funny in the head, with all the trouble we'd had, all the fights and everything. We had lost the trip to Auckland, and now they were starting about this match marriage again.

"What?" said Hakopa.

"No! Kaore! He's only young, and I'm older than him. Give him two years to grow up."

Then Mihi stood up and she started to talk to me.

"Listen, *e hine* . . . you are in my house! On your marae, all right, you're the boss, but this is my marae and I'm chief here . . . so listen. Everyone has agreed to have a taumau marriage between you and your cousin Eruera Kawhia. And I'm telling you, this is a better way than the pakeha engagement — that's too long! Who's to know that you could stay as good as you are? You might look at somebody else and that. So this is the Maori way. Tonight you and your cousin will sleep together. The room is ready for you, everything is prepared . . . the people have arranged it all."

Ah . . . then that time I started to shiver! I started to shiver, and I stood up and I thought, no, I'm not! I'm not going to give in to them.

Hakopa shouted at me, "Don't you stand up, girl, sit down! You heard what the old lady said. This is her marae and she's the chief. Don't be above yourself — sit down!"

I started to cry, and I sat down.

"Why don't you listen — we're not degrading you or anything, we are making you a chiefly woman."

"I don't want to be a chief, I want to go home!"

Mihi said, "That's enough. Stop crying, and don't say any more. We are honouring you."

She grabbed hold of my hand and took me to the bedroom.

"I want to go to the toilet!" I said. I was only pretending. So I got out and I ran outside to the toilet, and I sat there and started to cry. They were watching me, you know. I heard Kareti calling.

"Amy! Amy! Come on. We want you back here. You've been there long enough."

"All right, I'm coming."

You know what I was doing? I was looking round for my horse. It was tied under a pohutukawa tree at the back of the house before, but now I couldn't see it. I thought, if only I knew where my horse was, and the saddle and bridle, I'd get on that horse and go back home to Ruatoria. Then I saw the housemaid Susan, standing on the back porch looking at me. She turned around and went into the house. I thought, perhaps I could ask Susan to go and get the horse, and take it into the *quicks* [bushes]. She could tie it there and then whistle. When I heard her whistle, I'd know the horse was saddled and everything, and I'd just run there and nobody could catch me. So when Kareti went to the dining-room, I ran inside, and I found Susan was hanging on to a post there and crying. I put my arms around her.

"Susan! What's wrong? Are you sick?"

"No."

"What's the matter then?"

"It's that beggar!"

"Who's that?" I said.

"That blasted Dick! He's been playing around with me . . . him and I have been — you know. And now you're going to marry him."

"But he's at Te Aute."

"No he's not, he's here! I know, I'm telling you. Do you want to see him?"

"Yes."

She bent over and opened the door a bit, he was sleeping on the bed.

"There," she said, "that's the brute!"

And I looked at him — oh, he was only a young boy. And I saw his hair, yes, he had that stick-up hair — the other brothers had got curls. . . .

I said to Susan, "Look Susan, I tell you something now. You've been courting with this man, eh."

"Yes, the beggar!"

"That's all right, now you listen to me, you can *have* him, I don't want him. I tell you what. You go and get my horse for me, and saddle it up . . . See the bush of thick quicks down there? Take the horse there and when you're ready, blow a strong whistle. I tell you Susan, once I get on that horse, I'll get out of this place, they'll never catch me. Will you do that?"

"Yes."

"Don't go in the daytime though, they'll see you. Wait till it's dark."

"All right Amy."

"Well, I'll wait for you and listen."

It was getting dark, so I went to my room and started to pack my bag. I looked round for Kareti and Areta, but they'd disappeared. It was the first time they had left me. I felt lost, there was nobody around to talk to. I got my bag ready, then I opened the window and I thought as soon as I hear the whistle, I'll jump out and run down the road, straight to that bush of quicks. I was waiting for the whistle — no whistle, no whistle . . .

Hakopa came in.

"All right Amiria, you've got to sleep with your cousin tonight. Go on — get ready for bed. You can't wear a coat in bed."

I started to cry. He took my coat off, gave me my nightgown and made me put it on. Oh, Susan . . . you're a long time to whistle! When the old man left, I sat by the window holding my coat.

The next thing, Dick walked in the room. He had his pajamas on.

"Come on in the bed!"

He started to pull me to the bed.

"You keep your hands to yourself! You're not my husband yet . . . "

"I am though . . . "

So I jumped out of the window and started running. I was so hurt, I thought, I'm going to drown myself. I ran straight to the reef right out to this very far point. And not a sound of Susan. I ran till I got right to the very end. When I got there, waves were dashing up on the rocks, boom! boom! on the rocks. I called out to my grandmother.

"Nanny, Nanny! I want to go home, I don't want this to happen to me!"

Just then I heard Areta yelling, "Amiria, Amiria, Amy. Don't do that, Amy, don't, don't! It's all right we're going home . . . stop it . . ."

She pulled me back flat on the stones, and she grabbed hold of me. We sat there crying to one another, she was holding me.

"No, don't do that. Come on home. We're going back to Ruatoria. It's got to stop, this; it's no good, it's no good."

Then Kareti arrived too, and they took me right home. I asked them if they heard someone whistling.

"Did you hear anybody whistling, Addie?

""No."

"Nobody?"

And I asked Kareti.

"No."

I thought to myself, poor old Susan must have got caught.

They took me inside, and the old people had a good lecture at me. When the old lady came in — she was the one I got frightened of because of the way she talked — I just looked at her.

"Now stop being so stupid! Do you think we're trying to belittle you, to make you a slave? No. You know we are honouring you. And yet you behave like this. You're a *bad* girl. None of the old people want you now, you'll have no relations, nothing! You are making fools of us all. Now you must promise me to stop it — give me your hand . . ."

I shook hands with her.

"You've agreed now. So stop it!"

Kareti, Areta, and I went to bed together, but I fell off to sleep and they got up and walked away. He came in and slept with me.

It had to be that way. The next day it was something great to them. Everyone came to visit, to greet us and so on. But the thing that worried me — from that day to this day, I didn't know what happened to that horse. Someone told me that Susan got caught, and she got thrashed for it. And I think they took that horse back to Ruatoria.

[In accordance with Maori customs, the wedding was held later. Her mother was still upset and interrupted the services. Then the young couple went to live with his family on the Stirling estate and Amiria includes long discussions about her relationships with her new mother-in-law and her husband's relatives. Their first child, Lucy, was born there. Although Amiria was happy, she wanted her own place. She and her husband had learned to tend sheep, shear, and market the wool. Sheepherding is one of New Zealand's foremost commercial activities. So with the help of his family, Eruera and Amiria got their own place. When Lucy was four, Amiria "started carrying" again. The birth contractions had started; but the baby didn't seem to want to come out. Amiria was at home, her friend, Heni, a midwife, had come.]

Life on the Farm

The pains came and Heni got prepared, then the pains would go! After a while, Heni got wild with me.

"By . . . gosh!" She grabbed hold of me and shook me.

"I think it's you! You're holding that baby. Come on, let go! What's wrong with you?"

"It's not me, Heni."

"Oh yes it is. And if the baby's not born tomorrow, you'll have to go to Te Puia. Do you know what's the matter?"

"No — I don't . . . "

"You ought to know by now." She was growling at me. "Give that force! You're not giving that force. You're scared, that's what's wrong."

But I knew it wasn't me. The baby had been playing up like that; I kept getting pains and then they'd disappear.

In the end, Heni got tired of waiting. She said to me, "I've got a family too, you know. If you're going to play up like this with me, I'm going to leave you, I'll go home to get tea for my husband."

Then she turned to the old lady, "Tell your mokopuna to bring the baby. She's scared, that's what's the matter."

Mereana came and told me off.

"I'm telling you, Amiria, *bring* that baby. Go on! While Heni is still here. Hurry up!"

She took me and put me down on the floor on a mat, then she put her knee against my belly and just *hit* me there.

"Wait on, Heni, wait. The baby's coming now!"

I heard the baby coming. Heni came running back and the baby was born. Oh, I was glad. I was just resting back with relief, I was glad it was finished. The next thing I heard them crying.

"Heni! What's the matter? Is the baby dead?"

She looked around and shook her head.

"Why are you crying?"

She shook the baby and the baby started to cry.

"Oh, Grandma . . . why are you crying? The baby's born and you're crying . . . "

My grandmother took the afterbirth and said to me.

"You must wash this and look after it."

"Why? All that has to be buried, doesn't it?"

"No," she said. "This baby was born with a cap on his head and this is the cap [the amniotic sac]. You must look after the cap, so the baby will be all right. Otherwise, something terrible will happen to this child."

I got sick of all the Maori talk.

"Look, the baby is born, he's all right! Never mind about all that — those days are finished."

Heni came and kissed me, and Mereana took the baby and washed him. I didn't know she kept that afterbirth until years after; I went back one time and she showed it to me, it was like silk. I don't know what happened to it when she died.

That child was our son George. When I think back now and remember what happened to that boy, I can see it all. If only I had listened to her, he would still be alive today. But I was like a lot of young people, I couldn't be bothered with the old Maori ways.

[In the years that followed, the Stirlings did mixed farming in the Bay of Plenty on a farm called Otaimina. They milked cows, ran sheep, raised crops like potatoes, sweet potatoes, cabbages, and other vegetables. Six more children arrived. The couple were gradually drawn into Maori cultural life: remembering the genealogies, speaking the language, studying the art and helping build or restore the traditional meeting houses — marae — that were the heart of Maori traditional life. Because she was a trained nurse, people frequently asked for her help. Later, they returned the favors and helped her. Their son George won a scholarship to college. World War II started. The Stirlings entered the war effort with a passion. Amiria worked hard for the Maori Women's Welfare League and helped raise money for the Maori Battalion. She recalls those times as the days of plenty in the Bay of Plenty. "That was the beauty of those days." After the war George finished school and took a job helping Maori veterans with innovative agricultural techniques. But one day, George was killed in a road accident.]

Low in My Mind

When we arrived at the marae all the women started wailing; it was the most heart-breaking sound I've heard in my life. There was a dog howling in the background and it was Pete [George's dog], tied up at the back of the marae, jumping at his chain and crying his heart out. The body was put on the porch of the meeting-house, and all the people kept coming to *tangi* [grieve and weep] for George. In the end somebody let Pete loose and he came racing to the meeting-house and tried to jump on the coffin — I could hardly bear to see that dog. The people kept coming for days, and then George was buried. They shoveled dirt on his coffin and I cried out, "Oh son, the violets and freesias are blooming now — where are you . . . ?

That night the dog broke loose from his chain. Someone heard him howling in the cemetery, and they found Pete digging at the graveside, trying to find George, so they took him home and tied him up again. Later on the family told me that on the night George was killed, Pete had suddenly started to howl at about midnight and he cried for the rest of the night, they couldn't make him stop. Early the next morning the news about the accident came to Otaimina.

That's how our son George lost his life.

After George died I just couldn't bear the place, everything was too much of a memory of him to me. Even the dogs and the horses in the paddock and the fruit trees, they all made me feel sick. I started to get low in my mind and I didn't feel hungry and in the end I grew very weak. One day I collapsed in the house and it started to play up with me like that. They sent me to the doctor in Opotiki and he said that I had TB, I'd have to go to Waipukurau to get better.

Then I started to worry about the family; I knew I'd have to leave them for Eruera to look after and he already had the cows to milk and everything, and that made me feel worse.

One morning I was lying in the bed while the girls were doing the housework, and they must have all gone outside because it was very quiet. I fell off to sleep and I had a funny dream — I dreamt I was on a mountain. When I looked up it looked like Hikurangi with all the snow on top, but when I looked down it was black, as though it was floating in midair. I was about halfway down that mountain and I was slipping, you could see the marks where I'd been. I knew that if I wasn't careful I'd fall right off and that would be death, because it was black all around and the mountain was just standing there in the middle of a great big hole. I slipped a little way and I prayed to God in my heart that he'd give me strength to climb up again, but the grass was slippery and every time I put my foot on it I'd slide down again. I struggled to get back to the top of that mountain but I kept on slipping, and in the end I fell off. When I was falling I knew I was dead, so I called out, "Dear Lord, help me to get back, I want to stay with my family!"

A rock broke my fall, it was protruding from the side of the mountain and I knew that was the Rock of Ages from the song, "Rock of Ages, cleft for me . . ." I started to sing this in my heart, and there I was, hanging on to this rock. When I looked down — oh, it was jet-black down there. I knew that only Almighty God could save me now; if he wanted me to be saved, that rock would stay firm. I made one last struggle to climb up and the rock fell away. I thought, well I'm gone. I had a tangi to my family and I could feel myself going, I was lost and finished.

The next thing I heard the birds twittering, and that brought me back to myself. When I looked around I could see these birds singing in the air, and they seemed to be following me. I was flying too, I had big wings and I was flying in the air beneath the mountain. I looked up and saw the snow on the mountain, and I knew it was this world of ours; when I looked down I could see the sun shining onto dried grass, and that was the other world.

I still wanted to stay with my family so I tried to fly back, but the harder I flew the further the mountain went from me, and in the end I got tired of trying. I thought, well it's no use Amiria, you're for the other world now; you'd better fold your wings and start to walk. As soon as I folded my wings, I landed in a tree. I could see the other birds still flying around, and when I looked down I saw this beach — I'd never seen a beach like that before! The sand was like iron-sand and it was all mixed in with the water, so that when the waves dashed up there was more sand in them than water. I said to myself, "*E hika!* Where am I now? I've never seen a beach like this before, even in Ruatoria, Tuparoa, or the Bay of Plenty, I've never seen a beach like this."

"*Ko te kainga tuturu tenei . . .*"

I heard this voice talking and I looked up.

"What was that?"

"This is the last home; the place where people truly love one another. This is the final resting-place."

"The final resting-place?"

"Yes."

"Oh . . . Do you know an old lady called Mereana Mokikiwa?"

"I know her well."

"And what about my mother Ani — how is she?"

"She's well, we are all well here."

"Where is this place?"

"This is the Rerenga Wairua."

I thought, I'm going to get out of here! I tried to fly but I could only go around in circles so I thought, it's no use, I have to go down there on the ground. When I put my wings together, huh! I was on the ground, walking. I could hear people talking but I couldn't see them, and just then a pakeha woman called out to some children and I felt one of them brush past my legs.

"Hurry up, dears — come along!"

I looked around but I still couldn't see them, so I followed the sound of their voices and the next thing I saw this tiny little gate. Every now and again the gate would slam — bang! and after a while — bang! I thought I might as well go through that gate but when I tried it was too small for me.

I kept on trying, and in the end I turned sideways and managed to slip through. I heard these people still in front of me, and then I saw the church. I thought oh! — this is the first thing you've got to do, you've got to go to church; I must be really there now. The people were going in so I started to climb up the steps, and just as I was about to put my head inside I heard the minister start up a hymn. When I heard his voice I knew it was Te Aperahama Tatai Koto, a minister who used to be in Tuparoa — he had such a beautiful singing voice. I wanted to go in and listen, but the next thing, "Moo . . . oo . . . oo!!"

One of our working steers made a big noise and he woke me up. I looked out of the window and it was Reddy, he was leaning over the fence crying out to the cows in the milking-shed; he couldn't get to them because the gate was shut. I thought, oh Reddy, good on you, you've brought me back! If you hadn't called out, I might have been stuck in that other world forever.

[Because she is "low in her mind" after George's death, Amiria and Eruera decide to move away from their farm and resettle in Auckland. But this part of the story has one last piece.]

Before we came away to Auckland, our youngest son Kingi came to live with us at Otaimina. You see, when George was killed and I was sitting beside his body at the tangi, one of the women told me that my sister-in-law Edie had given birth to a baby the day before George's accident. I asked her, "What is the baby?"

"It's a boy."

When I heard that I felt that my son George had come back again, and all through the tangi I was hoping that I could get this baby; I knew it would help me to forget what had happened. When Edie came to Stirling Castle with the baby not long after, I asked her to call the baby after George, and she agreed. Then I said, "I would like to take the baby, Edie — you give that baby to me and I'll look after him."

"Oh no, no! You leave the baby with me, but it's all right, I will name him Kingi [King] George, after George."

Kingi George was the name given to our son by Mrs. Williams. He was born on June 3rd, and when Mrs. Williams heard about it she said, "Fancy that — June 3rd is King George's birthday! I'm going to ring Amy up and ask her to call the baby King George."

She rang me up about it and I said, "I'm very sorry, Mrs. Williams, but this baby has already been named. The old lady has called him Te Ariki-tapu-ki-waho, after one of her ancestors."

"Well, you can give him this name too, because he was born on King George's birthday."

Just to make her happy I agreed, and our son was christened Kingi George Te Ariki-tapu-ki-waho.

Anyhow, Edie said she would call her son Kingi George too, but she said, "I want to keep this baby, Amy. Later on maybe, when he's running around and you can feed him on *kumara* [sweet potatoes] it might be all right, but while he's a baby, I think I'd better look after him."

"It doesn't matter about the feeding, Edie; I fed my own babies with a bottle, I can look after him."

"Oh never mind, Amy, leave it, leave it . . ."

I didn't bother her again while I was sick, but when I came back from Auckland I really started to think about this baby. One day somebody said to me, "Did you know that Edie's gone to Te Puia?"

"What for?"

"Oh, she going to have another baby."

"Is she? What's looking after the baby?"

"Her eldest daughter, Maru."

I thought, here goes, I'm going to get that baby now. I rang Frank Walker and told him that I wanted a taxi to Te Araroa.

He came and picked me up, and away we went to Te Araroa. When we got there I walked into Edie's house.

"Hello Maru, how's everybody?"

"Oh, all right Auntie. Mum just had her baby the other day you know, she's still in the home."

"Where's Kingi now?"

"There he is, under the table."

The baby was crawling around and trying to stand up under the table so I grabbed hold of him and picked him up.

"Where are his clothes, Maru?"

"In the room. Auntie . . . what are you going to do?"

"I'm going to take this blanket and look after him. Just give me his clothes and a blanket."

She gave me all the baby's clothes and I wrapped him up in the blanket, and got in the taxi and went back to Otaimina.

When Edie came back from Te Puia, she couldn't see Kingi anywhere.

"Maru, where's Kingi?"

"Oh, Auntie Amy came here and took him away."

"Did she now!"

As soon as she was free Edie came to Raukokore and told me off for stealing her baby.

"But I *told* you Edie, I wanted that baby. If you'd had a trouble like mine and lost a dear son, you'd need some comfort too. I feel better now, because I've got someone to talk to when the kids are away at school . . . So you look after your baby and I'll look after mine, and we'll both be all right."

Edie wasn't very happy about it but she went away, and left Kingi at home with me.

[So the family moved to Auckland. Amiria got a job in a factory making hats and ties. She enjoyed her work, her house and living in Auckland, despite the discrimination against Maoris, which seemed to be more common in the city than in the country. Here are a few stories from her old age and some opinions about life. Amiria has earned them.]

Later Years

When I got to my pension age, I had to give up work. After that we had more time to go to *huis* [ceremonial gatherings], and we joined up with some of the clubs around Auckland too — the Pioneers', the Founders' Society, and the Old Folks' group down at Coronation Hall.

Once when the Festival was on, our Old Folks' president told me that there was a bus taking all the old people down to the Flower Show at the Town Hall; if I wanted to go I'd have to be down at Gundry Street on time. I wasn't going to miss out on that trip, so I got ready early in the morning and took a bus from Ponsonby to the Old Folks' Hall. When we got to Queen Street there were crowds of people standing outside, waiting to get in. Soon another bus arrived and a whole lot more people got off; the next thing the back row of the queue seemed to start pushing, and somebody shoved me and I banged into the woman in front.

"What did you do that for? It's no use pushing, you know we can't get to the box!"

"It wasn't my fault, somebody shoved me from behind."

We were growling at each other like that when something *banged* me on the head.

"Oh! What did you hit me on the head for?"

She looked up, then she started to laugh.

"Don't do that, or I might hit you on the head too . . ."

Another woman called out, "Mrs. Stirling, feel on the top of your head; up there!"

I put my hand up and I felt something move, then this thing dropped down on to my shoulder.

"Heck! What's this?"

When I turned my head, I saw a pigeon sitting on my shoulder. It hopped back on top of my hat, and everybody was so busy looking at me and laughing that they left the box free. I thought here's my chance, so I ran to the box and put my money down, and I bought my ticket. When I went to the doorman he didn't notice the pigeon at first; I think he thought it was a decoration on my hat until I bent over to put away my change and the bird flapped its wings, then he said, "Hey . . . you can't go in there with your bird — it's not allowed!"

"Well it's not my bird — and anyway I've got my ticket here, you can't put me out."

I walked inside and it was beautiful with all the waterfalls and lilies and ferns and flowers. The only trouble was that the other people thought I must be part of the show, so they followed me around.

"Can I stroke your bird?"

"How do you get it to sit there?"

"Please can I touch it?"

I said, "Oh no, I don't think you'd better, the bird might fly up and damage something."

I was sure that bird would fly away inside the Town Hall because it's very high up there, but it just sat on top of my hat. In the end I decided to sing a song to shift it, so I started,

Mehe manu rere ahau e	If I were a flying bird
Kua rere ki to moenga	I'd fly to your bed, dear
Ki te awhi to tinana	There to embrace you, dear
E te tau tahuri mai.	Oh my darling, turn to me.

The bird just sat up and flapped its wings, and all the people laughed. Then I sang,

Kei te moe to tinana	Your body is sleeping
Kei te wake to wairua	But your spirit wakes
Kei te hotu te manawa	You are sighing
E te tau, tahuri mai.	Oh love, turn to me.

It was no use, so I walked around and looked at all the flowers, then I thought if I go outside, that bird is bound to fly away. I went back out to Queen Street and I tried to shake my hat, "Go on birdie — you'd better go home now!"

No, the bird just sat there. I thought, well, if it wants to sit there I suppose it can do that, so I walked down to the Civic to catch the Ponsonby bus. When I climbed on, the bird moved, and the driver looked up.

"Hey! You! Wait a minute, you're not allowed in here with that bird!"

"How else am I going to get to Ponsonby? I haven't got any other transport." I walked to the back of the bus and sat myself down.

"I *mean* it, lady. If your bird flies around in here and something gets damaged, we'll sue you for it."

"Well if you want to do that you can sue the City Council, this is their bird, not mine."

I stayed in my seat and the bird didn't move. The children came to talk to him and they wanted to stroke his back, but I said, "No, you'd better not do that — you heard what the driver said."

When we got to Ponsonby I climbed out of the bus. Some of the children got smart and they grabbed some little stones and tried to hit the bird. One stone went straight into Lambournes and there were some cups in there; it hit one of those cups and it fell down and smashed. Luckily the woman in there knew me so she said, "Never mind, Mrs. Stirling."

She picked up the cup and put it in the rubbish bin so the manager wouldn't see it. I hurried off to the Building Society to pay for my shares, and when I went in the manager was laughing.

"*What* are you doing with that bird on your hat, Mrs. Stirling?"

"Well I don't know — it just flew and sat there."

He laughed like anything. . . .

After that I walked on down Ponsonby Road, and the next thing a woman tapped me on the shoulder.

"Excuse me, Madam — is that your bird sitting there?"

"No, it's not mine. It just flew and sat on my hat."

"That's funny . . . Can you tell me what does that mean to the Maori?"

"Well — what does it mean to the pakeha?"

"It means news, the bird has brought news."

"I hope it's good news; I don't want *bad* news."

"It can be either good or bad."

"What do I have to do about it, then?"

"Well . . . Just think of whatever comes into your head. If it's good, that's all right, but if it's bad, try to fix it up."

"Oh, thank you."

It was time to take the bird back to its home. When my taxi stopped I saw a big car parked outside; I put my hat down on the footpath and gave it a good shake, then I ran and hid behind the car so that the bird couldn't see me. When I looked up again, the bird had gone. I caught a bus and came home. The funny thing is my name is Amiria Manutahi, and *Manutahi* means one bird; Eruera told me that bird might have been my ancestor come back to life. . . .

One time when I was going down Queen Street there was some sort of a meeting going on, so I thought I might sit at the back and listen. This chap was talking about all sorts of things, and then he started having a go at the Maoris and their tangis [funerals].

"Now just look at the Maoris, when a man dies they have a tangi for two or three days before the body is buried! What I want to know is this — what's the use of sitting there and howling over that man when he's already dead? I'm looking at the waste of money involved. We've got the Crippled Children and the Blind and all that, so why waste money on a man who's already dead? They should learn to do it the pakeha way, just send a wreath and a card and that's it, then they won't be wasting all that money . . ."

I got so wild I couldn't hang on; I thought, right! and I stood up.

"Excuse me sir, I'm a Maori and you're talking about my people. You can't change our way of life, even if you take it to all your big men of the pakeha, you can't change us! The trouble with you pakehas is that you've got no *aroha* [love, compassion] like the Maori, your love is *money*. If someone dies you don't love that person, you just take a flower and give the widow a clip on the cheek and that's all. But that's not the Maori way — we don't care how much we spend! We take our aroha to the tangi, and a little bit of money too, and after we've had our tears we give the money quietly to the relatives, so they can pay their tangi debt. We press noses with them to show that love, and we stay with them so they don't feel lonely. It's not the pakeha way — a clip on the cheek, flowers, finish, it's gone! That's the light and easy way, but our way is too heavy I suppose. So don't you try to change us, because we were in this country first, and nobody asked you to come here and change our ways!"

Then I thought ho, I've gone a bit too far, so I sat down and then I went away. But now I'm glad to notice that the pakeha is coming to see the Maori way, because not long ago I went to a tangi at Tira Hou for a young Maori chap, and he must have been an orphan because there was a pakeha couple sitting beside the coffin with all their children. They were having a tangi exactly in the Maori way, sitting by the coffin and crying, and the children would go and kiss him. I asked the people, "Are those his parents?"

"No, but that chap had been living with them for about fifteen years before he died."

I was surprised to see that pakeha woman and her husband. I thought, well look, there's that aroha, the pakehas have got it now. I really appreciated it, and I had to go and speak to them in the end. It was blowing very cold that day so I made a bed for them inside the meeting-house, then I asked the woman to take the children and go and have a rest. I said, "Why don't you go inside? You can leave the coffin on the verandah, it's all right — but it's too cold out here for the children. Sitting on the verandah is all right for the Maoris, but . . ."

She shook her head and said, "No!"

"Are you going to sleep out here?"

"Yes."

Well look, I nearly howled myself; I thought, the pakeha . . . that's it, that's it! There's that Maori aroha, they've got it at last. And the next day when a group of pakehas came to marae, they did the same as the Maoris, they put money down on the marae as a gift; I could hardly believe it.

This young fella had been a sailor and he wanted his ashes to be thrown into the Waitemata Harbour, so the people came to ask me what to do with all these wreaths. Somebody had told them to take them to the hospital, but I said, ""Hey, wait a minute. You can't do that!"

"Somebody said it's better to take them there."

"No, it's not right! It might be all right to the pakeha, but it's not right to the Maori way of doing it. Those people in the hospital are there for their health's sake, they want to live a little bit longer; but those wreaths are for the dead. Now you're taking the dead man's wreaths to the living! It's as if you're saying, 'Come on, you come *this* way. You too, come on!' That's not right."

This man just looked at me.

"Listen here, those people are in hospital to gain their lives, they want to live. Why take the property of the dead and give it to them? If you want to give them flowers, well go and get some, but *not* off the coffin here, no! If I had a relative in that hospital I'd go straight there and stop any of these wreaths going into his room."

They must have had a talk about it because they put all the wreaths back on the coffin, and when they took the body away all the wreaths were there in the cars. So that fixed up that. I supposed they were looking at the waste, all those wreaths at five dollars or six dollars or ten dollars each, just to be thrown away. It was money again, worrying their minds. But the Maoris don't worry about money for the tangi — everybody brings their donation to the marae, and in the cities, a lot of tribes have formed associations to carry the cost.

Eruera started the Tai Rawhiti Association in Auckland about ten years ago, so that the east coast people could be buried at home when their time came. We didn't want a marae in Auckland because there's plenty of maraes at home, but the trouble is, there's nobody to look after them any more. If the milking was still on, the young people would still be there, milking cows and all that, but now — nothing. So now we're trying to think about putting trees on the land, and if the young people are interested in it, well and good.

Anyhow, the Tai Rawhiti Association helps us to save up our money for that last day; all the members pay so much, and we hold our socials at the university cafeteria, five dollars a ticket. Some people grumble about the money but I don't think they should grudge it, it's for a good cause. If you pass on, you don't have to worry, they can take you right back home to be buried and that's better. The old people call it *Te ukaipo*, the place where you fed at your mother's breast. . . .

I suppose I must be eighty now, and when I look back on my young days, the world is not the same; the *tapu*, the *wehi*, the *maoritanga* [the sacred customs of Maori culture] of those times has all gone. The people of today don't have the dignity of the old chiefs and chieftainesses, they've taken up too many of the pakeha ways. One step they're Maori, the next step they're pakeha, and that's the way they move around.

When I was young there were certain people in each area who were senior in their lines and everybody respected them. If any of those old people spoke to you, you had to listen, and that's how they managed our taumau marriage — you couldn't do it today.

As I say, the maoritanga is not so high up in standard today, any old way will do. Just look at the marae — it used to be a tapu place. When there was to be a hui, the senior man would call all the tribes and subtribes, and the local people would come to get everything ready.

It was almost like a church sort of place then, and if you took your children they had to go to the back, otherwise they might make too much noise and upset the man that's talking. But now it's so easy to go to the marae, and the children jump around all over the place. And the meeting-house was built to represent the ancestors, so it's very tapu, and that's why the old people never allowed drink inside. But these days, oh! they drink like anything. I was shocked to go to Te Poho-o-Rawiri a few years back, it used to be the most gracious meeting-house; but that night, look here! it was full of beer. I can't help saying this because I saw it and I was disgusted. If the old people came back and saw that, I'm sure they'd cause an earthquake to bring that house down.

And the young people of today can't speak their own language, but it's not their fault, I feel sorry for them. I remember what Apirana used to say, "Go to school by all means and get a pakeha education, but never forget you're a Maori. Put your language in your heart and keep it there, and teach it to your children, because the moment Maori is lost, the Maori people will disappear from this earth. Learn your language and your genealogy, and take your pakeha education with you, then you'll have two fists to fight with — a Maori one and a pakeha one. But if you leave your maoritanga behind, you'll just be a swagger and a mongrel, with no place you can call your own."

Now I see they're even taking the name of Waitangi Day away. It was Apriana who told us about that name. He said that when the first canoes came to this island the people went ashore, and that night they heard voices wailing in the bush. They searched around and they couldn't find anyone, but still they heard that wailing up in the air.

In the morning they discovered it was the sea, and the old people said it was the ancestors calling their last farewell to those who had arrived in the new land. So they named that place Waitangi — "wailing waters," for the farewell of their ancestors. But now I hear they're changing the name of Waitangi Day to "New Zealand" Day, the name that was given to this country hundreds of years later by Tasman. *We* are the people who discovered this country first, and when Tasman came our ancestors were already here. Why should we pass the name of this country over as a memory to him, instead of to our own people? Because as I say, New Zealand is Maori soil.

❖

A Last and Lasting Word

When Amiria had finished her story, it was published. She and Anne Salmond were proud of their collaboration and proud of the book that resulted. Anne had made a significant contribution to the anthropology and history of New Zealand and the Pacific. Amiria had the opportunity to choose the stories she wanted to tell, the way she wanted to tell them. It is quite clear that both of them had enlarged their lives and learned more than they had anticipated.

At some point in this long process, Amiria's husband, Eruera, asked Anne for the same kind of professional assistance. He wanted to leave a record of Maori life as he experienced and remembered it. He was determined to pass on his traditional knowledge and to explain to a younger generation the deeper meanings of tribal life. His book is not, however, autobiographical in the same way Amiria's is. Eruera wanted fervently to speak of cultural issues rather than personal ones. So their friend, the anthropologist, helped him write his book. It's called *Eruera: The Teachings of a Maori Elder; As Told To Anne Salmond* (New York: Oxford University Press, 1994). It is rare for a husband's book to follow his wife's. But then, it is rare to have such stories and such storytellers at all.

In the Spirit of Writing Women's Lives

By now it is obvious that women are helping each other write our lives. There also seem to be many different approaches to doing this. One of the talked-about and widely reviewed books in this vein in recent years is Ruth Behar's *Translated Woman: Crossing the Border with Esperanza's Story* (Boston: Beacon, 1993). The autobiography of a Mexican Indian woman, Esperanza, becomes her stories as seen from many perspectives; and then it becomes Ruth's story. In this tale nations, classes, cultures, languages, and genders are all borders to be crossed in the postmodern manner. This book has interested many readers and writers because Ruth Behar puts herself in as a character, a woman, an anthropologist, and a translated woman herself.

Many anthropologists have published collaborative autobiographies of women they met doing fieldwork and with whom they became friends. Three very moving and enlightening examples include Elizabeth Colson's *Autobiographies of Three Pomo Women* (Berkeley: Department of Anthropology, University of California, 1974); Alice Marriott's *Maria: The Potter of San Ildefonso* (Norman, OK: University of Oklahoma Press, 1948); and Judith Friedlander's *Being Indian in Hueyapan. A Study of Forced Identity in Contemporary Mexico* (New York: St. Martin's Press, 1981). Friedlander wrote this book as a dissertation. It is the story of Doña Zeferina, a poor peasant woman who happens to belong to a community where their collective pasts as "Indians" has vanished except in the minds of outsiders. Her life is largely spent tricking representatives of Mexico's non-Indian, Hispanic elite. She sums up her life, "A person must know how to defend herself."

Once again I note: one does not need to be an anthropologist to see the worth of helping another person tell her story. One such person worth noting is an oral historian, community organizer, and United Church of Christ minister named Fran Leeper Buss. While her family was living in northwestern New Mexico she met Jesusita Aragon, apparently the last of the traditional Hispanic midwives in the area. Jesusita was eager to tell her story; they collaborated and the result is *La Partera: Story of a Midwife* (Ann Arbor, MI: University of Michigan Press, 1980). This is a valuable story that would otherwise have vanished. But Fran's next one is far more politically and poetically powerful. Maria Elena Lucas was the oldest of seventeen children. She was a poor, Chicana farmworker, who wrote songs, poems, and diaries at night by flashlight. She became a fearless fighter on behalf of migrant workers. Then a nearly lethal dose of pesticide from a crop-dusting plane left her permanently disabled. Hundreds of hours of interviews and a loving reconstruction of this woman's life has given us *Forged under the Sun/Forjada bajo el sol: The Life of Maria Elena Lucas* (University of Michigan Press, 1993).

In the Spirit of Questioning

1. The growth of feminist spirituality in the last two decades has taught us about acknowledging suffering, particularly the loss of our children. Please notice all the events and interpretations about George's life and death that Amiria has focused on in her story. What other kinds of child loss are there? What are other kinds of frameworks do women use to understand and explain the loss of children?

2. Amiria is quite articulate about the loss of traditional Maori ways of living. She also notes the price that young people would pay to maintain those customs (a price she already paid), as well as the attractions or necessities of "modern" or postmodern lifestyles. Then she seems to conclude, even accept, that one cannot have both — the richness of traditional cultures and the freedom and individuality of contemporary urban life. Is she right? How do her experiences parallel those of many women and men around the world?

3. Another arranged marriage! "It had to be that way." That is all Amiria ever said about this dramatic story or her decades of married life. She never comments, complains, compares, or remarks on the personality or feelings of her husband. Doesn't this suggest that marriage across human cultures may be something more — or something less — than our current romantic fancies would have us believe? What are the implications of such stories for our lives?

4. Some people claim that anthropologists may be somehow exploiting native peoples — taking their stories, knowledge, or assistance and using them for our own personal or professional profit. Some people say that the colonial context is always about power and power differentials. If one believed that, how would one have counseled anthropologist Anne Salmond? To do it (that is, go ahead and record Amiria's story)? Do it differently? Don't do it at all?

Endnote to Chapter 6

1. This quote is from *Amiria: The Life Story of a Maori Woman: As Told to Anne Salmond* (Auckland: A. H. & A. W. Reed, 1976), 164.

This is the name of the writer Nawal el Saadawi rendered in formal Arabic. Many artists use this beautiful calligraphy to honor important titles, names, phrases, or sayings.

Artwork by Dr. Ahmad Massasati.

Nawal

"I Had to Find My Own Answer to the Question"

Often called "the Simone de Beauvoir of the Arab world," Nawal el Saadawi is an Egyptian psychiatrist, feminist, and writer. Although her life story is dramatic, as you will see, she has not written a straight-through, "this is my life," autobiography. Instead, she writes her life into all her books — whether they are novels, short stories, nonfiction, or memoirs.

For purposes of this chapter I have used two of her books. The first is *The Hidden Face of Eve.* This book is technically classified as nonfiction. But the passion Nawal brings to good analyses about women's lives in Egypt arises from her own life experiences, some of which are intensely recounted here. The second part of this chapter comes from her book *Memoirs from the Women's Prison.* Nawal went to prison because she writes books — books based on her experiences. Then she wrote a book about going to prison — also based in her experiences. Prison memoirs are a special form of autobiography that fascinate and repel us. Women rarely write them; this one is distinctive.

Nawal's bare-bones biography starts with her birth date, October 27, 1931, in Egypt. In 1955 she married a physician, had a daughter, and divorced him a year later. Then she married a judge, had a son, and divorced him. In 1964 she married for the third time, a writer and doctor. Meanwhile, she completed her medical degree at the University of Cairo in 1955 and a master's degree in public health at Columbia University in the United States in 1966. She worked as a doctor in rural health programs, in women's health programs, and for the United Nations. She cofounded the African Women's Association for Research and Development. She is also a practicing psychiatrist, and she writes.

In 1986 Nawal el Saadawi gave an interview to some of her colleagues. They asked: at what point in your life did you decide to become politically active? She answered:

> When I worked as a physician in rural areas. Then I started to be shocked by many things. And also by my life. I started to feel the conflict, as a wife. My first husband, a physician, didn't want me to work as a physician. He was jealous of my colleagues, and he told me: "You shouldn't meet those men." Can you imagine such a mentality? This shocked me, and it gave me insight into the problems of women: private life and public life. My second husband was a lawyer. When I published a short story in a magazine his colleagues in the Council of State told him: "Oh, it's a very courageous story. How well your wife writes." He came to me and said to me: "You shouldn't write. You have to choose between me and your writing." So I said to him, "Well, I choose my writing."[1]

So in the 1950s she wrote short stories; in the 1960s, novels. Then in the 1970s she began to write about women. Five books about the lives, the deaths, the health, and above all, the multiple oppressions of Arabic and Egyptian women poured out. The first one was called *Woman and Sex;* the response was immediate. As the first edition quickly sold out, the Egyptian authorities ordered the books removed from stores. But copies circulated and the ideas could not be suppressed.

> Shortly after it appeared, I realized that I was now sitting on the edge of a volcano, listening to its distant rumblings coming ever closer. And day by day the avalanche of letters, telephone calls, and visits from young and old, men and women, grew steadily, most of them asking for a way out of problems, most of them friendly or desperate, and a few, very few, menacing. . . . I had come to know more firmly than at any other time that the great majority of men and women in our society carry a thirst for greater knowledge and understanding, and a sharp hunger for further progress. However, it was natural that a small minority express their fear, or even panic, at words written by a pen sharp as a scalpel that cuts through tissue to expose the throbbing nerves and arteries embedded in a body.[2]

Nawal was a scalpel in the flesh of patriarchal Arab society. She had a distinguished career in public health, both in Egypt and abroad, until she spoke out about sexual aggression against female children, genital mutilation, prostitution, marriage, divorce, and adult sexual relationships. In 1972, she was dismissed from her post as Director of Health Education in the Ministry of Health in Cairo and prevented from publishing the journal, *Health,* of which she was editor-in-chief. She now says that if one mixes politics, religion, and sex, it may blow up.

Several themes surface in all her writings. First, she is jealous of her brothers for the privileges they had as males. For her this inequality eventually becomes the model for the double standard from which men benefit and women suffer. Second, she says that prisons exist everywhere; in fact, they may be seen as metaphors for women's lives under patriarchies. Third, women in the West must understand that Arab or Moslem societies, so-called Third World countries, or postcolonial nations, are not the only places where oppression and patriarchal rule occur. These are worldwide systems in which all of us participate and in which all women have second-class citizenship.

Her fictional works draw deeply from her realities as a woman living in male-dominated societies. They reflect a universal struggle for independence, love, and an authentic self. *The Circling Song* — published in English in 1989 — is a powerful novel about the anger, desperation, shame, and servility under patriarchy. *A Woman at Point Zero* is based on a true story of a prostitute sentenced to death for killing her pimp. It is the story of a woman's passage from incest to murder and finally, a kind of redemption. In *Two Women in One* a female medical student rebels against conformist values; the retribution is swift.[3]

The Fall of Imam is set on a fictitious male-dominated island; it satirizes the hypocrisy of the double standard, a topic that obsesses Nawal. Why are women supposed to be chaste and men allowed to be promiscuous? she keeps asking. But the questions provoked death threats from extremist religious groups. The same government that arrested her had to station armed guards around her house to protect her. From 1987 to 1989 she was hostage to fears that had no faces, guarded by police who suspected her of inciting women to rebel and riot.

Nawal writes in Arabic; then she tries to publish first in Egypt; but censorship is sometimes subtle and discouraging, sometimes blatant and forbidding. When the books cannot be published in Egypt, she looks elsewhere in the Arabic-writing world. Although Nawal's books are no longer censored in her homeland, they were banned in Egypt and other Arab countries for a long time. Despite the banning, they circulated silently and secretly through the Arab world. Later they were translated into Danish, Dutch, Finnish, French, German, Italian, Japanese, Norwegian, Portuguese, Swedish, Urdu, Persian, and other languages.

The Hidden Face of Eve was Nawal el Saadawi's first publication available in English. Although the book is an oft-quoted analysis about women in history, women in Arab history and literature, and women in Egypt, the opening chapter, entitled "The Mutilated Half" is autobiographical. It is, as you will see, an extraordinary account by any measure.

The Question That No One Would Answer

I was six years old that night when I lay in my bed, warm and peaceful in that pleasurable state which lies half way between wakefulness and sleep, with the rosy dreams of childhood flitting by, like gentle fairies in quick succession. I felt something move under the blankets, something like a huge hand, cold and rough, fumbling over my body, as though looking for something. Almost simultaneously another hand, as cool and as rough and as big as the first one, was clapped over my mouth to prevent me from screaming.

They carried me to the bathroom. I do not know how many of them there were, nor do I remember their faces, or whether they were men or women. The world to me seemed enveloped in a dark fog which prevented me from seeing. Or perhaps they put some kind of cover over my eyes. All I remember is that I was frightened and that there were many of them, and that something like an iron grasp caught hold of my hand and my arms and my thighs, so that I became unable to resist or even to move. I also remember the icy touch of the bathroom tiles under my naked body, and unknown voices and humming sounds inter-rupted now and again by a rasping metallic sound which reminded me of the butcher when he used to sharpen his knife before slaughtering a sheep for the *Eid* [the four-day festival during pilgrimage season].

My blood was frozen in my veins. It looked to me as though some thieves had broken into my room and kidnapped me from my bed. They were getting ready to cut my throat, which was always what happened with disobedient girls like myself in the stories that my old rural grandmother was so fond of telling me.

I strained my ears trying to catch the rasp of the metallic sound. The moment it ceased, it was as though my heart stopped beating with it. I was unable to see, and somehow my breathing seemed also to have stopped. Yet I imagined the thing that was making the rasping sound coming closer and closer to me. Some-how it was not approaching my neck as I had expected but another part of my body. Somewhere below my belly, as though seeking something buried between my thighs. At that very moment I realized that my thighs had been pulled wide apart, and that each of my lower limbs was being held as far away from the other as possible, gripped by steel fingers that never relinquished their pressure. I felt that the rasping knife or blade was heading straight down towards my throat. Then suddenly the sharp metallic edge seemed to drop between my thighs and there cut off a piece of flesh from by body.

I screamed with pain despite the tight hand held over my mouth, for the pain was not just a pain, it was like a searing flame that went through my whole body. After a few moments, I saw a red pool of blood around my hips.

I did not know what they had cut off from my body, and I did not try to find out. I just wept, and called out to my mother for help. But the worst shock of all was when I looked around and found her standing by my side. Yes, it was her, I could not be mistaken, in flesh and blood, right in the midst of these strangers, talking to them and smiling at them, as though they had not participated in slaughtering her daughter just a few moments ago.

They carried me to my bed. I saw them catch hold of my sister, who was two years younger, in exactly the same way they had caught hold of me a few minutes earlier. I cried out with all my might. "No! No!" I could see my sister's face held between the big rough hands. It had a deathly pallor and her wide black eyes met mine for a split second, a glance of dark terror which I can never forget. A moment later and she was gone, behind the door of the bathroom where I had just been. The look we exchanged seemed to say: "Now we know what it is. Now we know where lies our tragedy. We were born of a special sex, the female sex. We are destined in advance to taste of misery, and to have a part of our body torn away by cold, unfeeling, cruel hands."

My family was not an uneducated Egyptian family. On the contrary, both my parents had been fortunate enough to have a very good education, by the standards of those days. My father was a university graduate and that year (1937) had been appointed General Controller of Education for the Province of Menoufia in the Delta region to the North of Cairo. My mother had been taught in French schools by her father who was Director-General of Army Recruitment. Nevertheless, the custom of circumcising girls was very prevalent at the time, and no girl could escape having her clitoris amputated, irrespective of whether her family lived in a rural or an urban area. When I returned to school after having recovered from the operation, I asked my classmates and friends about what had happened to me, only to discover that all of them, without exception, had been through the same experience, no matter what social class they came from (upper class, middle, or lower-middle class).

In rural areas, among the poor peasant families, all the girls are circumcised, as I later on found out from my relatives in Kafr Tahla. This custom is still very common in the villages, and even in the cities a large proportion of families believe it is necessary. However, the spread of education and a greater understanding among parents is making increasing numbers of fathers and mothers abstain from circumcising their daughters.

The memory of circumcision continued to track me down like a nightmare. I had a feeling of insecurity, of the unknown waiting for me at every step I took in the future. I did not even know if there were new surprises being stored up for me by my mother and father, or my grandmother, or the people around me. Society had made me feel, since the day that I opened my eyes on life, that I was a girl, and that the word *Bint* (girl) when pronounced by anyone is almost always accompanied by a frown.

Even when I had grown up and graduated as a doctor in 1955, I could not forget the painful incident that had made me lose my childhood once and for all, and that deprived me during my youth and for many years of married life from enjoying the fullness of my sexuality and the completeness of life that can only come from all round psychological equilibrium. Nightmares of a similar nature followed me throughout the years, especially during the period when I was working as a medical doctor in the rural areas. There I very often had to treat young girls who had come to the out-patient clinic bleeding profusely after a circumcision. Many of them used to lose their lives as a result of the inhuman and primitive way in which the operation, savage enough in itself, was performed. Others were afflicted with acute or chronic infections from which they sometimes suffered for the rest of their days. And most of them, if not all, became the victims later on of sexual or mental distortions as a result of this experience.

My profession led me, at one stage, to examine patients coming from various Arab countries. Among them were Sudanese women. I was horrified to observe that the Sudanese girl undergoes an operation for circumcision which is ten times more cruel than that to which Egyptian girls are subjected. In Egypt it is only the clitoris which is amputated, and usually not completely. But in the Sudan, the operation consists in the complete removal of all the external genital organs. They cut off the clitoris, the two major outer lips (labia majora) and the two minor inner lips (labia minora). Then the wound is repaired. The outer opening of the vagina is the only portion left intact, not however without having ensured that, during the process of repairing, some narrowing of the opening is carried out with a few extra stitches. The result is that on the marriage night it is necessary to widen the external organ by slitting one or both ends with a sharp scalpel or razor so that the male organ can be introduced. When a Sudanese woman is divorced, the external opening is narrowed once more to ensure that she cannot have sexual relations. If she remarries, widening is done again.

My feeling of anger and rebellion used to mount up as I listened to these women explaining to me what happens during the circumcision of a Sudanese girl. My anger grew tenfold when in 1969 I paid a visit to the Sudan only to discover that the practice of circumcision was unabated, whether in rural areas, or even in the cities and towns.

In spite of my upbringing and medical education, in those days I was not able to understand why girls were made to undergo this barbaric procedure. Time and again I asked myself the question: "Why? Why?" But I could never get an answer to this question which was becoming more and more insistent, just as I was never able to get an answer to the questions that raced around in my mind the day that both my sister and I were circumcised.

This question somehow seemed to be linked to other things that puzzled me. Why did they favour my brother as regards food, and the freedom to go out of the house? Why was he treated better than I was in all these matters? Why could my brother laugh at the top of his voice, move his legs freely, run and play as much as he wished, whereas I was not supposed to look into people's eyes directly, but was meant to drop my glance whenever I was confronted with someone? If I laughed, I was expected to keep my voice so low that people could hardly hear me, or better, confine myself to smiling timidly. When I played, my legs were not supposed to move freely, but had to be kept politely together. My duties were primarily to help in cleaning the house and cooking, in addition to studying since I was at school. The brothers, however, the boys, were not expected to do anything but study.

My family was educated, and therefore, differentiation between the boys and girls, especially as my father was himself a teacher, never reached the extent which is so common in other families. I used to feel very sorry for my young girl relatives when they were forced out of school in order to get married to an old man just because he happened to own some land, or when their younger brothers would humiliate and beat them for no reason at all, except that as boys they could afford to act superior to their sisters.

My brother tried to dominate me, in turn, but my father was a broadminded man and tried as best he could to treat his children without discriminating between the boys and girls. My mother, also, used to say that a girl is equal to a boy, but I used to feel that in practice this was often not the case.

Whenever this differentiation occurred I used to rebel, sometimes violently, and would ask my mother and father why it was that my brother was accorded privileges that were not given to me, despite the fact that I was doing better than he at school. My father and mother, however, never had any answer to give me except: "It is so . . ." I would retort: "Why should it be so?" And back would come the answer again, unchanged: "Because it is so . . ." If I was in an obstinate mood, I would repeat the question again. Then, at the end of their patience, they would say almost in the same voice: "He is a boy, and you are a girl."

Perhaps they thought that this answer would be enough to convince me, or at least to keep me quiet. But on the contrary it always made me persist more than ever. I would ask: "What is the difference between a boy and a girl?"

At this point my old grandmother, who very often paid us a visit, would intervene in the discussion, which she always described as being an "infringement of good manners," and scold me sharply. "I have never in all my life seen a girl with such a long tongue as you. Of course you are not like your brother. Your brother is a boy, a boy, do you hear? I wish you had been born a boy like him!"

No one in the family was ever able to give me a convincing answer to my question. So the question continued to run around restlessly in my mind, and would jump to the forefront every time something happened that would emphasize the fact that the male is treated everywhere and at all times as though he belongs to a species which is superior to that of the female.

When I started to go to school, I noticed that the teachers would write my father's name on my notebooks, but never that of my mother. So I asked my mother why, and again she answered, "It is so." My father, however, explained that children are named after their father, and when I sought to find out the reason he repeated the phrase that I knew well by now: "It is so." I summoned up all my courage and said: "Why is it so?" But this time I could see from my father's face that he really did not know the answer. I never asked him the question again, except later on when my search for the truth led me to ask him many other questions, and to talk to him about many other things that I was discovering on the way.

However, from that day onwards I realized that I had to find my own answer to the question that no one would answer. From that day also extends the long path that has led to this book.

[Here Nawal talks about the universal female experiences of moving from child to menstruating woman. Arab women, she says, are treated like children — kept in ignorance, in fear and in intimidation.]

Obscurantism and Contradiction

Women, therefore, tend to nurture their ignorance and simplemindedness so that society continues to look upon them as being virtuous and of good reputation. Parents also encourage ignorance in their daughters, and want them to be simple and naive, to remain "blind pussy cats" as the Egyptians would say. For a "blind pussy cat" is what an average Egyptian man would consider the kind of girl best suited to be a wife.

This cult of ignorance does not apply to matters related to sex and men alone, but is advocated in so far as all matters related to the female body are concerned. Arab girls are therefore brought up in an environment of darkness and silence concerning everything related to the body and its functions. They are often seized with nervous shock, therefore, on the day when, opening their eyes in the morning, they perceive a trickle of red blood between their thighs and a scarlet stain on the white sheet beneath their buttocks.

It would be difficult for anyone to imagine the panic that seized hold of me one morning when I woke to find blood trickling down between my thighs. I can still remember the deathly pallor of my face in the mirror. My arms and legs were trembling violently and it appeared to me as though the disaster which had frightened me for so long was now a fact. That somehow, in the dark of night, a man had crept into my room while I was sleeping and succeeded in causing me harm. This eventuality had never left my thoughts, and each night, before going to bed, I used to close the window overlooking the street as tightly as possible.

An amusing aspect of this situation is that on the previous day at school we had been given a lesson on the subject of *bilharzia*. This is a parasitic disease that infects the urinary tracts of rural folk in Egypt. At one of its stages in the life cycle, the parasite lodges in the soft tissues of a water snail, and is released into the water of streams and canals where it penetrates the body by piercing the skin of the legs. One of the symptoms of this disease is blood in the urine, and it occurred to me that I might have become infected with it, which would explain the red trickle emanating from the opening between my thighs.

I was then ten years old and thought that, if this was so, all I had to do was to wait until the disease cured itself. But the flow of blood did not stop. On the contrary, it increased from hour to hour, and on the following day I was obliged to overcome the fear and shame that possessed me and speak to my mother. I asked her to take me to a doctor for treatment. To my utter surprise she was calm and cool and did not seem to be affected by her daughter's serious condition. She explained this was something that happened to all girls and that it recurs every month for a few days. On the last day when the flow ceased, I was to cleanse myself of this "impure blood" by having a hot bath. Her words echoed in my ears "monthly condition," "a hot bath" to rid me of the "impure blood." I was therefore to understand that in me there was something degrading which appeared regularly in the form of this impure blood, and that it was something to be ashamed of, to hide from others. So I stayed in my room for four consecutive days, unable to face anybody. When I opened the door on my way to the bathroom, I would look around to make sure that nobody was in sight, and before returning I would wash the floor carefully as though removing the marks of a recent crime, and under my arms and between my legs, several times, to make sure that no smell of this impure blood remained.

These incidents are typical of the life of Arab girls who are brought up in an atmosphere of sexual fear and kept in ignorance of their reproductive organs and of the natural physiological functions carried out by different parts of the body. Girls are made to feel the difference between themselves and boys from early childhood. A brother can go out and play and jump around. But a girl must remain indoors, and if her skirt rises just one centimetre above the prescribed level, her mother will throw threatening glances at her and put her to shame.

Her thigh is a source of evil, a taboo that must be hidden from sight. From a young age a girl is made to feel that her body is something impure, obscene, and must remain invisible, unseen. Newspapers, magazines, and the mass media instil religious conceptions that portray the female body as an obscenity that should be hidden carefully. Only the face and palms of the hand should appear, and, for this reason, many girls take to the wearing of veils.

Yet despite these rigid and orthodox teachings which deny sex in the life of a girl and aim at moulding her into an asexual being, a parallel and contradictory educational process is going on all the time which seeks to make her an instrument of sex and a mere body which should be adorned and made beautiful so as to attract men and arouse their desire. A girl is trained, again from early childhood, to be almost wholly preoccupied with her body, her hair, her eyelashes, and clothes, at the expense of her mind and thoughts and her future as a human being. Arab girls are reared for the role of marriage which is the supreme function of women in society; whereas education, work, and a career are considered secondary matters which should in no way divert her from her primary functions as a wife whose job is to cook, serve her husband, and look after her children.

As a child I had to struggle against the whole family so that I could be permitted to read and develop my mind. I used to refuse cooking and cleaning in the house and insist on going to school. I would rebel against long hair, coloured ribbons, and plaits, and wonder why my mother paid so much attention to my clothes and dresses. I used to surpass my brothers at school and gain high marks, yet nobody seemed to be happy or think of congratulating me. Yet if I once cooked a bad meal, everyone would criticize me.

The moment I took refuge in my own small world of illustrated books and coloured pencils, my mother would drag me to the kitchen and mumble: "Your future lies in marriage and you must learn to cook." Your future is in marriage, marriage! That ugly word that my mother would never tire of repeating until I hated it with all my being. No sooner pronounced, I would imagine before my eyes a man with a swollen belly full of food. The smell of the kitchen for me was the smell of men. So I learnt to hate the smell of men, and the smell of food.

For me, everything my mother said seemed to be contradictory. How come that she should always be warning me about sex and men, and yet always be so careful about my appearance and clothes, with the sole aim of making me more desirable to them? I was mortally afraid of men, and used to avoid them like the plague. I believed that proximity to a man could only bring shame and be a danger to my reputation as a good respectable girl. Yet, at the same time, I felt deep inside me a tremendous force that attracted me to the opposite sex. The passionate songs full of yearning and love, or the films which we saw now and again, only served to increase my obscure desires. Many a time I would conjure up a scene in my mind in which an unknown man would hold me in his arms, and at the very next moment I would be overpowered by a feeling of guilt and shame, a feeling that was magnified by the pleasure I derived from these daydreams. I could not understand myself or assimilate the inherent contradictions in my thoughts and actions. Inside me there would be a burning flame and, on the outside, a picture of cool indifference.

[This ends the autobiographical sections from *The Hidden Face of Eve* Holding these questions and experiences fiercely inside her, Nawal grew up. She went to college and medical schools, married, bore and raised two children. She wrote books. Then one day, something happened.]

I heard a knock at the door.

I was sitting at the small desk in my bedroom, absorbed in writing a new novel. The clock hand pointed to three. It was the afternoon of Sunday, 6 September 1981.

I ignored the knock. Perhaps it was the concierge, or possibly the milkman, or the man who does our ironing. Or it could be anyone else, but if no one were to answer the door, the steps would surely recede.

When I sit down to write, it is the small household tasks, or the sound of the doorbell or telephone, which torture me. I can be rid of the telephone by pulling the cord from the wall, but the door . . . am I to rip the door from the wall?

This novel is tormenting me. I've freed myself completely to write it, letting everything else go for its sake. It's intractable, like unattainable love. It wants me, my entire being, mind and body, and if it can't have that it will not give itself to me at all. It wants all or nothing — it's exactly like me. To the extent that I give to it, it gives to me. It wants no competition for my heart and mind — not that of a husband, nor a son or a daughter, nor preoccupation with work of any sort, not even on behalf of the women's cause.

I began working on this novel in the autumn of 1978. At that time, I was in Africa working as a consultant to the United Nations. My home base was Addis Ababa, but my work obliged me to travel frequently from one African nation to another. For the first time in my life, I saw the sources of the Nile in Ethiopia and

Uganda. As a child, I had imagined what Lake Victoria must be like; now, its smell and the colour of its water reminded me of Egypt, my homeland, which I carry inside me wherever I go. The streams emerging over the boulders of Ethiopia supply the water for small rivers the colour of the Nile, the tone of my skin. The features of Addis Ababa's inhabitants resemble those of my ancestors, my father and my aunts in the village of Kafr Tahla.

The second knock at the door.

I was still seated, ignoring the knocking, just as I was paying no attention to the car horns from the street below. I've travelled all over the world, but I have never seen the likes of Egyptians for exerting the same pressure with their hands on the car horns as they do with their feet on the accelerator. My flat is on the fifth floor, but the car horns still sound like screams, like a continuous wailing.

My flat in Addis Ababa, which overlooked foothills of green, was a quiet place, one of utter tranquility, unbroken by voices or car horns. But still the novel spurned and resisted me. I could write scientific studies, draft agreements, write books on women's issues — everything except the novel, this particular novel. It is a strange business: the more I distance myself from Egypt, the further the novel travels from me. No sooner do I land at Cairo Airport, and breathe in the odours of dust and people's sweat, the car horns and pale, fly-laden children's faces, the queues of women in their black *gallabiyyas*, and the broken, exhausted eyes of the men, than the novel comes ever nearer.

I was searching for a writer who has written a great work of literature while absent from the homeland. My mind would tell me it was possible, and I would travel.

I did not travel by choice: I was looking for another homeland. Since the winter of 1972, I had been feeling estranged in my own country. Why? Because I had written a book containing new ideas and because in one of the lectures I gave in the College of Medicine at Ain Shams University in Cairo, I had stood up and given my views on women, society, medicine, literature, and politics — for I don't isolate any one of these topics from the others.

I have written only what my mind dictates to me, and I have expressed only my own opinions in front of the groups of men and women students. In this instance, the lecture hall was filled with hundreds, or thousands, of them and all were happy. The lecture ended with a profound and scientifically based discussion, and I returned home.

What followed that lecture, however, astounded me.

The Internal Security police summoned me and interrogated me. The Minister of Health had become angry. The Physicians' Syndicate had become angry. The publishing houses and the mass media were angry with me.

My name joined the government's blacklist.

When the authorities get angry with a writer, they can prevent that writer from publishing and can stifle the writer's voice so that it won't reach anyone. A writer cannot mount to the pinnacles of literature, and stay there, unless the authorities approve.

Everything in our country is in the hands of the state and under its direct or indirect control, by laws known or concealed, by tradition or by a long-established, deeply rooted fear of the ruling authority. One day, I asked a leading literary man working at a major daily Cairene newspaper, *Al Ahram,* "Why do you tell me one thing and write something else?" He replied, "'If they fire me at *Al Ahram* will you support my children and pay for their schooling?" Fearing servility, people became servile.

Most people here, even writers and philosophers, are civil servants.

It has been many years since I have read a great literary work, or heard of a single philosopher. I worked in the United Nations in order to free myself from the government, but I discovered that the apparatus of the United Nations is like that of the government, and the United Nations' experts fear for their monthly salaries just as all civil employees do. Moreover, the United Nations is led by men from the upper classes and the wealthy First World nations, while women from the Third World slide to the bottom of the heap.

The third knock at the door.

It must be the concierge, I thought, but I will not open the door for him. This concierge respects none of the residents of the building except for its owner. He would never consider knocking on the landlord's door three times, or with this violence. People in Egypt have changed. The only ones who are respected any more are those who own blocks of flats or office buildings, dollars, open door firms, farms producing Israeli chickens and Israeli eggs, or American chewing gum.

I resigned from the United Nations in the autumn of 1980 in order to end my self-exile and return to Egypt. However, my exile not only continued in Egypt — it grew. In government service, my exile grew too. So I wrote my letter of resignation in the winter of 1981, stating that in Egypt everything foreign had taken on greater value than anything Egyptian, even human beings.

The fourth rapping, and the fifth, and the knocking on the door went on and on. This can't possibly be the concierge. However much he scorns tenants, his audacity wouldn't go this far.

I got up and went to the door. Long black shadows behind the glass pane, and the sound of heavy breathing. A shiver ran over my body. I was all alone in my flat. My husband had left before dawn for his village, near Tanta in the Delta to the north of Cairo. My daughter and son had gone out and would not return before nighttime.

Thieves, perhaps. But thieves don't knock on doors.

Hesitant and apprehensive, I did not open the door. There's no security or peace of mind these days. I spoke up from behind the door in a voice which I made sure was loud and confident: "Who's there?"

A strange voice answered: "The police."

The earth spun round for a moment, and I imagined that an accident had happened to my son or daughter, or my husband as he was on his way back from the village. But the voice was hostile; it did not give the impression that this was an accident report.

With shaking fingers, I opened the little opaque glass pane set in the door. My eyes widened in alarm: a large number of men armed with rifles and bayonets were out there, sharp eyes piercing the narrow iron bars, as a rough voice said in a tone of command: "Open the door!"

A dream, perhaps? Reality mingling with imagination, the world of the conscious with the realm of the unconscious. My mind still did not believe that any of this was really happening.

"Who are you?"

"Open the door. That's an order!"

My imagination, no doubt about it. From childhood to this day, no one had ever spoken to me in such a tone of voice — neither my father nor my mother, nor anyone who had come into my life or knocked at my door.

Never in his life did my father give me a command. He discussed everything with me, even the existence of God. As for God, well, I engaged him in discussion, and God had to convince me of what he was saying.

Anger was gathering in my throat. "What order?"

"The police!"

"You're not wearing police uniforms."

From behind the armed band stepped an officer wearing a police helmet and a white jacket. On each shoulder, a bit of gold or brass glittered, and his white teeth gleamed in a polite smile.

"Please open the door."

"Why?"

"We have an order to search your house."

"I want to see this order before I open the door."

"We don't have it with us at the moment."

"Absolutely out of the question for me to open the door to you without seeing a warrant from the office of the Chief Prosecutor. That's the law."

"You must open the door."

"I won't open it until I see the warrant from the Prosecutor."

I shut the pane. My whole body was shaking, and my heart was knocking violently beneath my ribs.

But the knocks on the door became more vehement. A nightmare, perhaps. I opened my eyes, trying to wake up, but I discovered that I was already awake and standing on my own two feet in the sitting room. The door was shaking under the violent knocking.

I managed to move my feet, forwards, backwards. I wandered back and forth through the three rooms, not knowing what to do.

[Nawal is arrested and put into prison. She does not know why, what she has done or what will be done to her. But she discovers that a number of women, feminists, professors, writers, journalists, and colleagues are also in prison. In fact she meets most of the opposition to Sadat's government there.]

Prison

Among the women and girls, I lived a communal life. I recaptured my happiness as a student at secondary school. Rejoicing, growing angry and fighting, mending our differences, feeling delight at the smallest things, and growing sad for the simplest of reasons. Tears appearing in our eyes even as we smiled, and smiles breaking through while we still wept. From the disagreements among us in prison, one would have thought oceans separated one from another, and that each of us was an island unto herself. The dispute might grow yet more intense, but soon we would draw together, there would be harmony among us, and we would close ranks, a solid line facing the single power which had put us behind bars.

Nur was the only Christian among us. She had been arrested among the groups of Copts and other Christians they'd taken in. She was a girl of about twenty, delicate and shy, who had no connected whatsoever with the political work or the sectarian rift — for such were the accusations which were applied to anyone belonging to an oppositional group. We used to ask one another why, if the state was accusing those it was keeping in the prisons of instigating a sectarian rift and spreading hatred and malevolence among and between sectors or the populace, why, then, had they placed everyone together in a single cell? Why did they lock up the Muslim activist with the Christian, and "the left" with "the right"? Were the authorities hoping that some of us would destroy others, inside the prisons?

It was the complete opposite of this which happened, however. Within the group, harmony reigned. Inside the prisons, mutual understanding between all strands of the opposition were achieved.

Suddenly, a new order was issued: separation of Muslims from Christians, and the imprisonment of each group in isolated cells.

One morning, the head prison official in charge came in to our cell, calling out the name of the Christian girl, "Nur."

"Bring your clothes and come along with me."

Her face went pale.

"Where are you taking her?" we asked in unison.

"We've had an order to separate Christians from Muslims."

"Why? You can't lock her up alone far away from us!" We stood in closed ranks, to prevent her from being taken away, but he pulled her out by force. As she sobbed, we hugged her, one by one.

Solemnly, we sat down together without saying a word. In that silence we understood the truth of the matter. The latest imprisonment regulations had not been issued in fear of sectarian discord, but rather in dread of national unity.

The hardest part of any disaster to bear is its beginning, and the most momentous event in the life of a prisoner is the unexpected transferral from one life to another, from habits of a lifetime to new patterns which must be learnt. The hardship increases to the extent that the individual has been living a life of contented ease, or has been pampered, always expecting others to serve.

But I have become accustomed to serving myself. I work a lot and eat sparsely; I bathe in cold water in the wintertime and have taken regular physical exercise since I was a child. I realized early that I needed two strong arms with which I could defend myself when necessary — in the street, or in a bus, whenever any man would try to turn my being into a female body which he could grab from behind or from the front.

While a student at the university, when my female colleagues were priding themselves on the softness of their hands, the smallness of their feet, the gentleness of their small bodies, and the laxness of their weak muscles, I *was* proud of my tall stature and my strong, taut muscles. How had that happened? I don't know. I sensed within myself a rejection of the notion of weakness as "feminine" or of femininity as weakness. I have never used powder on my face. However I *was* used to washing my face every morning, brushing my teeth with toothpaste, and doing my morning exercises, then exposing my body to the gushing water of the shower.

I opened my eyes that first morning in a gaol and found no water in the tap, no toothbrush or toothpaste or soap or towel or shower. The toilet was a hole in the ground, minus door and flush, overflowing with sewage, water, and cockroaches.

We began our life in prison by repairing the state of the toilet. That was the first point of agreement and it was the beginning of a common ground among all cellmates, veiled and bareheaded.

It is fortunate that the human digestive system does not distinguish between right and left, or between one religious outlook and another. Whatever the difference in thought or politics between one individual and another, their need for the toilet is identical.

Our first meeting in the cell was attended by all inmates. In fact, Boduur, who had refused at first to join even one session with those whom she labelled "atheistic infidels," was the most enthusiastic of any of us about this meeting. I had not seen her so worked up even when praying or reading the Qur'an [the holy scriptures of Islam]. I learned later that she was afraid to enter the toilet because of the cockroaches, and if it had not been for the intense constipation which was nearly killing her, she would have gone on like this forever.

Fawqiyya also was very enthusiastic about this first meeting. Like Boduur, she boycotted the toilet, not out of fear of the cockroaches but because she was unable to squat over that hole in the ground.

We all suffered this toilet problem together, and we all feared the cockroaches and insects, but for Boduur and Fawqiyya the problem was acute.

I thought at first that the constipation problem was the sole reason for Fawqiyya's enthusiasm about the meeting, but I came to understand subsequently that she loved to hold meetings, or rather she had become addicted to the practice of organizing meetings. She had also become used to speaking in literary Arabic, articulating her words clearly and emphatically, and taking the chairperson's place.

In prison, chairs are one of the things which are prohibited. We used to sit on the ground. During the first few days it seemed that Fawqiyya missed chairs and speakers' platforms. After that, she created an imaginary dais from a top bunk, to which she would ascend with great difficulty. After the bed fell as she was sitting on it, she would sit on the lower level, and finally became inured to sitting on the ground. But she never did get accustomed to crossing her legs or folding them beneath her while sitting. Like Boduur, she seemed to be against working her muscles, not because it was a taboo or because the Qur'an said something about it, but because of losing time in muscle movements for which she could see no obvious benefit or result. We used to laugh, asking her "Don't you believe in the use of any muscle in your body other than your tongue?"

In the first meeting, we began to distribute jobs and responsibilities among ourselves so we could achieve a human existence inside the cell. We took a collective decision to stand firmly together in facing the prison administration, in order to achieve fulfillment of the following demands:

1. Repair of the toilets and water taps; installation of a shower in one of the toilet enclosures so we could bathe.
2. Fumigation of cockroaches and insects, whether the sort that bite or not.
3. Obtaining bread from the market — *khubz mulki* — instead of the ordinary prison/military bread which is infested with worms and termites.
4. Closing up the gap in the wall between us and the mothers' cell to block out the voices which were irritating us day and night.

We had discovered that the strange voices, the shouting and wailing and howling and sobbing, were all coming from the cell of mothers imprisoned with their children who had been born in prison. Three hundred mothers, and three hundred children, inside one cell the size of ours, with nothing to separate us from them but half a wall — one which did not even reach the ceiling. If the mothers stopped quarrelling and shrieking then the children would start howling, and if the children ceased, the mothers began . . . and so forth, day and night.

If there exists a hell on earth it must be the mothers' cell at Barrages Women's Prison. By comparison, our cell came to seem like the epitome of comfort and tranquility. God's paradise on earth, and all the problems we faced were relative ones indeed. We were fourteen women in a cell, with a space of floor on which we could stretch out our bodies and extend our legs. At least we could walk between the beds.

Over the ground, my fingers sketch letters and interlacing circles. My hand trembles with anger, and my heartbeat quickens. If my fingers had not come to know the pen, perhaps they would have known the hoe. The pen is the most valuable thing in my life. My words on paper are more valuable to me than my life itself. More valuable than my children, more than my husband, more than my freedom.

I prefer my place in prison to writing something which has not originated in my mind. The sincere word demands a courage akin to that needed to kill — and perhaps more.

My fingers chisel the letters in the dirt. I contemplate the words which are circling round my head. What appeared to me as certain a moment ago I see now as surrounded in the fog of doubt. To this moment, I don't know why I am in prison. I have seen no investigator or prosecuting attorney or lawyer. I heard the *shawisha* [orderly] say that she heard they were saying I entered prison because of my writings . . . my crime, therefore, comes under the rubric of crimes of opinion.

Is free opinion a crime? Then let prison be my only refuge and my final fate!

But does free opinion really merit the hardship of prison? The fatigue and hunger and illness and the harsh life in this tomb-like cell? My father, my mother, and my acquaintances — all of them — believed that I would be the cleverest of physicians and the greatest of writers . . . that I was created for success, and for arriving at the top. It would have been possible; I could have been like that — I could have obtained the highest position and title, lived in a veritable palace, owned a yacht, and married a prince or a great ruler.

But since childhood I have abhorred rulers and authority — ever since I saw my mother rebel against my father when he raised his voice against her, and ever since I heard my father cursing the king, the government, and the British.

I was a child; my mother imagined that I did not see her rebellion, and my father thought that I did not understand what he was saying, or that I would forget as I grew older . . . but I did not forget.

I had imagined prison to be solitude and total silence, the isolated cell in which one lives alone, talking to oneself, rapping at the wall to hear the responding knock of one's neighbor. Here, though, I enjoyed neither solitude nor silence, except in the space after midnight and before the dawn call to prayer. I could not pull a door shut between me and the others, even when I was in the toilet.

If Boduur ceased quarrelling with her colleagues, she would begin reciting the Qur'an out loud. And if Boduur went to sleep, Fawqiyya would wake up and begin to discuss and orate. If Fawqiyya went to sleep, Boduur would wake up to announce prayer time and the onset of night.

One night, the quarrel between Boduur and one of her comrades continued until dawn, ending only when Boduur fainted after she'd been hit by violent nervous convulsions. She tore at her hair and face with her fingernails, screaming until she lost consciousness.

As soon as the *shawisha* had opened the cell door in the morning, I called out to her. "I want to be transferred to a solitary cell. I don't want to stay in this cell any longer."

But the prison administration rejected my request. I came to understand that in prison, torture occurs not through solitude and silence but in a far more forceful way through uproar and noise. The solitary cell continued to float before me like a dream unlikely to be realized.

Since childhood, I've had a passion for solitude. I've not had a room in which I could shut myself off, for the number of individuals in every stage of my life has been greater than the number of rooms in the house. But I have always wrested for myself a place in which I could be alone to write. My ability to write has been linked to the possibility of complete seclusion, of being alone with myself, for I am incapable of writing when I am unable to give myself completely to solitude.

After midnight, when the atmosphere grows calm and I hear only the sound of sleep's regular breathing, I rise from my bed and tiptoe to the corner of the toilet, turn the empty jerry can upside down and sit on its bottom. I rest the aluminum plate on my knees, place it against the long, tape-like toilet paper, and begin to write.

❖

Freedom and Prison

Why did Nawal el Saadawi go to jail? Here is her answer. In early September of 1981, the government of then President Anwar Sadat made public accusations against people perceived to be part of the opposition to the government. The language of accusation was unusually vague; some citizens were accused of promoting "sectarian strife" and of participating in extremist religious movements. Political life in Egypt was volatile; the roundup of dissidents grew in numbers and in hysteria.

Saadawi and a number of her female colleagues were arrested and held under a so-called Law for the Protection of Values from Shame. This piece of legislation prohibited dissent and provided for extensive periods of detention. Under existing Egyptian laws, those detained could apparently be held without specific charges or legal recourse. Nawal was an obvious target. An outspoken feminist, she wrote books about women and sex. Her alleged "crimes against the State" were apparently encouraging, even instigating, women to sexual freedom and immorality.

Nawal el Saadawi was arrested on September 6, 1981. Her imprisonment attracted publicity as women throughout the Arab world, Europe, the United States, and Asia campaigned for her release. As prisons go, it was not the worst. Nor was she there a long time. As autobiographical writing about imprisonment, it is rare and outstanding.

Nawal is philosophical about going to prison. She says, "Imprisonment in my country is always possible for any person who thinks and writes freely. Most of the men and women I know have been in prison at one time in their life."[4] Her husband, Sherif Hetata, was in jail for thirteen years because of his intellectual and political rebellions. He says, "The comradeship of prison is like no other."

For Nawal the lessons and choices of prison centered on writing. When she had no tools with which to write, she wrote in her head. By the time she reached the outer limits of her capacity for remembering, a prostitute smuggled a stubby eyebrow pencil and a small roll of toilet paper in to her. She remembers those moments as intensely happy — a victory over authority, steel bars, and marauding cockroaches. The sheer act of writing defines her life.

> Writing: such has been my crime ever since I was a small child. To this day writing remains my crime. Now, although I am out of prison, I continue to live inside a prison of another sort, one without steel bars. For the technology of oppression and might without justice has become more advanced, and the fetters imposed on mind and body have become invisible. The most dangerous shackles are the invisible ones, because they deceive people into believing they are free. This delusion is the new prison that people inhabit today, north and south, east and west. Now that I have traveled to most of the countries on the globe, I have discovered that this thing called "democracy" is nothing more than a veil — as are the words "God," "religion," "peace," and "justice" — used to conceal the vilest sorts of force, murder, oppression, and exploitation.[5]

If she was to be in jail because she wrote, then write she would. Above all she says, "Writing to me is like breathing. I must do it to live."

President Anwar Sadat was assassinated on October 6, 1981. Saadawi was released on November 25, 1981. She and her colleagues believe these events are related and had it not been for the shooting, they would probably have remained in jail with unpredicted consequences.

After she was released from prison, Nawal began to travel more and more. The book that followed is called *My Travels Around the World* (London: Minerva, 1992); it is a series of journeys reported from eyes and tongue uniquely free of Western sensitivities. But she was still an exile. "I am no longer on the blacklist. But I am on the so-called *grey list* I can publish some of my work in Egypt. But the regime is not happy with what I write. I always belong to the opposition. . . . At least I can travel." And write. Nawal el Saadawi no longer lives in Egypt.

The Matter of Books: Books That Matter

Nawal el Saadawi wrote *Memoirs of a Woman Doctor* just as she graduated from medical school; she had read no feminist literature. Nothing like Women's Studies existed at that time. She merely wanted to express the experiences and feelings of a woman who is a doctor at work and a wife and mother at home. Sounds reasonable, even familiar, doesn't it. But the book was controversial. It was thought to be a revolutionary feminist novel; it was censored and cut. She says it is only a love story, a novel, not an autobiography. Not in a conventional way, perhaps. But it is certainly vintage Nawal el Saadawi and well worth reading, even emulating. It was translated from the Arabic by Catherine Cobham (San Francisco: City Lights, 1989).

October 6, 1981, was a turning point for many people. Ask the wife of President Anwar Sadat of Egypt. Jihan Sadat's autobiography begins with the date her husband was shot and turns back to the high points in her husband's career. She also speaks of being wife and widow, of loving her country, and how little understood Egypt as a nation is. Her life story, juxtaposed against her husband's career, is called *A Woman of Egypt* (New York: Simon and Schuster, 1987). This book is certainly a contrast to others noted here and reminds us that women, even women from the same time and the same place, fit no single mold.

Occasionally I need to be reminded of the extraordinary varieties of women in the world as well as the fact that feminism and fascinating women go together in unexpected places and at unexpected times. Imagine an Egyptian girl, born in 1879, who grew up in a wealthy household, a member of the last generation of women who lived under the harem system. Her relatives did not plan this life for her, but Huda Shaarawi became a feminist and a leader in the first women's nationalist demonstrations and organizations. She was, at various times, president of the Egyptian Feminist Union and the Arab Feminist Union. She called herself an Egyptian, an Arab, an international feminist, and a lifelong activist. Just her account of living in a harem is worth the reading. Her autobiography is called *Harem Years: The Memoirs of an Egyptian Feminist, 1879–1924*. It was translated, edited, and put into context by Margot Badran (New York: The Feminist Press, 1986).

Besides Nawal el Saadawi, the best-known woman writing about Arabic or Islamic women is probably Fatima Mernissi. She grew up in a harem in Morocco and became a sociologist. Her books are often considered a "must-read" for Western women who need or want to know more about the ancient struggles for women in Islam. But not every sociologist and excellent writer such as Mernissi will or can write an autobiography too. Hers is very special: *Dreams of Trespass: Tales of a Harem Girlhood*. The evocative photographs are by Ruth V. Ward (Reading, MA: Addison-Wesley, 1994).

Another book that complements Nawal's is *My Life Story: The Autobiography of a Berber Woman,* by Fadhma Amrouche. Born in Algeria, Amrouche was a singer and poet, a woman whose life reflected the conflicts between colonist and colonized, Berber and Arab, women and men in North Africa. She did not dare show her husband the memoirs she wrote in 1946. She felt free to publish them only after he died. Dorothy Blair translated her book and wrote the introduction (New Brunswick, NJ: Rutgers University Press, 1989).

Margot Badran, whose name appears as editor or translator for several of the books mentioned here, completed degrees in Middle East Studies at Harvard and Oxford. She and Miriam Cooke met each other at Oxford in the 1970s. They collaborated on an anthology of writings by women who are both Arabs and feminists. Women such as Nawal Saadawi, Fatima Mernissi, or other writers from the more than twenty sovereign states that stretch from Morocco to the Arabian peninsula had influenced their own thinking. So they wanted to bring these exciting voices to Western audiences. The result is a major contribution to women everywhere, *Opening the Gates: A Century of Arab Feminist Writing* (Bloomington: Indiana University Press, 1990).

A Woman Writing Life

1. Nawal el Saadawi wrote a prison memoir that did not make her captors look good. She appears to be more powerful and empowered than ever. Shouldn't repressive regimes take notice of the power of women's words? Shouldn't the rest of us?

2. Nawal discovered an unexpected sisterhood in prison. This must mean that there are many unexpected places where sisterhoods form amd flourish. How can we find them, create them, hear about them, tell about them?

3. We have heard the saying, "The pen is mightier than the sword." Nawal says that prison is no punishment for a writer, that she must write to breathe. Can telling our stories ultimately mean freedom for women?

4. Nawal had a searing personal experience with genital mutilation. Can Western women join her crusade against this practice? Should we? Are equally horrible things being done to girls and young women in our own culture?

5. These seven chapters present many models for living, listening to, reading, and writing women's lives. Where does one go from here?

Endnotes to Chapter 7

1. Fedwa Malti-Douglas and Allen Douglas taped this conversation, August 15, 1986, in Cairo, Egypt. It was published in *Opening the Gates: A Century of Arab Feminist Writing,* edited by Margot Badran and Miriam Cooke (Bloomington: Indiana University Press, 1990). The quote is from page 398.

2. From the introduction to Nawal el Saadawi, *The Hidden Face of Eve* (London: Zed Press, 1982), 2.

3. Citations for books by Nawal el Saadawi: *The Circling Song* (London: Zed Press, 1989); *A Woman at Point Zero,* translated by Sherif Hetata (London: Zed Press, 1983); *Two Women in One* (Women Translation, 1991); *The Fall of Imam* (Portsmouth, NH: Heinemann, 1990). These are only four of her novels; others are also available in English.

4. *Contemporary Authors,* New Revised Series, Volume 44:126.

5. This quote is from the "Afterword," a new section added to her prison memoirs, which were republished in 1994 by the University of California Press, page 200.

ACKNOWLEDGMENTS

CHAPTER 1

From "The Autobiography of a Fox Indian Woman" by Truman Michelson, 40th Annual Report of the Bureau of American Ethnology, 1918–1919. Printed in 1925. National Anthropological Archives, Smithsonian Institution.

CHAPTER 2

From *A Daughter of the Samurai* by E. I. Sugimoto. Copyright 1925, 1928 by Doubleday, a division of Bantam Doubleday Dell Publishing Group, Inc. Used by permission of Doubleday, a division of Bantam Doubleday Dell Publishing Group, Inc.

CHAPTER 3

From *Discretions* by Mary de Rachewiltz. Copyright 1971 by Mary de Rachewiltz. By permission of Little, Brown and Company.

CHAPTER 4

From Mary F. Smith, *Baba of Karo: A Woman of the Muslim Hausa.* Copyright 1955 by Yale University Press.

CHAPTER 5

From Oscar Lewis, Ruth Lewis, and Susan M. Rigdon, *Four Women: Living the Revolution, an Oral History of Contemporary Cuba.* Copyright 1977 by the Board of Trustees of the University of Illinois. Used by permission of the author and the University of Illinois Press.

CHAPTER 6

From *Amiria: The Life Story of a Maori Woman* as told to Anne Salmond. Reprinted by permission of Reed Publishing Ltd., Auckland, New Zealand.

CHAPTER 7

From Nawal el Sa'adawi, *The Hidden Faces of Eve.* Copyright 1982 by Zed Books Ltd., London, England.

❖

The extracts are reprinted from pages 1–5; 40–43; 116–117; and 128–129 of *Memoirs from the Women's Prison* by Nawal Sa'adawi, translated from the Arabic by Marilyn Booth, first published in English by The Women's Press Ltd., 1986, 34 Great Sutton Street, London EC1V ODX, are used by permission of The Women's Press Ltd.